Business Process Management

This book is for:

- Technology-savvy CEOs, EVPs, Directors and the senior executive management of companies interested in improving business processes in the enterprise who are considering investing in BPM, workflow automation, EAI or related collaborative technologies.

- Technology-savvy line-of-business managers in marketing, sales, manufacturing, quality assurance, human resources, customer relationships, accounting, financials and other operations concerned with improving efficiencies through business process automation.

- CIOs, application software managers and network managers of companies seeking new ways to respond to the collaborative needs of their internal and external customers.

- CTOs of business software and e-commerce companies interested in incorporating BPM and workflow automation to differentiate their products and services while increasing the value proposition to their customers.

- Business process and Six Sigma consultants interested in new solutions and technologies to improve the productivity of their corporate clients.

- Members of the investment community interested in understanding the dynamics of the burgeoning BPM market.

- MIS and IT educators interested in imparting knowledge about a new breed of products to their students.

Companion Software

Business Process Modeling and Analysis (BPMA) is the first step on the road to business process management. BPMA can be used by business process owners to design, model, optimize and document business processes. To bring these concepts to life, a free copy of business process modeling and optimization software, with samples, can be downloaded from the Internet to illustrate the benefits of using such software for designing and optimizing processes before they are automated using a BPM solution.

Interested readers can download this software tool from *www.practicalbpm.com* by using the Access Code CQN1952. A sample process and a document describing how to use the software for process optimization can also be downloaded.

Web site: www.practicalbpm.com

Business Process Management

A Practical Guide

Rashid N. Khan

Meghan-Kiffer Press
Tampa, Florida, USA, www.mkpress.com
Advanced Business-Technology Books for Competitive Advantage

Publisher's Cataloging-in-Publication Data

Khan, Rashid.
  Business Process Management: A Practical Guide / Rashid Khan, - 1st ed.
    p. cm.
      Includes appendices and index.
      ISBN 0-929652-32-0 (paper)

      1. Reengineering (Management) 2. Technological innovation. 3. Strategic planning. 4.
      Management information systems. 5. Information technology. 6. Information resources
      management. 7. Organizational change. I. Khan, Rashid. II. Title

HD58.87.S548 2003   2002106051
658.4'063–dc21   CIP

Book's Web site: http://www.practicalbpm.com

Published by Meghan-Kiffer Press
310 East Fern Street ☐ Suite G
Tampa, FL 33604 USA

Company and product names mentioned herein are the trademarks or registered
trademarks of their respective owners.

Meghan-Kiffer books are available at special quantity discounts for corporate
education and training use. For more information write Special Sales, Meghan-
Kiffer Press, Suite G, 310 East Fern Street, Tampa, Florida 33604 or e-mail
books@mkpress.com

MK
Meghan-Kiffer Press
Tampa, Florida, USA
Publishers of Advanced Business-Technology Books for Competitive Advantage

Printed in the United States of America.   SAN 249-7980
MK Printing 10 9 8 7 6 5 4 3 2 1

This book is dedicated to the memory of my mother, Mustafai Khanum, and to my father, Nisar Ahmad Khan.

Table of Contents

road to BPM. This chapter discusses the role of BPMA and how it can be used to design, model, optimize and document business processes.

This chapter describes the major capabilities of a BPM server and tools for administering the server.

This chapter discusses the design tools that are needed for developing complex BPM applications.

The workflow client is the "inbox" used by workflow participants. In this chapter the key requirements of a workflow client are discussed and differentiated from the e-mail inbox that readers are most familiar with.

This chapter discusses business process monitoring and metrics and how they can be used to improve organizational performance.

This chapter discusses the technologies and techniques that are used by BPM solutions to integrate with other applications.

This chapter discusses the impact and significance of the Internet on BPM. It describes Web Services technology and its importance to BPM.

This chapter presents two live BPM installation case studies and offers insight into some tangible and intangible benefits of adopting BPM.

This appendix provides a framework for evaluating and categorizing the large number of BPM products on the market today.

Preface

This book provides a clear and concise explanation of Business Process Management (BPM). It is a practical book with very little theory, and written so that any businessperson or student can understand BPM and the practical way it uses technology to change the way organizations work.

This book is for anyone interested in an in-depth understanding of a new way of running a business in the Internet Age. Just as factory automation revolutionized the manufacturing of hard goods in the 20th century, BPM is poised to dramatically change the way 21st century organizations collect, review, analyze and distribute information for the purpose of efficiently serving their customers.

BPM enables an organization to create automated "production lines" for processing information by leveraging modern software technology, the power of the network, and, in recent years, the ubiquity of the Internet. Automated information production lines enable the modern organization to reduce the time and the cost for delivering information, goods and services to customers, while at the same time increasing accountability and metrics-driven performance improvements. Like a production line that effectively integrates workers and machines, BPM binds workers and line-of-business information systems in a process that moves work at the speed of the modern network. BPM is essential for creating an agile organization capable of real-time response to business need.

One goal of this book is to de-mystify BPM and differentiate it from workflow automation and enterprise application integration (EAI). Workflow automation, an important subset of BPM, has been around for more almost two decades. However, for years it existed in isolation. The cost and complexity of early solutions thwarted widespread adoption. Even in the technology-savvy IT community there is much confusion about workflow automation, and how it relates to and interacts with other technologies. For the lay businessperson, coping with the constant deluge of new technologies and products spawned by the information revolution, workflow automation is a perplexing subject to comprehend. This is ironic, since every businessperson today participates in or manages business processes that are the very target of workflow automation. The introduction of new buzzwords such as "e-process," "knowledge management," and "work management" has further confused the subject. The emergence of EAI, the second subset of BPM, has caused even more confusion about BPM. EAI is essentially a technical means of connecting fragments of function-specific information systems to achieve a broader business purpose, such as connecting a payroll system to a sales system in order to handle sales commissions for sales people. While both workflow and application integration technologies have had a great impact on how companies support their operations with automation, BPM takes the whole affair to another level.

Propelled by rapid advances in software technology, the pervasive growth of the Internet and new business-oriented Internet standards, BPM is moving quickly to the business mainstream. It is, therefore, imperative for anyone concerned with improving productivity in a modern organization to understand the basic facts about this technology and how it is changing the way we do business.

This book took three years to write on a part-time basis working on weekends and evenings. Many individuals contributed to the success of this project. Special thanks are due to Hank Barnes and Ken Bagnal for reviewing the early drafts and providing valuable feedback. Peter Fingar has patiently reviewed the final drafts and gave a lot of good advice and suggestions to guide me through the process. Louis Criscuolo gets credit for all illustrations, the book cover design, and also carefully copy-editing the material. Finally, without the loving willingness of my daughters Nadia, Nushmia and Saffa to leave me alone, it could not have been completed.

Rashid N. Khan
September, 2004

Chapter 1

A Brief Introduction to Business Process Management

---

busi☐ness (b ĭz' n ĭs) proc☐ess (prō' sĕs')

n. A business process is a sequence of tasks that are performed in series or in parallel by two or more individuals or computer applications to reach a common goal.

busi☐ness (b ĭz' n ĭs) proc☐ess (prō' sĕs') man☐age☐ment (măn' ĭj-mənt)

n. Business process management is the discipline of modeling, automating, managing and optimizing a business process through its lifecycle to increase profitability.

What is Business Process Management?

Every organization is defined by the many different business processes that describe the way it conducts its business. Some of the processes are mission critical and essential to the success of the organization and its competitive advantage. Others may not be mission critical, but still important for the stakeholders of the organization. These business processes are the nervous system of the organization. Like the human nervous system, business processes collect information about the status and needs of the internal employees and external customers of the organization and process it into meaningful actions that can satisfy these needs. The health of business processes is as vital to the success of an organization as the health of the nervous system is to the success of the human body. Speed of response and clarity of decision-making are the two most important measures of the health of business processes as well as the human nervous system.

Business process management (BPM) uses a fascinating technology designed specifically to manage business processes. These new BPM systems are rapidly coming to the forefront of business innovation because of the dramatic potential for improving the productivity and agility of organizations. BPM addresses the problems and challenges faced by every businessperson in every organization. Despite this broad applicability, BPM and its underlying technology is still shrouded in mystery. The goal of this book is to de-mystify BPM so that business readers in every organization can understand the technology behind it, then start to explore its vast potential as educated consumers.

Organizations have numerous business processes that involve people as well as automated systems. A business process can be simply defined as "a sequence of tasks that are performed in series or in parallel by two or more individuals or computer applications to reach a common goal." Common examples of business processes that are readily recognizable include:

- *Order Processing* that dictates how customer orders will be received, entered, manufactured, shipped and invoiced.
- *Claims Processing* that specifies how an insurance company will receive, review and process claims.
- *Performance Reviews* that define how, when and by whom employee performance will be reviewed.
- *Customer Complaints Processing* that describe the mechanisms for handling complaints issued by customers.
- *Loan Processing* that defines how a bank will process loan applications and the rules and approvals that must be obtained.
- *Purchase Order Processing* that lays out the rules and paperwork that must be processed in order to control the acquisition of goods and services.

These business processes define the tasks, the rules, the people and the automated systems engaged in delivering goods, services or information to the employees and external customers and partners of the organization.

A BPM system is a software product category and technology used for automating these types of business processes. There are seven major facets of BPM:

1. Design and document processes using software tools to improve the understanding of the process and to develop a plan for improvements.
2. Convert paper-based business processes into electronic processes that eliminate paper forms, file folders, documents and the inefficiencies associated with these.
3. Integrate business processes with a variety of computer applications to automate entire processes (or steps of processes), thereby eliminating human involvement.
4. Incorporate control features that ensure the integrity of the process and compensate for human or system failure.
5. Increase the speed of response and reduce lag, or dead time, that is inherent in business processes today.
6. Provide real-time feedback about the status of processes.
7. Measure the time and cost of the processes so that they can be optimized.

Overview

The first four chapters of this book introduce the reader to BPM and some of it major benefits. Chapters 2 and 3 discuss the two major component technologies of BPM: workflow automation and enterprise application integration (EAI). Workflow automation and EAI are distinct technologies with very different histories; they evolved as solutions for different problems at different time frames in the history of business computing. To clarify these differences and understand these technologies, these chapters discuss their evolution, unique characteristics, and impact on productivity.

Chapter 4 follows with a discussion of the profound impact of a new Internet technology called Web Services, and Moore's Law that is forcing workflow automation and EAI product categories to converge. It is indeed the blending of these technologies that is a major contributor to the confusion about business process management. The convergence of workflow automation and EAI, coupled with the development of business process modeling and reporting, has given birth to BPM that enables organizations to manage their business processes over their life cycle. By understanding the similarities and the differences, this book strives to provide a clear understanding about BPM, workflow and EAI.

The remaining chapters of this book provide an in-depth explanation of the features and functions of a BPM system from a business perspective. The goal is to help the reader become an educated consumer of this powerful new business approach and technology.

This book also discusses the underlying benefits of BPM that have propelled it as one of the most important product categories for enhancing the productivity of modern organizations. However, the focus of this book is not on the benefits of BPM (which are compelling). Many other authors have done an excellent job of enunciating the benefits of BPM and how it can be used by organizations to increase revenue, reduce cost, improve customer service, and increase responsiveness and agility. Instead, the focus is to provide business readers a solid understanding of the technology behind BPM, why it is important to them, and what they need to know if they are going to be educated consumers of this technology.

Chapter 2

Workflow Automation

Workflow automation deals with the automation of business processes that are people-centric. There are a number of software applications designed for *workflow automation* versus *enterprise application integration* that focuses on data collection with some built-in *flow* characteristics. It is important to know the difference between these two application types in order to fully comprehend the essential requirements of a workflow automation product.

The Evolution of Workflow Automation

Workflow automation software belongs to the broad category of products called *groupware*. Thus, to understand workflow automation one must understand groupware and its impact on the modern organization.

With the widespread use of the personal computer at home and in the office, personal productivity software packages such as spreadsheets, word processors, graphic design tools and databases have become ubiquitous. These products are designed to improve individual productivity, and they have had a revolutionary impact on how we work. Since its introduction in the early 1980s, personal productivity software has created *islands of automation* that improve individual productivity, but do not do much to improve the overall productivity of groups or teams working together. In modern organizations and societies the ability to work together, share and collaborate is essential. Workflow automation is a subset of the broad category of products called *groupware*, whose goal is to unite the human *islands of automation* so that they can work together effectively.

Groupware is a relatively new technology. It was made possible by the growth and widespread use of the computer Local Area Network (LAN) in the second half of the 1980s. By networking computers together, the LAN connected the *islands of automation* created by personal productivity software. This generated a demand for solutions to enable groups of people to work together and share information over the LAN, giving birth to *groupware* as the software designed to improve productivity of groups of people working together. The word "groupware" was first coined by Lotus Corporation to position its new product, Lotus Notes, introduced in 1988. Lotus Notes was the first widely publicized groupware solution that rode the coattails of the highly popular Lotus 1-2-3 spreadsheet. Lotus Notes was a revolutionary new product that allowed users to share documents and folders for collaboration across the network. Like all revolutionary new products that establish a new paradigm, Lotus Notes posed a challenge to the Lotus marketing team to describe and position it. The Lotus marketing team coined the word *groupware* for software that enables groups of people to work together.

In the early days of personal computer networking, LANs were limited to departments or individual company sites. This meant that groupware was also generally restricted to a departmental or a site solution. As LANs were complemented with Wide Area Networks (WANs), the reach of groupware extended to multiple locations. Groupware started becoming an enterprise-wide solution. With the growth of the Internet as a network that spans the globe and reaches remote locations, the potential for groupware as the technology that will revolutionize society has increased dramatically.

Working together is fundamental to modern organizations. There are numerous ways in which people work together, making the potential market size for groupware enormous. It is, therefore, not surprising that almost every software vendor is focused on some aspect of groupware. Growth of the groupware market is no longer constrained by technology. Computer processing power continues to increase with decreasing cost. The Internet continues to expand rapidly as the electronic network provides an excellent *highway* on which to build groupware solutions. Today, the growth of group-ware is constrained primarily by the need for product developers to under-stand the complexities of human interactions and the need for flexibility. Human beings work with each other in complex ways that are not always logical. Their patterns of working together change frequently and in ways that are not predictable. To be successful, a groupware product must be able to adapt and support the variety of human interactions.

The following section analyzes how people work together to provide a better understanding of the complexities and unique needs of each mode of interaction, and to better understand the relationship of groupware to workflow.

Categories of Groupware

There are three primary ways in which people work together or inter-act with each other in groups:

1. *Communication:* People communicate with each other by sending infor-mation, requests or instructions.
2. *Collaboration:* People collaborate with each other by working together on joint projects.
3. *Coordination:* People coordinate with each other as participants in

structured or semi-structured processes. Coordination is workflow.

Communication, collaboration and coordination are the "3Cs" of groupware, another phrase coined by Lotus to describe the modalities of working together [1].

Groupware products fall into three broad categories that accommodate these modalities of working together. These three categories are briefly discussed below.

Communication Products

Communication products enable users to quickly and easily communicate with each other. Communication is mostly ad hoc; there is no structure or process. Successful communication products share the following general attributes:

1. Communication products must be quick, convenient and easy to use. Otherwise they will not be suitable for ad hoc communications.
2. They must be very low cost. Otherwise they will not be widely used.
3. They must be widely used. Otherwise they are not an effective means of communication.

Examples of communication software products include e-mail, chat programs, fax solutions, computer telephony and video conferencing. Video conferencing is still relatively expensive and more difficult to use. Therefore it is not as widely accepted as the other means.

Collaboration Products

Collaboration involves *knowledge workers* working in teams on projects such as producing reports, creating marketing collateral, designing complex products, or participating in research. Collaborative groupware products cater to the needs of individuals working together on joint projects by:

1. Providing a document repository where the collective work of the team is stored and easily accessible to all participants. For collaboration the *document repository* is the key since it is the repository of the collective knowledge of the collaborators, and dictates the format in which their work is saved and presented.
2. Providing a means for knowledge workers to locate and access documents with security and appropriate access rights.

3. Making collaboration easy and non-intrusive. Otherwise, the product will hamper the creativity that is the principal contribution of knowledge workers.

Examples of collaborative groupware products include Lotus Notes, document management systems, *team room* solutions such as Documentum's eRoom, and other multi-user applications such as Computer Aided Design (CAD) or graphics design applications.

Coordination Products

In addition to communicating and collaborating, individuals also work together by participating in structured or semi-structured processes involving more than one individual. These processes include reviews, approvals, processing orders, handling applications and many others. Groupware designed for coordination is workflow automation and accommodates certain needs:

1. The *process* is the essence of workflow or coordination. Workflow products enable an organization to easily and effectively design, deploy, monitor and measure business processes.
2. Processes can be *structured or semi-structured*. They can never be purely ad hoc. Indeed, if there is no structure or logic to a process it cannot be automated.
3. Workflow is *proactive*. The purpose of a workflow automation solution is to push tasks toward reaching a goal or outcome.

Every organization has a large number of business processes. Coordination, or workflow, is prevalent in every organization in some way, shape or form. Companies that have provided significant workflow products to the market include IBM, Staffware, FileNet, and Ultimus among others.

The relationship between groupware, coordination (workflow), collaboration and communications is graphically illustrated in Figure 2.1.

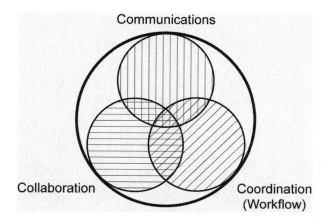

Figure 2.1. Groupware consists of Communication, Collaboration
and Coordination (Workflow)

Workflow Defined

A simple definition of a workflow process is: "A sequence of *structured or semi-structured* tasks performed in *series or in parallel* by *two or more individuals* to reach a *common goal.*"

Note that this is very similar to our previous definition of a business process. The key difference is that workflow applications have focused most of their efforts on automating processes that involve people. System-to-system processes have been addressed by EAI technologies that will be discussed in the next chapter.

The italicized words or phrases in the definition signify the five essential elements of a workflow:

1. Workflow is a *sequence* of tasks indicating the plurality of things that must be accomplished. One task alone does not constitute a workflow.
2. The sequence of tasks is *structured or semi-structured*. This signifies that there is some logic to a workflow. The tasks are not performed on a purely ad hoc basis.
3. Tasks can be performed in *series or in parallel* based upon the logic of the business process.
4. There must be at least *two or more* individuals involved as players performing different tasks. If one individual uses an application or form to enter information into a database, that does not constitute a workflow.

Work must flow from one individual or application to another individual or application.

5. The sequence of tasks must have a purpose of reaching a *common goal* or outcome. This emphasizes that workflow is geared towards producing results. Merely linking together unrelated tasks into a series of steps does not make a workflow.

Figure 2.2 is a sketch for a simple purchase requisition workflow process for a small company. In this example, any employee can initiate a purchase requisition by filling out a form. This is the first step, or task, that must be performed. The supervisor of the employee must then approve the purchase requisition, as represented by the second step in the process. If the supervisor disapproves the purchase, then an e-mail message is sent to the employee informing him of the reasons. If the supervisor approves the purchase, and the amount is less than $1,000, the purchase order is sent to the buyer since the supervisor is allowed to approve items costing up to $1,000. If the amount is more than $1,000, the purchase order is sent to the company controller who checks for funds availability and makes a recommendation. It is then sent to the general manager of the company who can approve or disapprove the purchase. Again, if the general manager disapproves it, an e-mail is sent to the employee who requested the purchase; if the general manager approves the request, it is routed to the buyer. The buyer can either place an order via telephone and the process ends, or the buyer can ask for a printout of a hard copy and mail it to the supplier.

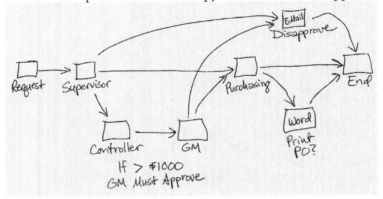

Figure 2.2. A Sketch of a Simple Purchase Requisition Process

This simple example illustrates the essential elements of a workflow. The purchase requisition workflow is a *sequence* of tasks such as the initial request, supervisor approval, e-mail notification, general manager approval and purchasing. Each step in the process represents a discrete task.

The sequence of tasks is *structured or semi-structured*. The tasks are carried out in accordance with certain logic or rules. For example:

a. The initial request must always be approved by the initiator's supervisor.
b. If the amount is more than $1,000, the general manager must approve it.
c. If the request is denied, the requestor must be notified via e-mail.

The tasks can be performed in *series or in parallel* based upon the logic of the business process. In this example the e-mail notification is sent in parallel, or at the same time the buyer is requested to place the order.

There must be at least *two or more* individuals involved as participants performing different tasks. There are several people involved in the purchase requisition workflow: the employee, supervisor, buyer, general manager and controller. In this example we also have two applications involved, namely e-mail and Microsoft Word.

The sequence of tasks must have a purpose of reaching a *common goal* or outcome. In this example the purpose of the workflow is to either approve and buy the requested item, or deny it and inform the requestor of the reasons it was denied.

By understanding the definition and reviewing this simple example, other important attributes of a workflow can be observed:

1. A workflow has rules that define the structure of a process.
2. The workflow uses *roles and relationships* that dictate who will perform each task in a process. The general manager is a *role* that approves purchases for items greater than $1,000. The employee's supervisor is a *relationship* that must initially approve the request.
3. The workflow has numerous exceptions that are too complex to represent graphically. For example, the buyer may not have enough information to purchase the item and may have to return the order for clarification. The supervisor may not be at work on a given day and the employee must get the order approved quickly in order to meet a customer's requirement.
4. Every workflow benefits from some form of status monitoring. For

example, the employee who initiated the purchase order request needs to know where it is, especially if it is late.

5. Every step in the workflow has a time and cost associated with it. Only by measuring the time and cost can an organization hope to make their business processes more efficient and streamlined.

Based on the definition and this simple example, it is easy to think of other examples of business processes in every company or organization that fall in the workflow category. Some of them are listed in Table 1.1, but the number and type of workflow processes vary from organization to organization. Suffice it to say that there are a large number of workflow processes, and every organization has its own flavor of each.

Table 1.1. Typical Workflow Processes

Order Processing and Fulfillment	Change Orders
Performance Reviews	Purchase Requisitions
Capital Appropriations	New Hire Processing
Defect Tracking and Resolution	New Product Development
Document Approval Routing	Leads Management
Medical/Insurance Claims	Customer Care Processes
Expense Reports	Return Material Authorizations
Warranty Management	Invoice Processing
Employee Self-Service Processes	Correspondence Tracking

Workflow vs. Workflow Automation

There are numerous companies and software packages that claim to offer workflow capabilities. The IT press and analysts often report that there are over 100 workflow products. Similarly, a quick search of major search engines on the Internet for *workflow* will produce many listings for the category. If there are so many products and companies offering workflow it leads one to ask the following questions:

1. Why has workflow technology not gained more prominence?
2. Why is the use of workflow not more widespread?
3. How do you find the right product for your workflow needs from among the myriad of products?

The answer to these questions lies in clarifying the confusion between *workflow* and *workflow automation*.

Workflow is the simple routing of work from one person to another. One can attach a document to an e-mail and send it to someone for review and make some decisions. Thus work has *flowed* from one to the other person. From a strict linguistic point of view it is correct to say that this is *workflow*. However, everyone will agree that it is not *workflow automation*. The e-mail sender does not know when it reached the recipient; when the recipient completed the task; how long the recipient took to complete the task; what happened after the recipient completed the task; what if the recipient did not check her or his e-mail and the task is still not done; and so on. E-mail therefore enables or facilitates workflow; but it does not automate workflow. Automation means the proactive control of the entire workflow process from instantiation to completion. It also means the ability to monitor the status of a workflow, handle exceptions, and generate metrics to improve the performance of the system. Workflow automation manages, drives and controls the flow of work in order to promote accountability and rapid decision-making.

Like e-mail, there are a large number of software applications which can do simple routing of information or documents from one person to another. These include applications such as Microsoft Exchange, Lotus Notes, Document Management Systems, intelligent Web sites, network management systems and others that have some rudimentary form of messaging or information routing to the recipients based upon roles, rules and events. These applications have workflow features, but they are not *automating workflow*.

The next section outlines the ten essential capabilities that a software package must have in order to meet the basic requirements of workflow automation. Comparing the 100-plus software packages that are touted as *workflow automation* products against these requirements will reveal that there are only about 10 to 15 that make the cut.

Essential Requirements for Workflow Automation

Workflow automation systems must provide the following minimum features and capabilities. The italicized words or phrases in each requirement described below signify the important concept of the requirement.

1. *Graphical Workflow Representation:* A means of graphically displaying

workflow process maps that define the flow of work and the tasks that must be performed from start to finish.

2. *Roles:* It is essential to have the ability to assign tasks to *roles* or *job functions* so that the workflow design does not have to be changed each time a user changes job function or responsibilities. Advanced solutions also provide integrated organization charts and the ability to assign tasks based upon reporting relationships.

3. *Rules:* The ability to embed complex business rules in the workflow definition without the need for programming or scripting makes it easy to design workflow processes.

4. *Exception Handling:* The ability to handle exceptions that are ubiquitous in every organization. For example, the ability to reassign a critical task from one user to another if the user is absent because of an emergency and his computer is password protected.

5. *Monitor:* The ability to monitor the status of workflow incidents is important. Ideally, this ability should be available to each workflow participant for incidents they have participated in, and to a centralized workflow administrator for all workflow incidents.

6. *Metrics:* It is necessary to be able to produce workflow metric reports so business managers can measure the time and cost of workflow processes. Metrics can then be used to modify business processes based upon their cost-effectiveness and timeliness.

7. *Integration with Third-Party Applications:* Workflow involves not only users but also third-party applications that perform tasks. These include spreadsheets, word processors, databases, ERP systems, accounting software, document management/imaging systems and many more. A workflow automation system must provide an effective and seamless means of integrating with a variety of third-party applications.

8. *Proactive:* The ability to move workflow forward on a proactive basis is essential. The workflow solution must inform users of new tasks, warn them of late tasks, and be able to re-route tasks to other users in abnormal situations.

9. *Database Connectivity:* Every workflow process either uses information from databases to enable users to make decisions or feeds information into databases. In many cases, they do both. A workflow automation solution must provide seamless database connectivity.

10. *Workflow Inbox:* A software application that lists all the tasks that a user has to perform and allows the user to perform them is necessary. As will be discussed in Chapter 11, "Workflow Client: The End-User Experience," the requirements for a workflow inbox are far greater

than what a simple e-mail inbox can provide.

Conclusion

Workflow automation developed as a technology for the automation of people-centric processes. It was made possible by the emergence and widespread adoption of computer networks. Workflow automation solutions offer many of the benefits of business process automation. Workflow automation has some similarities with enterprise application integration (EAI), which deals with the automation of system-centric processes. However, there are major differences between workflow automation and EAI. The confluence of workflow automation and EAI, coupled with the realization that business processes are assets that need to be managed over their lifecycle, has led to the emergence of business process management (BPM).

Chapter 3

Enterprise Application Integration

Workflow automation and Enterprise Application Integration (EAI) are distinct technologies with very different histories. They evolved as solutions for different problems during different time frames in the history of business computing. While workflow automation and EAI have some similarities, there are major differences between the two. By understanding their similarities and differences, the stage is set to develop a clear understanding about business process management (BPM) in relation to both workflow and EAI.

The Evolution of Enterprise Application Integration

EAI evolved because of the need to automate the movement of data between applications and computers. It is different than workflow automation, which focuses on the movement of data between people.

EAI emerged after the hey-day of the mainframe-based computing that was dominated by IBM. IBM and other mainframe vendors sold integrated and proprietary systems. When a company purchased an IBM mainframe, they also purchased everything needed to run the mainframe. This included not only the processors, disks, printers and other hardware, but also the software and applications such as databases, accounting, manufacturing and human resource applications. These applications were integrated out-of-the-box. There was no need for integration. However, there also were no best-of-breed applications and not many options for customers to choose from.

Two technology disruptions changed the IBM mainframe-dominated computing landscape. The first was the emergence of increasingly powerful minicomputers, followed by personal computers and servers. The second was the development of UNIX and other operating systems to power this new breed of computers, followed by the rise of Microsoft Windows. These new technologies contributed to the development of application software and other programs by independent software vendors (ISVs) that did not run on mainframes. Companies now had a choice. As software from the ISVs matured, it encroached upon the domain of the mainframe. Starting first from small departmental applications, ISV software grew into mainstream applications. This trend accelerated with the development of client/server technology that resulted in the emergence of major new ISVs such as Oracle, SAP, PeopleSoft, Siebel and numerous others.

The emergence of the ISVs fostered tremendous competition, choice and the rise of best-of-breed applications in each category. Instead of buying all their applications from IBM, companies now could mix and match. In order to meet their needs in each application category (database, manufacturing/MRP, financial/accounting, HR management, etc.), customers could purchase from any ISV who they determined had the best solution in the category. This was a major step forward for companies and a boon for the ISVs that engendered competition and innovation that drove the software industry in the late 1980s through the 1990s.

The emergence of the best-of-breed applications developed by competing ISVs resulted in the creation of new challenges. The most serious of these challenges was the emergence of function-specific *application silos* that evolved in more or less isolation with other function-specific applications. The ISVs focused on innovation, new features and increasing the performance for their own applications with little or no regard to how these applications would interact with other applications developed by other ISVs. In the competitive environment and the quest of delivering best-of-breed solutions, the ISVs created their own data formats, communication protocols, user interfaces and terminology. As companies adopted and deployed these applications they became *silos* or *islands of automation* as illustrated in Figure 3.1.

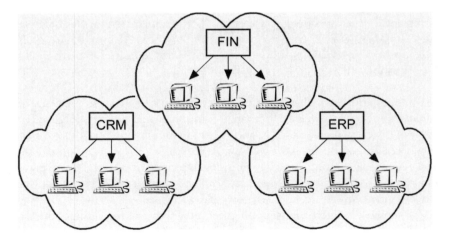

Figure 3.1. Enterprise Applications are Islands of Automation

While the functionality inside the application was tightly integrated and seamless, there was little or no capability for interaction with other applications that were also deployed in the organization. This evolution was more or less similar to the emergence of best-of-breed personal productivity applications such as word processors and spreadsheets. The latter improved productivity of individual users who worked as *islands of automation*, whereas enterprise applications improved the productivity of department or specific solutions without any concern for how they would interact with other applications.

In the beginning the lack of interoperability between enterprise applications was not a major impediment to the growth of best-of-breed applications. Companies were focused on automating specific departmental functions such a human resources, accounting, finance, or sales force automation. Most companies were organized along departmental lines and their functions did not span departmental boundaries. However, several things changed this situation:

- After deploying the initial wave of departmental solutions, companies realized that simply automating departmental functions limited the opportunities for improving company productivity. In many cases, the same data had to be entered into different systems. Likewise, the information necessary to measure corporate performance was often present in multiple locations, resulting in inefficient manual efforts to generate reports.

- Beginning in the early 1980s, businesses experienced successive waves of quality and productivity improvement initiatives. These started with Total Quality Management (TQM), which was quickly followed by ISO 9000, reengineering, downsizing and finally Six Sigma. These initiatives created an acute awareness among business thought leaders that business processes span departments, and that to improve productivity required the improvement of inter-department processes. To improve and streamline these processes it was important to interconnect the *islands of automation* to facilitate the seamless flow of information. The emergence of e-business concepts in the late 1990s extended the need for interconnection to include disparate systems owned by suppliers and other trading partners so that they could also be included as important role players in the business processes.

The first attempts to integrate the silos were *point solutions*, as illustrated in Figure 3.2. After deploying best-of-breed applications, a company would develop specific and proprietary interfaces between the applications. This was a very expensive proposition for two reasons:

1. The cost of developing custom integrations was very high. Each application had to be interfaced with every other application that it needed to interact with, and this was a complex and costly endeavour.

2. The switching cost was prohibitive. Once a company integrated its applications, they could not justify switching their applications, or sometimes even to upgrade to newer versions of the individual applications.

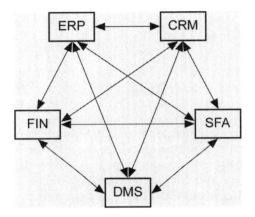

Figure 3.2. Point Integration Solution

EAI products emerged in response to this need for integration. Early EAI solutions were simply adaptors or connectors that enabled specific applications to integrate with other applications. However they quickly evolved to provide complete solution frameworks for integration. The common technique used by EAI products is to provide a unified integration framework or platform that addresses these four key requirements of integration:

1. *Interface Standardization:* Every application has its own methods of allowing third-party applications to exchange information. These methods are in essence the *language* that is used to communicate with the application. EAI products provide interface standardization by offering a single, unified interface and connectors for each application that map and convert the proprietary interface of the application to standard interfaces. It therefore provides a *common language* and *adaptors* from the proprietary language to the universal language. This is graphically illustrated in Figure 3.3. EAI is a translation layer between a given application and

third-party applications. Third-party applications can provide a single connector to the integration platform. They can then integrate with all other third-party applications that have connectors for the integration platforms. EAI vendors, working in conjunction with ISVs, developed a large number of connectors for a variety of applications commonly used by their customers.

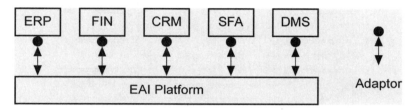

Figure 3.3. Using an EAI Platform for Integration

2. *Data Transformation:* Every application saves information internally in it its own format. Some applications save information in binary, others in ASCII text, and perhaps others in formats that are unique to their requirements. If one application can communicate with another through standardized interfaces, it is still important that the data from the transmitting application be converted into the format understood by the receiving application. This is accomplished through data transformation and is an important function provided by EAI products.

3. *Mapping:* Applications use different terminology. One might use the word "order" and another might use the term "purchase order" to identify the same information. When these applications exchange information with each other, it is important to *map* or associate information fields in one application with corresponding fields in the other that represent the same information. In some cases, the mapping may also involve decomposing the information into constituent parts that can be paired with equivalent pieces of information in the other application. For example, one application might retain "Address" as a piece of information, and assumes that the address includes Street Address, City, Zip Code, State and Country. The other application may have specific and somewhat different information elements for each component of the address. Mapping is a capability provided by EAI products that facilitates association between different pieces of information and decomposing information so that it can be interchanged meaningfully. Mapping and decomposition is graphically illustrated in Figure 3.4.

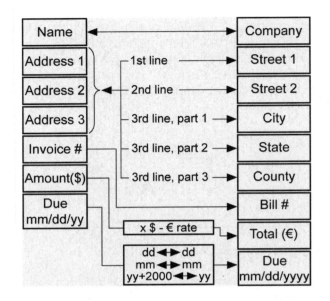

Figure 3.4. Mapping, Transformation and Decomposition

4. *Synchronization:* There are a variety of ways in which software applications interact with each other. First, an application may simply be looking for data from another application. Second, the application may be sending data to the other application and receive an acknowledgement that the data has been received. Third, one application may be sending data to a second application, and at the same time asking the other application to take some specific actions with the data and then send some resulting data back. In all these cases there may be some latency between the request and the response. EAI tools provide the means to synchronize the interaction between applications. In some cases the interaction may be synchronous, i.e., a calling application makes a request and waits for the called application to respond. In other cases the integration may be asynchronous, i.e., the calling application makes a request and then proceeds without waiting for a response. When a response becomes available, the calling application is notified and it can take appropriate action based on the response.

By providing standard connectors and adaptors and a means of data transformation, mapping and synchronization, EAI applications provide a framework for a variety of applications to interact with each other. Each application only needs to provide an adaptor or connector to the EAI platform. Once this is available, the application can theoretically be interfaced with any other application that has a connector for the EAI platform. EAI, therefore, provides the glue that binds the islands of automation created by function-specific enterprise applications, and plays a role identical to what groupware and workflow automation play for combining human islands of automation.

It is important to note that even though EAI platforms provide a significant amount of functionality and ease the task of integration, the integration is not simple and "out-of-the-box." EAI products are fairly expensive and require a considerable amount of consulting services from specialized companies known as systems integrators to ensure that complex enterprise applications can be integrated and work together.

EAI and Business Processes

Once companies have integrated their applications, the next obvious challenge is that in many cases a piece of information needs to be routed to different applications as a part of a structured process. For example, a company may have a Sales Force Automation (SFA) application that it uses to manage the selling team and its processes. When a new order is received, the name of the customer and the order information has to be moved from the SFA application to the customer relationship (CRM) application. Some parts of this information may also need to be sent to the ERP system and the accounting system. If the order amount is more than $5,000 (for example), the credit department may need to be notified so that it can obtain credit approval. Furthermore, if some exception is encountered in the process, such as an incorrectly configured order, people may need to get involved to handle the exception. When the product is actually shipped, all the systems have to be updated with a variety of information. All of this involves a process that moves data between systems as a part of a specific and well-defined series of activities. Such a process is graphically illustrated in Figure 3.5. High-end EAI solutions by vendors such as Web Methods and TIBCO provide a business process engine that controls the routing of information as directed by a well-defined process map.

Several characteristics are immediately obvious about the application integration process:

1. It involves a series of tasks that are performed in series or in parallel.

2. In most cases each task is performed by an application.
3. If there is an exception that requires human intervention, a task may be performed by an individual.
4. Business rules are associated with the processes that dictate the routing or flow.

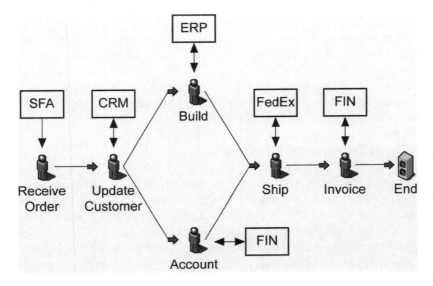

Figure 3.5. An EAI Business Process

These characteristics reveal that there is a great deal of similarity between workflow processes and EAI-driven processes, with the notable exception that one deals primarily with applications and the other with people. This similarity causes casual observers to confuse EAI and workflow, and lump them into a generic BPM category of products. Experience has shown that the challenges associated with automating human interactions and automating system interactions are very different. At the same time, technology trends are minimizing the gap between these systems and forcing a convergence.

The Benefits of EAI

EAI products help organizations in many ways:

1. The most important benefit of EAI is that companies no longer need proprietary, point-to-point integration. Instead they can deploy an EAI platform that can integrate their best-of-breed applications for which adaptors are most likely available and provided by the vendors of those applications.
2. The use of standard adaptors and EAI also means that if the vendor upgrades the application, the customer can upgrade to the new version without the cost of re-writing the integration code.
3. Even if some of the applications do not have an adaptor for the EAI platform they have selected, they have to develop a proprietary connector to this application. Once this adaptor is developed, integrating with the other applications becomes somewhat easier.
4. EAI platforms provide flexibility to companies that deploy these solutions. These companies are no longer tied to specific best-of-breed applications. They can switch to other applications as long as these new applications have adaptors for the EAI platform. Of course, this must be done with due diligence because not only are enterprise applications expensive by themselves, but also the cost of integrating a new application, even with an EAI product already installed, is still significant.
5. EAI solutions provide process management capabilities that enable companies to automate Straight-Through Processing (STP) as a part of a business process. Straight-Through Processing refers to moving data between systems without any human involvement. This capability means that not only are applications integrated, but also the movement of data between applications is automated as a part of a well-defined business process. For these reasons EAI provides many of the benefits that are associated with BPM systems.

Workflow Automation versus EAI

The many similarities between EAI and workflow automation stem from the fact that both types of products deal with business processes. EAI's goal is to execute business processes that span applications, whereas workflow automation is targeted at people-centric processes. The most helpful way to overcome the confusion resulting from these similarities is to compare and contrast between the two. Their seven major differences result from the different problems that they are trying to solve:

1. *Speed:* EAI systems move data between applications. Therefore they

have to work at very fast computer speeds. A delay of a few seconds could cause significant bottlenecks in application-centric processes that typically involve very high volumes. On the other hand, workflow automation products move information between people. They have to work at the speed of people. A delay of a few seconds in moving a task from one person to another will not be noticeable, because in real life people interact with one another with response times measured in minutes, hours or even days.

2. *User Interface:* EAI products do not require any human user interface for the participants in the processes that are computer applications. Applications interact with data, and not with human-friendly interfaces. Workflow automation applications, on the other hand, deal with people. The user interface and presenting data in a useful and user-friendly fashion are major challenges of workflow automation solutions.

3. *Number of Participants:* A medium-sized organization does not have a very large number of applications that need to be integrated through EAI. If there are 20 applications that would be a lot. Thus the number of participants who play roles in an EAI process is limited. Business processes handled by workflow automation solutions, by contrast, involve large numbers of people that can easily run in to the hundreds. Each of these participants has different roles and relationships that impact the logic of business processes.

4. *Exceptions:* Applications are generally available when they are needed. They do not take vacations, go off on holidays, or want to reassign their work to some other application. An EAI solution, therefore, does not have to handle a large number of exceptions resulting from their lack of availability. People, on the other hand, can be absent from work for a variety of reasons, and in many cases want to consult with others or reassign their tasks to others. A workflow automation solution, therefore, has to deal with a large number of process-specific and people-centric exceptions.

5. *Business Rules:* EAI processes have a substantial number of business rules that dictate the flow of information among various applications as defined by the process. Workflow automation systems have many more business rules because people participate in a process with different roles, responsibilities and skill levels. Workflow automation solutions have to have complex business rules engines to handle this diversity.

6. *Data Transformation and Mapping:* Data transformation and mapping is a basic requirement of EAI. Without this capability an EAI product would have limited value. However, data transformation and mapping

is not a basic requirement of workflow automation. In a sense, the user interface presented by a workflow automation solution serves the purpose of data transformation and mapping in a workflow automation solution. The user interface translates and maps the information into a form that makes sense to the user.

7. *Primary Value Proposition:* The primary value proposition of an EAI solution is application integration. Organizations invest in EAI solutions because they want to integrate their applications. Process automation comes after the integration. On the other hand, the key value proposition of workflow automation is process automation. Integration with applications is important but is subservient to process automation.

These differences between EAI and workflow automation solutions are summarized in Table 3.1. Understanding these differences makes it possible to differentiate between the two product categories. At the same time, newer BPM systems provide technology to address both human-centric workflow, application integration and more, thereby offering new possibilities for business.

Table 3.1. EAI versus Workflow Automation

	EAI	Workflow Automation
Speed	High	Moderate
User Interface	None	Extensive
Number of Participants	Small	Large
Number of Exceptions	Small	Large
Number of Business Rules	Moderate	Large
Data Transformation/Mapping	High	Low
Primary Value Proposition	Integration	Process automation

Conclusion

EAI is aimed at connecting the islands of automation represented by the silos of enterprise applications such as ERP, CRM and HR. It also accomplishes this by automating processes that dictate the flow and logic of data between these applications. While EAI and workflow automation appear similar on the surface, under the covers they are very different. The emergence of powerful Internet technologies such as Web services and the increasing processing power of computers and software are forcing these product categories to converge under the banner of Business Process Management.

Chapter 4

The Emergence of BPM

The BPM system is a new product category that combines EAI and workflow automation, and then extends them with two other categories: Business Process Modeling & Analysis, and process metrics. The evolving IT architecture of a modern organization leverages BPM to overcome the technical and business shortcomings of previous architectures. Understanding the most significant benefits of BPM help to explain why BPM is not a fad. It is destined to become even more prominent than other enterprise applications such as ERP, CRM and HR, all of which have become the mainstays of modern organizations.

The Convergence of Workflow Automation and EAI

Six major technology trends are forcing a convergence of EAI and workflow automation and giving rise to BPM:

1. Moore's Law: The first trend is the continued and unabated applicability of Moore's Law. First postulated by Gordon Moore of Intel Corporation, Moore's Law states that the computing power of processors will double every 18 months. This relentless improvement in processing power and speed has had a dramatic impact on all aspects of the computer and information technology industries, and EAI and workflow automation are no exceptions. Increasing processing power and speed means that relatively low cost servers can be used for deploying solutions capable of a very high number of transactions. Coupled with the development of server clustering (the ability to run many servers in parallel to perform the same tasks), Moore's Law is marginalizing speed or transaction volumes as a differentiator between EAI and workflow automation systems. Workflow automation systems designed and optimized for human-centric processes are now able to perform at speeds that are suitable for application-centric processes that were in the past relegated to EAI systems. Speed or transaction volume is no longer a feature that differentiates EAI from workflow automation.

2. Web Services: The second major trend is the emergence of Web Services as technology that has the potential of fundamentally reducing the cost and complexity of integrating disparate applications. In brief, Web Services technology promises to become the predominant method for applications to interact with each other, reducing the value proposition for expensive and proprietary EAI products as integration platforms. The result will be that workflow automation and EAI will converge into a single technology. With the availability of Web Services technology, workflow automation products will not have to rely on EAI to deploy application-centric business processes. To maintain their value proposition, EAI vendors will reposition their products to incorporate workflow automation applications.

3. Business Processes as Assets: The third trend is the realization among business managers that business processes are valuable corporate assets needing to be managed just as other business assets. Business processes have a lifecycle spanning their design, deployment and improvement. This trend started with the focus on Total Quality Management (TQM) in the 1980s. TQM was followed by ISO 9000 in the early 1990s that explicitly focused adopting organizations on the need to document their processes, and to ensure that the organization and its employees follow these processes. ISO 9000 was followed by the re-engineering wave championed by Hammer and Champy [5] among others, and stressed radical change in business processes. In the late 1990s, organizations led by GE and Motorola adopted the Six Sigma methodology that also focused on modeling, analyzing and improving processes in a continuous, iterative manner. All this energy focused on business processes has left an indelible impression in the minds of business leaders and managers that business processes are important, and they need to be managed and improved over time. As some business processes were digitized using solutions such as workflow automation and EAI, the concept of developing software to manage the lifecycle of these business processes was simply a natural progression.

4. Limitations of Embedded Workflow: In the late 1990s enterprise applications such as ERP, CRM and document management systems (DMS) began to incorporate simple workflow functionality into their core components. Several analysts predicted that workflow would simply become a part of these enterprise applications rather than a separate software entity. This was at a time when most workflow automation companies were very small in comparison with large enterprise software companies such as SAP and PeopleSoft that were setting the trend. The workflow functionality added to the enterprise application packages was designed in response to customer requirements and geared to improve the core functionality of these systems. This approach was adequate to handle the business processes embedded in these applications, but not for general-purpose workflow automation of all types of business processes. As a result this form of embedded workflow was very difficult and costly to expand outside the "silo" of the host application. One consequence was that if an organization deployed five enterprise applications for different functions, the organization ended up having to manage five workflow automation systems.

As a combination of applications working together, a BPM system requires a variety of different skills to manage. It is challenging enough to manage one such robust BPM system. It is extremely difficult and very expensive to manage multiple BPM systems to handle business processes as shown in Figure 4.1.

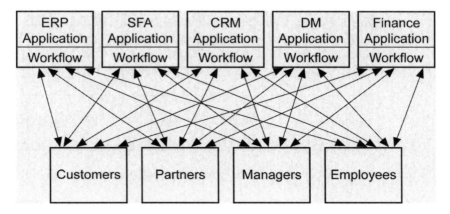

Figure 4.1. Embedded Workflow Is Difficult to Manage

It quickly became apparent to analysts and architects alike that what the organization needed was a robust BPM platform for managing business processes independent of the enterprise applications. At the same time, the BPM system must be able to interact with all of the enterprise applications as well as the employees, customers and partners of the organization. This separating out of business process management from enterprise applications is illustrated in Figure 4.2.

5. Process Modeling and Analysis Software: In parallel with the development of EAI and workflow automation, design and model business process software of all types has grown tremendously over the last decade. Process modeling software enables business owners and analysts to model and optimize business processes. It allows them to statistically evaluate the performance of their process under various scenarios, and change the design to optimize the processes for their unique scenarios. Advanced solutions such as ARIS from IDS Scheer go even further and model the resources available to the organization so that they can pinpoint bottlenecks in the processes or the resources of an organization. Process modeling software is a natural progression for BPM systems since it allows non-technical business people to define and optimize their processes before they are automated. Process modeling is the first stage in the business process lifecycle.

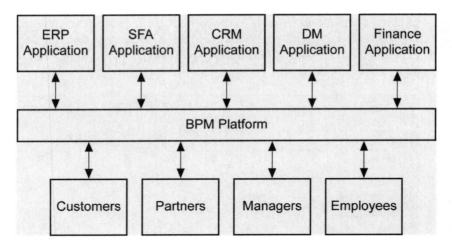

Figure 4.2. Standalone BPM Platform

6. Business Process Reporting Software: The capabilities and use of report generation and business intelligence software have increased tremendously in the past ten years, driven by the widespread use of SQL databases for saving business information. Because it is important to measure the performance of business processes, the emergence of sophisticated reporting and business intelligence software was also a natural addition to the capabilities offered by EAI and workflow automation solutions. It enables business people to understand the workload and performance of live running business processes.

The consequence of these six trends has resulted in the emergence of BPM systems as an integrated collection of applications that work together to manage business processes over their lifecycle as they are used or supported by both people and applications. Figure 4.3 illustrates the four major components of a BPM system: Business Process Modeling and Analysis (BPMA), EAI, workflow automation and business process reporting.

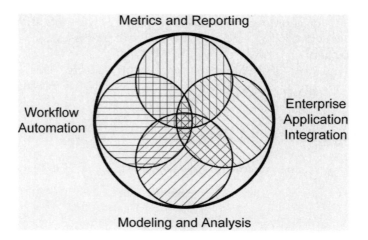

Figure 4.3. Major Components of a BPM System

BPM Defined

The definition of a business process combines the definitions of work-flow and EAI processes to cover all types of processes that span people as well as applications:

A business process is a sequence of tasks that are performed in series or in parallel by two or more individuals or applications to reach a common goal.

The definition of Business Process Management evolves from the definition of a business process:

Business Process Management is the discipline of modeling, automating, managing and optimizing business processes throughout their lifecycle to increase profitability.

Three things should be emphasized in this definition:

1. BPM is not only a product; it is also a discipline. It involves not only software applications, but also people. These include process owners, analysts, IT designers, developers and business users with different skills. Furthermore, BPM involves a methodology and a process-focused culture that exposes the dependence of all participants to each other in the process chain. The software part of BPM is referred to as a "BPM system."

2. BPM involves a number of activities that are important at different stages in the life of a business process. These activities are performed by people with different skills. While workflow automation and EAI

systems focus primarily on the *automation* of processes, a BPM system extends the scope to the *lifecycle management* of processes, including their automation.

3. The end goal of BPM is to improve profitability. This is an all-encompassing goal since profits can be increased by increasing demand or reducing cost.

Business Process Lifecycle

The lifecycle of a typical business process is illustrated in Figure 4.4.

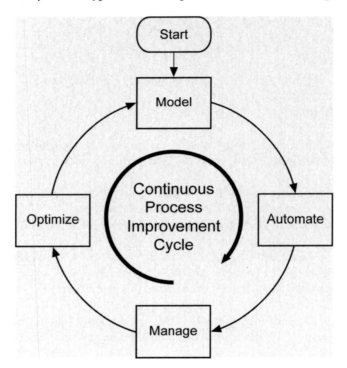

Figure 4.4. Business Process Lifecycle

It starts with someone coming up with the idea of defining a process to accomplish tasks that are performed again and again by a team of people and applications working together. The various stages of the lifecycle are as follows:

1. *Modeling:* The first stage is the design of a business process. This is generally the responsibility of business manages who own processes. In this stage the process is defined and a process map, or flow chart, is created. This effort is focused on documenting the process so that all who play a role in the life of the process will have a clearer understanding of its rules, responsibilities and purpose. In many cases, it is also advantageous to analyze and optimize the process before it is put to use.

2. *Automation:* In the second stage of the business process lifecycle, the process is automated so that it can be executed electronically instead of relying on paper and manual effort. At this stage IT designers are involved to convert business requirements defined in the modeling stage into a deployable application. If other systems are involved, this stage also involves developers who will develop integration using standards such as Web Services, XML or by custom coding or writing adaptors. Before the system is deployed, it must also be tested by quality assurance personnel.

3. *Management:* In the third stage of the process lifecycle, the automated process is deployed on the IT systems of the company and the participants, both people and automated systems, can actually start playing their roles in the live business process. This stage in the lifecycle also involves process managers who monitor the system and are available to handle any exceptions.

4. *Optimization:* The last stage of the business process lifecycle is optimization. In this stage, business owners and analysts use software tools to capture metrics from the BPM system that provide information about costs and performance bottlenecks. They can then use these metrics to optimize the process by changing resources or changing the definitions or rules that govern the process.

The last stage is not the end of the life of the business process. As depicted in Figure 4.4, after the process is optimized it goes through the same steps again in the cycle of continuous improvements. A variety of individuals participate in the various stages of the process lifecycle. Chapter 10, "BPM Process Development," provides a detailed discussion of the lifecycle by focusing on the software that a BPM system provides for the users at each stage.

The Benefits of BPM

Business process management offers numerous tangible and intangible benefits to organizations. As the technology improves and matures, the magnitude of the benefits will increase. Thomas M. Koulopoulos, an early thought leader in the workflow space, titled his book *The Workflow Imperative* [2]. According to Koulopoulos, the benefits of workflow automation are so compelling that adoption of workflow is not an option. It is necessary for the survival of every organization. These same benefits carry over and are extended by BPM. Numerous other industry observers and analysts have documented the many tangible and intangible benefits of BPM [3], [4], [5]. The most significant practical benefits are summarized below.

1. Speed.

When Bill Gates titled his book *Business @ the Speed of Thought* [6] he was thinking, in part, about business process management. While the title of the book is somewhat of a hyperbole, BPM does indeed increase the speed of business processes significantly. To understand how the speed of a business process is increased the process can be decomposed to determine the time it takes to complete each step. For example, consider Figure 4.5.

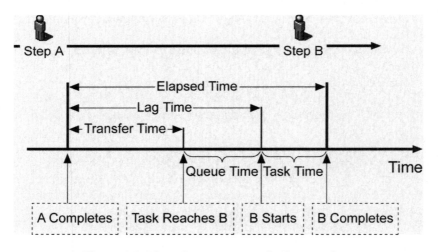

Figure 4.5. Time Components of a Process Step

Figure 4.5 represents two steps of a business process and shows the various components of time from the instant Step A is completed to the instant Step B is completed:

1. *Transfer Time:* Without business process automation, a business process relies upon paper forms, folders and documents that are transferred manually or via mail from the user who completes Step A to the user who completes Step B. The time consumed for doing this is called transfer time. Transfer time is dead time. It does not add any value to the business process. By facilitating electronic transfer of forms and documents, BPM does indeed reduce transfer time to zero.

2. *Queue Time:* When the task reaches the user for Step B, it will likely sit in the in-basket, or the task queue, of the user until the user gets around to working on it. This is called the queue time and is also dead time because no work is being done and no value is being added to the process. Business process management cannot eliminate the queue time. However, it can help to reduce it in a number of ways. A BPM system can provide e-mail notification for new tasks as a heads-up to the user. If the user does not perform a task in a timely fashion, it can also send late notifications via e-mail. In cases of extreme neglect, a task can be escalated and brought to the attention of a supervisor who can take corrective actions. These alerts are difficult and costly to implement without BPM.

3. *Task Time:* This is the actual time that the user at Step B takes to perform the task. This is the only productive time where the user is adding value to the process by making a decision, reviewing information or adding information. BPM cannot eliminate this time, but can help reduce it by (a) providing only information relevant for the task, (b) facilitating electronic access to information or documents needed to perform the task, and (c) providing electronic verifications to ensure that the information entered by the user is complete and consistent. This reduces task time by ensuring that the process does not have to return from a downstream step due to inconsistent or incomplete information.

The sum of the transfer time and queue time is sometimes also called the *lag time*, since it is a measure of the lag, or delay, between the completion of Step A and the start of work on Step B. By adding the transfer time, queue time and task time for each step in a business process the total time for completing the entire business process can be determined.

Analysts who study business processes report that lag time represents 90% of the total time consumed by a typical business process, while the remaining 10% is consumed by the task time, as depicted in Figure 4.6.

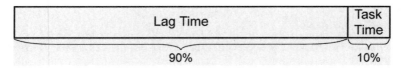

Figure 4.6. Lag Time versus Task Time

For example, when one applies for a mortgage at a lending institution, it may take two to three weeks for the loan to be processed. It is hard to imagine that during these two weeks the lending institution's staff was working 100% of the time on the application. Most of the time it was being routed from one step to another (transfer time), or waiting in the inbox (queue time) of the loan processors.

Figures 4.7 and 4.8 illustrate the most significant benefits of BPM. Figure 4.7 demonstrates that even if you improve the task time by 50%, the overall process time for the business process will only improve by 5%.

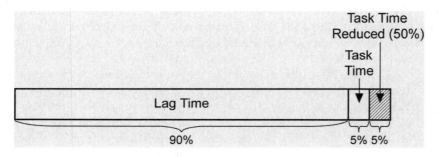

Figure 4.7. Reducing Task Time by 50% Reduces Overall Time by Only 5%

On the other hand, if you can improve the lag time by 50%, the overall process time will decrease by 45%, as shown in Figure 4.8.

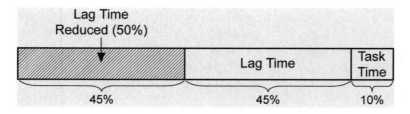

Figure 4.8. Reducing Lag Time by 50% Reduces Overall Time by 45%

Personal productivity software such as word processors, spreadsheets, and e-mail do indeed improve the task time. However, the impact they have on the overall process time is often insignificant. BPM systems attack the lag time, and the impact on the overall business process is dramatic.

The Lag Time Anomaly. The managing director of a large oil refinery, though an oil executive and not an IT person, is a strong champion of IT and fervently championed new technology. Under his leadership the company had only recently made the switch from mainframes to desktop computers. However, the managing director was a bit discouraged that even though his company had invested a significant amount of money for providing desktops to everyone in the company, tasks still took the same amount of time, and perhaps maybe even a bit longer. To his chagrin, he could not report observing any improvements in productivity that could justify the investments the company had made.

This is a classic example of the lag time anomaly. By investing purely in personal productivity solutions, the company attacked task time that contributed only a small percent of the overall problem. In fact, the introduction of desktop computers and office automation software probably slowed things down as the staff went through the learning process on how to use the new tools. What the company failed to do was to understand their business processes and deploy technology to reduce the lag time, and thereby perceptibly improve overall process time to completion.

2. Satisfaction Through Feedback

Being a control freak is a mark of humankind—the human brain and the nervous system are the most elegant and responsive of control systems. Everything that people do is based upon feedback and control. People eat until they are satisfied. They try to cool themselves until they no longer feel hot. If they touch something hot, they immediately try to end the contact so that they will not burn. They take actions to satisfy their needs, and their nervous systems provide instant feedback. If the need is not satisfied by their actions, they are either frustrated or miserable. They seek instant gratification. The longer the delay the greater is their misery or frustration.

When people deal with organizations, their desire for instant gratification is put to the test. They interact with organizations because they have some need that they wish to satisfy. Since they do not easily differentiate between interaction with the physical world around them and dealing with an organization, they have the same expectations for instant gratification when they deal with the latter.

Dealing with organizations necessitates dealing with the business processes of the organization. People request information, order goods or services, issue complaints or seek employment. If the organization responds quickly, they are satisfied even if the response may not be what they are seeking (and vice versa). All these interactions touch the business processes of the organization.

By reducing the lag time, BPM speeds up the business processes of an organization. It enables an organization to quickly and effectively provide feedback to internal employees and external customers. It also facilitates the completion of the processes in a timely fashion that is consistent with the feedback expectations engrained in humans. By providing fast response, BPM systems help satisfy the need for instant gratification that is directly proportional to the satisfaction of customers and employees.

3. Parallelism

When business processes are implemented manually, the most common practice is to route tasks sequentially to various participants. This happens despite the fact that many steps in the process could be performed in parallel. There are two reasons for the reliance on sequential routing:

1. It is easier and convenient to control a business process if it is sequential rather than parallel. The more parallel steps there are the more difficult it is to control.
2. Manual business processes rely on paper forms and documents. Information carried on paper cannot be easily split into many parallel paths, then recombined at the end.

BPM systems enable the performance of tasks in parallel by removing these two limitations. A modern BPM system has no difficulty controlling and synchronizing a large number of parallel steps. Electronic information can be easily split into components and sent to a number of individuals or applications that can perform the tasks in parallel. When tasks are completed, the information can be re-combined and used in subsequent steps.

Parallelism can significantly reduce the process time for many business processes. This is illustrated by a simple example of a request review process. Let us assume that after a request is initiated by someone (the Initiator), it must be reviewed by three other individuals (Review A, B and C), and then is sent to the manager for final approval (the Approval step). The typical manual way of implementing such a process is to do it serially as shown in Figure 4.9.

Initiate   Review A   Review B   Review C   Approval

Figure 4.9. Request Review Process Implemented in Series

The three Review steps could actually be done in parallel, but the process is not implemented in parallel since it is difficult to coordinate parallel steps when conducted by people. The total time to complete the process is the sum of the time consumed by all five steps. Figure 4.10 illustrates the same process, but steps A, B, and C are now implemented in parallel by using a workflow automation system that makes it very easy to coordinate parallel steps.

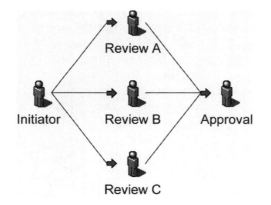

Figure 4.10. Request Review Process Implemented in Parallel

It is easy to see that the process time is reduced by the sum of the smaller two of step A, B or C. Business processes should be designed with parallel steps whenever practical in order to reduce process time.

4. Process Integrity, Accountability and Visibility

One of the major challenges facing organizations today is the sheer volume of business processes. As organizations grow, become global, and serve a larger number of customers, the burden of processing a large volume of process incidents increases proportionally. If the processes are not automated and rely upon human intervention, the response time as well as the integrity of the processes suffers. People make mistakes. The greater the volume the greater is the chance of making mistakes. Similarly, the chances of mistakes increase in proportion to the complexity of the rules that control the processes.

One of the biggest advantages of business process management is the elimination of manual intervention in business processes for the purpose of enforcing rules. Computers are ideal for rules-based decision making as long as the rules have been carefully and correctly defined. Once the rules have been defined, a BPM system can ensure that the business process performs according to the rules without bias. This makes it possible for an organization to handle increasing volume consistently and reliably.

Managers are trained to *manage by exception*. Computers are even better at handling exceptions as long as the exceptions and the resulting actions can be defined. A BPM system enables companies to *automate the exceptions* as much as possible so that the business process itself can handle them. Business process management helps change the role of management from handling exceptions to providing a higher level of value-add by refining and owning the rules that control business processes, and consequently the value that these processes deliver to the organization.

ISO 9000 was one of the most significant quality initiatives of the late 20th century, and is still a widely used quality methodology in many industries, especially manufacturing. The essence of ISO 9000 is best expressed by the slogan "Say what you do, and do what you say." Business processes define what organizations do, and BPM ensures that they do what they say by automating and managing the processes. Thus it is not surprising that some BPM products were developed as a response to ISO 9000 initiatives, and evolved from there.

5. Process Optimization

BPM not only automates business processes, it also provides the ability to measure the time and cost of each step in a business process. This enables a modern BPM system to generate process metrics based on actual data. While business process re-engineering tries to optimize business processes by a priori estimation of the time or cost budgets of various steps in a process, a BPM system captures this actual data. The real-life data can then be used to optimize the business process in several ways:

1. Process metrics enable the owners of the business process to assess the

overall cost of the business process and compare it with the benefits delivered.

2. Metrics enable management to determine the time and cost of the business process in specific departments of the company. This provides management a measure of the productivity of the organization.
3. Metrics can be used to add or remove resources allocated for performing the tasks that belong to the business process based on actual performance as compared to expectations.
4. Metrics may also be used to establish realistic expectations for the beneficiaries of the process. Establishing realistic expectations generally translates to higher satisfaction.

The Six Sigma methodology for process improvement is another widely used methodology in many leading corporations. The essence of Six Sigma is the concept of DMAIC, or Design, Measure, Automate, Improve and Control. When Six Sigma is applied to business processes, as opposed to manufacturing processes, the success of these initiatives is strongly related to the ability to automate these processes using BPM. Modern BPM systems provide the tools for design, measurement, analysis, improvement and control of business processes. The role of BPM tools for Six Sigma initiatives is discussed in detail in Chapter 8, "Business Process Modeling and Analysis."

6. Incorporate Customers and Partners

Business process management relies on electronic means of implementing business processes and using the power of computers to control them. One of the powers of the electronic media is that it enables a business process to reach outside the organization and permit customers and partners to actively participate. With the rapid emergence of BPM over the Web and the ubiquitous reach of the Internet, there are endless possibilities for collaboration and teamwork with customers and partners without distance being an impediment. This again shortens the cycle time and helps bring customers and partners closer to the organizations. They are not merely silent players whose satisfaction depends on how a faceless organization manages its business processes. Instead, they become active participants in a team through automated business processes that provide the comfort of feedback, and quick gratification through reduced process time.

As participants in a company's business processes, customers and partners can provide numerous benefits to the organization:

1. They have empathy for the needs and constraints of the organization.
2. They become more actively engaged in processes that are of value to the organization.
3. They are tightly integrated in the web of the organization. As such they perceive themselves not as adversaries, but as team players and collaborators; employees focus on the same goals as the organization.

7. Organizational Agility

The modern business environment is very dynamic and competitive, and it will continue to become more so as the Internet and globalization continue to expand. For organizations to succeed in this environment, it is important their business processes be able to adjust rapidly to new requirements and to the pressure of change. It is very difficulty to change business processes that depend entirely on human effort to ensure their performance and integrity, and the single most important contributor to this inertia is the necessity and cost of introducing change.

Business process management provides an excellent means for achieving organizational agility. Business processes are automated using software that is readily configurable. When processes change it is relatively easy to change the rules, roles and relationships that define these processes. As BPM technology evolves, it will become even easier to modify these processes in response to changes in the competitive environment or business strategy. One can foresee a day when business processes will evolve using adaptive learning technologies and more powerful business engines that facilitate change in rapid response to external or internal stimuli.

Conclusion

BPM is dramatically changing the paradigm of how organizations conduct their business. It is an essential technology for companies seeking to increase their productivity and competitiveness in the 21st century. Modern BPM systems are complete solutions that combine and extend key elements of workflow automation and EAI to support any business process in the enterprise which involve people as well as systems. Organizations worldwide are already using BPM for agility, responsiveness to customers, and providing visibility and accountability to business processes of all types.

Chapter 5

Inside Business Processes

A business process is a sequence of tasks performed in series or in parallel by two or more individuals or applications to reach a common goal. In each business process there is the notion of flow and structure that controls the flow. A process map is a bird's eye view or flow chart of a business process that represents it graphically. Process maps used in BPM are, however, more than simple flow charts. While the graphical representation of a process flow is important, it is not sufficient to fully represent a process. To do that, many more details are needed. This is akin to zooming into areas of the map of a city to get more and more detailed information about the structure and functions of the major objects in the city. Process maps encapsulate a variety of other pieces of information that are necessary to automate the process. Looking inside fully developed process maps can reveal how they are used by BPM solutions to encapsulate business processes and how the various components relate to each other to completely define the process. Such exploration also reveals the salient properties and features of process maps that are necessary to represent real life business processes. This chapter explains conceptually how any business process can be rendered into a process map.

The chapter concludes by discussing some important features of process maps that are necessary for handling exceptions. Handling exceptions is one of the major hidden challenges of BPM since they generally surface only after an organization is well on its path to automation, but are the major causes of complexity. Exceptions are what make business process automation a real challenge.

Process Maps

A process map is a graphical representation of a business process. It describes the step-by-step sequence of tasks that have to be performed in order to take one case, or incident, of a business process from initiation to completion. The purpose of a well-defined process map is to graphically illustrate the essence of the business process. By simply looking at it one should be able to determine the purpose and overall flow of the process.

The process map for the sample business process sketched in Figure 2.2 is presented in Figure 5.1. As the map shows, it is remarkably similar to the sketch in Figure 2.2. However, the similarity is misleading because there is a lot of process logic that is encapsulated inside a process map. By itself, the process map defines the default flow of the business process under normal conditions. The map shows that after a user initiates an incident by completing the Request step, the next step is the Supervisor step. After the Supervisor step the process takes one of three paths depending on whether it has been approved and the amount of the purchase. Likewise, if the recipient of the Supervisor step returns the incident because of incorrect or incomplete information, the process will go back to the Request step. The *flow*, or the sequence of steps after the Supervisor step, is readily apparent.

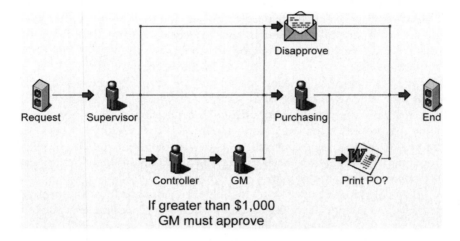

Figure 5.1. Process Map of Simple Purchase Requisition Process

From this simple example it can be discerned that a process map is made up of the following components:

1. *Steps:* A step represents a discrete task in the process that is performed by an individual, group of individuals, a sub-process or a computer application. In reality, more than one task may be performed at the same step. The exact breakdown or granularity of the tasks performed at each step is a decision best made by the process designer or analyst. The important point is that a step represents one or more tasks that are performed together before the process can move on to the next step. Since a step or task in a process can be performed by individuals, applications or other processes, steps can be of three different types: user steps, application steps or sub-process steps. In Figure 5.1, the Request, Supervisor, Controller, Purchasing and GM are user steps since individuals perform these tasks. The Disapprove and Print PO steps are automated application steps that are used to send an e-mail notification

and print the purchase order using third-party applications. The attributes of different step types are discussed individually later in this chapter.

2. *Links:* Links join steps together to indicate the flow of the process from one step to another. Links provide directional information. They originate at one step and end at another. This indicates that when the originating step is completed, the destination step is activated and the work flows from the originating step to the destination step. In Figure 5.1, the Request step is linked to the Supervisor step to represent the fact that when the Request step is completed, the Supervisor step will be invoked. Links also signify the default path that the process will take when any step is returned. For example, a user may receive a task but cannot complete it because of the lack of some information or the need for clarification. The user will want to "return" the process instead of simply aborting the case. As discussed later, business rules may be used under some special conditions to change the default path of the process as it proceeds forward or returns.

3. *Junctions:* Junctions are *dummy* steps. They do not represent a task. However they perform very useful functions in process maps since they can be used to represent *forks in the road* where a process path splits into multiple paths, or multiple paths converge into one. In some BPM solutions, junction steps can have *event condition tables* associated with them. These condition tables essentially represent the rules that dictate the path that the process will take based upon conditions that have been defined for the business process. The use of junction steps for effective process design will be discussed in a later section.

4. *Anchors:* Anchors are graphical artifacts that are used to change the direction of links in a process map. Their sole purpose is to provide a clear representation of the process. In the example in Figure 5.1, anchors are placed at several points to straighten the links and improve readability of the process map. Anchors are also useful for combining multiple process paths into one path to make it easier to represent complex process maps. Figure 5.2 and 5.3 illustrate this benefit. Figure 5.2 shows a section of a process map that has four steps: A, B, C and D. After the completion of any of these steps, the process has to activate all three of the following steps: E, F and G. The sheer number of links makes the map unnecessarily complex in appearance.

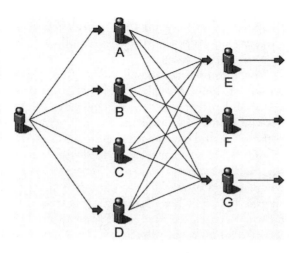

Figure 5.2. A Process Map Without Anchors

By using anchors, the process map can be greatly simplified as illustrated in Figure 5.3.

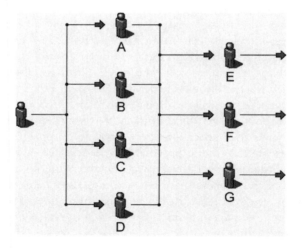

Figure 5.3. A Process Map With Anchors

5. *Labels:* Labels uniquely identify each step in a process map. They can also be used to display annotations on the map for explanations or clarifications.

6. *Conditions:* Every business process must deal with special conditions and exceptions. The number of special conditions and exceptions increases with the size of the organization. A process map uses conditions to enable process designers to effectively encapsulate business rules and exceptions. Conditions are discussed separately in this chapter because of their importance.

7. *Process Variables:* Process variables are the pieces of information related to a process that a BPM solution uses in order to make decisions or take actions. Business processes deal with a wide variety of data in different formats. A majority of the business data routed by a BPM solution is contained in other systems that are connected to the BPM solution, such as databases, electronic document management systems, and record management systems. However, business processes must have easy and real-time access to a subset of this information that can be used to make decisions about routing and flow that is *context aware* and based on the business information that is being routed or gathered. Process variables provide a mechanism for doing this and making routing decisions dynamic and sensitive to real-time business information. Process variables will be discussed in more detail in this chapter.

8. *Forms:* Electronic forms provide the user interfaces for the participants of business processes. Modern BPM solutions route information to the participants. Forms are the *windows* that enable users to review the information, enter new data or make decisions. It should be noted that EAI systems do not use forms because the participants in EAI processes are computer applications rather than individuals. For EAI systems, the equivalent functionality is provided by data transformation and mapping that allows information provided by one application to be transformed and mapped to corresponding information fields in third-party applications. Data transformation and mapping is discussed in Chapter 3, "Enterprise Application Integration."

User Steps

User steps represent tasks in a business process that are performed by people using electronic forms or documents. A user step can be assigned to one user or a group of users. In the latter case, all members of the group may be required to perform the task in applications that require polling. For example, in a Quality Control process that is partially shown in Figure 5.4, the QA Audit step is assigned to the group QA Auditors. All QA auditors will receive the same electronic forms that they can use to input the results of their audits. The following step, labeled Final Approval, is assigned to one person who will review the results of the individual audits.

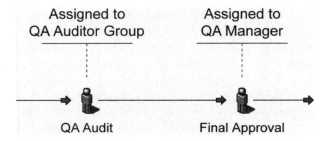

Figure 5.4. Parts of a Quality Audit Process Using Groups

Properties of User Steps

User steps have properties designed to make the BPM solution flexible. Some common properties are:

Recipient: This property specifies the user or group that will perform the task represented by the step. The ability to route the task to the right individual is one of the most important characteristics of a BPM solution. There are numerous ways of specifying and determining the recipient of a step. Because of the importance of routing workflow, Chapter 6, "Smart Ways of Routing Work," is devoted to this subject.

Time Limits: Modern BPM solutions allow process designers to define time limits for each step in the process. The solution ensures that if a time limit is exceeded, appropriate notifications or warnings are sent to the recipients or their supervisors (most commonly by e-mail). Advanced solutions also allow tasks to be escalated and re-routed to others when they become overdue. The purpose of a BPM solution is to ensure timely completion of processes. The ability to specify time limits ensures that tasks are performed on a timely basis.

Time limits can either be relative or absolute. Relative time limits specify the acceptable time for a task to be performed before it is escalated. For example, the relative time limit for a step may be specified as two days. When the step is activated, the software calculates the time when the step will become late by adding two days to the time when the step was activated. On the other hand, absolute time limits allow the process to be designed such that the time limit can be changed dynamically for each instance for meeting customer expectations. As an example, the initiator of a customer order process can enter the delivery requirements of the customer placing the order. The software can then calculate and assign absolute times for each step in the process so that the overall process can be completed in time to meet the customer's delivery requirement. This feature enables the step completion times to be established on the fly and change dynamically.

Advanced BPM solutions offer two level of late notifications and escalations. The first level is a warning to the recipient that the task will become late after a specified grace period. The second level is the actual escalation.

Delay Time: In many business processes it is necessary to delay a step by a specific time interval, or hold it until an absolute time. This is typically used when a process activity has to be synchronized with delays that are external to the process. For example, in a Loan Application process, after a credit report is requested, it might take an external credit agency several days to generate the credit report. Therefore, the application review activities may need to be suspended for several days pending the arrival of the credit report. A BPM solution can enable this by providing a "delay time" property that can be used to specify an absolute or relative time that the step is delayed before it is activated.

Conditions: Every business process has special conditions or exceptions that dictate the behavior of the process. Step conditions allow process designers to incorporate the rules governing these conditions and exceptions. Because of the importance of step conditions, they are discussed separately in this chapter.

The First Step: A Special Case

The first step in a process is a special case. The completion of the first step causes a new instance of the business process to be started. In order to support this capability, the first step has some additional properties that are useful for process design:

Initiation Rights: The right to initiate a business process may be reserved for a subset of the employees of the company. Not everyone may be allowed to start new instances. By definition, the recipients of the first step have the right to initiate new incidents of the process. Business process designers can specify an individual or a group that can complete the first step, and therefore only these recipients can cause new incidents to be started.

Anonymous Users Initiation: A company may want a large number of unknown users to be able to start a business process instance. For example, a government organization may develop a business process to allow members of the general public to issue request for services from its Web site. For such applications it is necessary to assign the first step to an *anonymous user* who is not identified *a priori.* Such users may need some unique method of identification and authentication that the BPM solution must be able to provide.

Application Initiation: In some cases a business process has to be started by another application. For example, a company may have an accounts receivables process that has to collect money from delinquent accounts. This process has to be triggered automatically by the accounting software when it determines that an account is delinquent. A BPM solution has to provide flexible means of starting processes from other applications. This will be discussed further in Chapter 13, "BPM and Application Integration."

Periodic Initiation: For many business processes it is necessary to start a new incident periodically. For example, time sheets must be completed biweekly and sales forecasts may be required at the start of each month. Instead of relying on users, it is much better for the BPM solution to do this automatically. Therefore, modern BPM solutions provide a method of specifying periodic initialization. If configured for periodic initialization, the BPM solution initiates new incidents of the process automatically at the specified periodic intervals.

Application Steps

Application steps represent tasks that are performed by third-party applications without human intervention. Some analysts refer to such steps as Straight Through Processing (STP) since they do not require any human involvement. A business process that is composed entirely of application steps is sometimes called an STP process. EAI business processes are composed almost entirely of application steps with only a few steps dealing with exception handling that are user steps. Since application steps do not involve people, a company can realize maximum return on investment by using application steps for as many tasks as practical.

When an application step is invoked process information is transferred to the third-party application along with specific instructions. The application then performs the tasks it is instructed to perform and returns information to the business process. These steps therefore provide a means of using business applications such as spreadsheets, word processors, e-mail, accounting, ERP and databases in business processes.

Properties of Application Steps

Application steps have properties designed to make them more useful and flexible for automating business processes. These include the following:

- *Recipient:* A BPM solution may offer agents or connectors for different desktop or enterprise applications. This property would specify the application agent or connector that will be invoked at a step in the process.
- *Location:* A business process may need to invoke a third-party application at different locations. For example, in an e-commerce fulfilment process, the shipping order for a particular item has to be printed at a different location depending on the warehouse the part is located in. The "location" property is used to specify this location.
- *Time Limits:* Like user steps, it is often necessary to allow process designers to define time limits for each application step in the process. This is useful in order to avoid stalling a process because of the failure of a third-party system. The BPM solution ensures that if the time limit is exceeded, appropriate notifications are sent to the process manager. Time limits can be either relative or absolute as discussed for user steps.
- *Delay Time:* In many cases it is necessary to delay a step by a specific time interval, or hold until an absolute time. This is typically when the activity has to be synchronized with delays that are external to the process. A BPM solution provides a "delay time" interval that can be used to specify an absolute or relative time that the step is to be delayed.

Sub-Process Steps

In many business processes it is often necessary for a *parent* process to call a *child* process. There are two reasons for this. First, one process may need to invoke another process that is owned by a different organization. In our example, the Purchase Order process shown in Figure 5.5 has to call a Parts Receiving process that is owned by the shipping and receiving department. Second, a business process may simply be too big. In this case it may be necessary to *chunk*, or break up a complex process into manageable sub-processes.

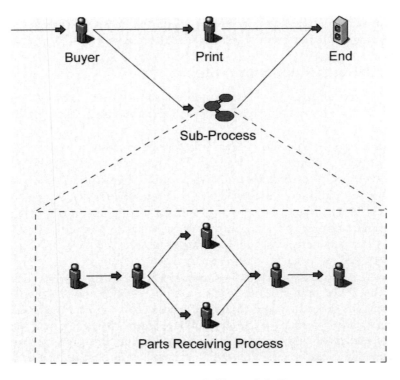

Figure 5.5. A Process Calling a Sub-Process

A sub-process step is used to represent and invoke a series of tasks that are performed by a sub-process. The sub-process may consist of one or more processes since sub-processes may call other sub-processes. When a parent process calls a sub-process, a new incident of a sub-process is invoked in response. Data from the parent process is passed to the sub-process that uses it for routing and decision-making. When the sub-process is complete, data from the sub-process is returned to the parent process.

Properties of a Sub-Process Step

Sub-process steps have properties that include the following:

- *Recipient:* This is the name of the sub-process that will be invoked at this step. It must be the name of another valid process.
- *Type:* Sub-processes may be invoked synchronously or asynchronously.

If a sub-process is invoked synchronously, the parent process waits at the sub-process step until the sub-process has been completed. In the asynchronous case, the process continues with subsequent steps without waiting for the sub-process to complete. This provides greater flexibility in automating business processes.

- *Repeat Count:* In many cases it is desirable to launch a sub-process multiple times, a feature also called "repeating sub-processes." An example of one such business process is provided below. The "repeat count" specifies the number of instances the sub-process will be invoked by the sub-process step.

A common business process is used to illustrate the use of "repeat count," and there are many examples of other business processes that have the same requirement. Every company has some form of Performance Review process for all employees on an annual or bi-annual basis. In many companies the normal process is that every month all employees whose anniversaries fall in that month are reviewed. This process actually consists of two separate processes:

1. At the start of the month, a Human Resource staff member creates a list of all employees whose anniversaries fall in that month. This list may have none, one or many employees.
2. For each employee in the list, the performance review process is initiated.

To implement this process requires the use of repeating sub-processes and may be implemented as illustrated in Figure 5.6. It consists of two processes: the Monthly Review List process and the Employee Review process, which is invoked by the former as a repeating sub-process. The Monthly Review List process is configured for periodic launch. It starts automatically on the first day of each month. The second step of this process is a Database step. In this step a database query is used to generate a list of all employees whose reviews are due in the current month, pertinent employee information and the name of their supervisors. The third step of the process is a repeating sub-process step. In this step, an Employee Review process is launched for each employee on the list.

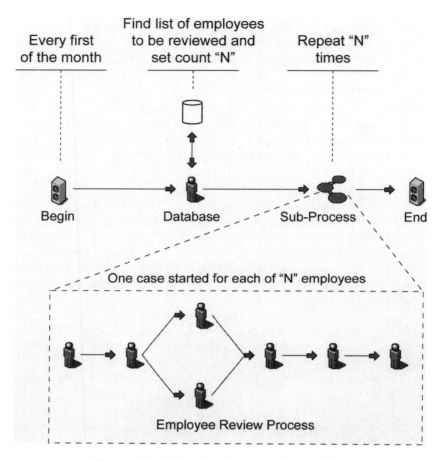

Figure 5.6. Calling Sub-Processes Repeatedly

Junction Steps

Junction steps in a business process are *dummy* steps since they are constructs to denote steps in a process that do not represent any task. Even though they do not represent any tasks, they can be very useful when developing sophisticated business processes. The four major benefits of junction steps are that they can be used to implement process joins, splits, conditions and iterations. These are described below.

Joins

In many process designs it is often necessary to join a number of parallel process paths into a single path. This can always be accomplished by using an ordinary user step at the junction point. However, doing so will invoke a user task. If the steps immediately after the join are to be determined based on a condition, it is not practical to use a user step for this purpose. Consider the process in Figure 5.7 as an example.

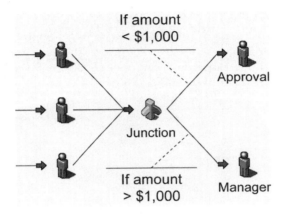

Figure 5.7. Using Junction Steps for Joins

This process has three paths which converge into a single path. When the three paths are joined, the process needs to activate the Approval step if the amount is less than $1,000 and the Manager step if the amount is more than $1,000. Such a process cannot be designed simply by placing a user step at the junction point. This is a good example where a junction step can be used as a process join. The Approval and Manager steps are immediately following the junction steps and can be invoked based on any conditions.

Splits

Splits are the reverse of joins. In many cases it is necessary to split a single process path in to a number or parallel paths. Junction steps can be used to implement such splits as shown in Figure 5.8. Again, while a user step could also be used to implement a split, the ability to use a junction steps provides additional flexibility that does not require a user step.

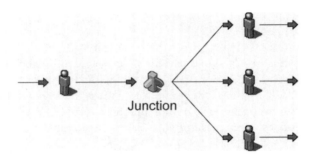

Figure 5.8. Using Junction Steps for Splits

To illustrate the power of using junction steps for joins and splits, consider the process illustrated in Figure 5.9.

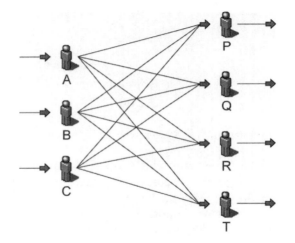

Figure 5.9. Process Map Without Splits and Joins

When any of the steps A, B or C are completed, it is desired that steps P, Q, R, and T be invoked. Since any of the first three steps can invoke the latter four steps, the resulting process map represents spaghetti if we do not have junction steps. However, by using junction steps as shown in Figure 5.10, the three parallel paths from step A, B, C and D can be joined by the junction steps, and then split to the four paths represented by steps P, Q, R and T.

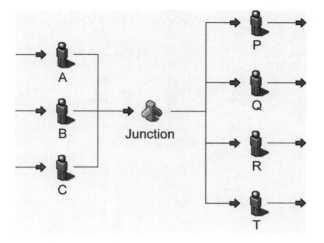

Figure 5.10. Process Map Simplified by Splits and Joins

Conditions and Actions

Some advanced BPM solutions allow junction steps to have conditions and actions. This means that a junction step can be invoked on a conditional basis. Furthermore, when a junction step has been executed, it can invoke other actions on a conditional basis. The ability to invoke other actions from within a junction step on a conditional basis provides the capability to implement complex logic and actions through the intelligent use of junction steps.

Iterations

In many process design situations it is necessary to invoke a collection of steps on a conditional basis. When these steps have completed, it is necessary to return to the point from where the collection of steps was invoked and proceed from there. Junction steps provide a good mechanism of implementing iteration as shown in Figure 5.11. Here the steps to be called on an iterative basis from various points in the main process are preceded by junction steps, then followed by another. Conditional logic within the junction steps controls the iterations in the step. When the iteration is complete, control returns back to the main process thread.

Since junction steps do not involve any tasks, they do not have recipients or completion times associated with them. However they may have "delay time" as a property, allowing these steps to be synchronized with other events similar to user steps and application steps.

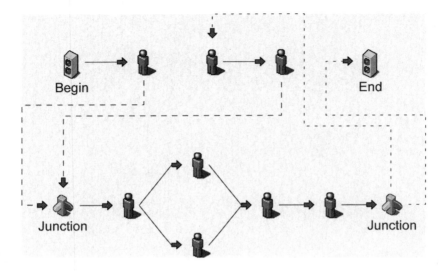

Figure 5.11. Using Junctions for Iterations

Process Variables

The purpose of business process automation is to route the right information to the right resource at the right time, so that the resource can make decisions or take actions. BPM is all about routing information in its many forms. Data, documents and images that appear as information externally to individuals are internally represented in a business process as process variables. These variables can contain actual data, pointers to database records, or reference numbers to electronic documents, images, voice and video files. A modern BPM solution must be proficient in two tasks:

1. Route variables to the various steps where the information contained or pointed by variables can be displayed, manipulated, or acted upon.
2. Provide a mechanism for acting upon the variable values in order to make decisions about the subsequent routing of the process. In other words, the BPM solution must be able to make decisions based upon the value of the variables. This is how an automated business process becomes *context-aware* and intelligent so that it can make decisions and interpret and enforce business rules without human intervention.

Process variables can be categorized into several different types depending upon the routing mechanism used by the BPM solution. The broad categories are:

- *Local Variables:* These are variables that are specific to one step in a business process. They are used for information retention and calculations at the step and are not transmitted to other steps.
- *Global Variables:* These are variables that are common to the entire business process. They are transmitted from one step to another. At any step they can be ignored, used or updated, based upon the requirements of the step.
- *System Variables:* These are variables that contain information generated by the BPM solution. These may include information such as the name of the business process, incident number, summary and priority.
- *Status Variables:* These are also variables generated by the BPM solution that typically provide information about the status of process steps. For example, at a particular step it may be important to determine the status of another step.

Process variables are sometimes used improperly as repositories for business information that the process is handling. This is improper for two reasons. First, process variables are generally transient and kept in memory in a binary data format that is optimized for speed and not easily accessible to external applications. If process variables are used as the sole repositories for business data, the data may not be readily available in real-time to external applications that could benefit from that data. In case of the failure of a BPM solution, it is possible to lose important business information. Second, the recommended method of saving business information is to use enterprise repositories such as databases, electronic document/image management systems, or electronic records management systems that are optimized and designed for saving such information. Process variables can be linked to content in these repositories so that information can be used, routed and updated during the course of the process, and also be available outside the BPM solution in real-time. This information can be also used through process variables to make decisions about routing business processes. The important point is that critical business information should be saved in enterprise repositories where it really belongs and associated with business processes through variables that carry pointers to the information.

Different BPM solutions have different methods of handling variables that optimize the performance of the software and maintain consistency with its design methodology.

Dealing with Exceptions: Event Condition Tables and Actions

Business processes in every organization are replete with rules, exceptions or special conditions. As the size of the organization increases, so does the number of exceptions. A BPM solution provides a method of incorporating these exceptions by taking actions based upon run-time conditions. Examples of scenarios that need to be handled on a conditional basis include the following:

1. Certain steps in a business process may need to be invoked only if certain conditions are true. For example, a supervisor must always review a new purchase requisition, but a manager must also review it if the amount exceeds a particular value or if the department's budget has been already exceeded.
2. Business processes generally move forward. However in certain situations a process might move backwards, or even sideways. A user might return a step because of the absence of some information without which the user cannot make a decision. In this case, it is most likely that the process will move back to the previous step. However, under certain conditions it may be desirable to move the process back to some prior step instead of simply the previous step. Conditions are used to determine the behaviour of the process under these situations.
3. When a step is completed, the process will generally move on to the next step in the process map. However, under certain conditions, it may be desirable to skip the next step and branch to some other step(s).
4. When a step becomes late, a BPM solution will generally send late notifications to the recipient or the recipient's supervisor. However, for some time-critical steps it may be advantageous to take the step away from the recipient and automatically reassign it to some other individual so that the process can be escalated.

Three capabilities are required for handling such exceptions and special conditions. First, the BPM solution has to provide a means of trapping process events. These events include the following:

- *Activate:* This event occurs when the step is ready to be activated. It can be used to determine if the conditions required to activate the step are satisfied, or to provide a mechanism of performing certain actions and pre-processing before the step is activated.
- *Complete:* This event occurs when the step is completed. It can be used to perform post-processing or determine the activation of subsequent steps based on decisions or actions taken in the step.
- *Late:* This event occurs if the step is late due to inaction by the recipient. This event can be used for escalation or other corrective action.
- *Return:* This event occurs if the recipient of the step decides to return the step because of lack of information, incomplete or incorrect information. This event can be used to decide to bypass previous steps in case a step is returned under some specific conditions.
- *Resubmitted:* This event occurs if the recipient resubmits a step that has already been completed because of new information or change in external conditions. For example, this can be used to implement process roll-back.

Second, for each of the events the BPM solution provides a *condition table* for specifying and evaluating conditions based upon the values of process variables. When an event occurs, the condition table is used to interrogate the value of the process variables and the status of the process to determine if particular conditions in the table are true.

And finally, the BPM solution provides a means of defining actions that are to be taken when the conditions are satisfied. Some possible actions may include the following:

- Abort a step
- Abort an incident
- Activate a step or steps
- Activate a script or Web Service

Each step in the business process is associated with events as described above. For each event there is a set of conditional statements that allows the process designer to specify conditions that must be evaluated. For each condition statement that is true there is a corresponding action(s) to be taken. When an event occurs, the conditional statement is evaluated and a corresponding action is taken.

Electronic Forms

Electronic forms are the user interfaces of business processes. As discussed earlier, the purpose of a BPM solution is to route the right information to the right user at the right time so that the user can make decisions or take actions. Electronic forms are the means to display the information and enable the participants to make decision or take actions.

A BPM solution borrows the metaphor of paper-based forms and files in certain ways, but is different and more powerful. It is important to understand their differences and similarities. In non-automated business processes, a file folder is typically used to route information about a case or incident that needs to be resolved by the process. The file folder may include a number of drawings, documents, images and other structured or unstructured data. It also contains a cover form that has summary information about the case, the decisions made so far, and the input of various participants in the process. As the file folder travels to various individuals in the course of the process, each participant can add their own decisions or input on the form, or take actions as may be required by the instructions provided. Each participant may also review the documents and drawings attached in the file folder to support the decision or seek clarifications.

A BPM solution provides similar capabilities for human participation. It provides the process designer the tools to create electronic forms that are used to display and input summary information, decisions and actions by each participant. Furthermore, it provides the means of attaching documents to the business process, and binds these forms with databases. Participants use the form to view the data associated with the task, and also use it to open the attached documents. Electronic forms should be used to present summary information, decisions and actions within a workflow process. They should not be used for embedding a large amount of data, documents or images. Detailed information is most efficiently handled by incorporating pointers to data, documents and attachments in the electronic forms and providing a mechanism to display them to the participants on demand.

The difference between electronic forms used in BPM and paper-based forms used in manual routing is that paper-based forms are static. They cannot be changed dynamically depending on the person who is performing the task, or the task at hand. Due to their static nature, paper-based forms are designed to contain all information and associated instructions for participants in the process. They tend to be large with some sections marked "For Official Use Only," others marked "For Use by Human Resource Only," and yet others that can be used by this or that department only. That is why paper forms tend to become large, cluttered and difficult to design and manage. Furthermore, it is impossible to prevent information designed for one group or individual to be viewed by another group or individual unless one takes special precautions by breaking the manual process into non-overlapping multiple processes. This becomes difficult to design and manage.

Electronic forms used in BPM have no such restriction since they can be totally dynamic. Each step in an automated business process can have its own electronic forms that display only the information and instructions necessary for performing the tasks at that step. This means that the forms are smaller, concise and to the point and therefore easier to use. Furthermore, any information that is confidential (or not appropriate for the task or the recipients of the task) can be hidden, thereby providing a higher degree of security and information integrity. Many new users of process automation, and indeed several early vendors, came to the incorrect assumption that the fastest way to automate business processes is to automate the routing of existing paper-based forms. Paper forms were designed to work within the constraints of static forms and the restriction on how they could be routed. Carrying these limitations over to electronic forms undermines many of the benefits of workflow automation.

Electronic forms used in workflow automation need all the features of electronic forms used for other purposes. These include ease of use, ease of navigation, aesthetics, flexibility through smart components like list boxes, combo-boxes, buttons, validation and data masking. However, electronic forms have some other the key requirements when used for business process automation, as described below.

Web Based

Everyone in an organization is likely to participate in workflow processes. The Web browser has become a part of every desktop, laptop and many mobile devices, and is used as the primary interface for a large number of Web-based applications. The widespread use of the Web browser as a standard interface stems from the fact that it does not require loading a client-side application on every desktop. If a Web-based application does require any special components, they are automatically downloaded and configured. Upgrades are equally transparent. Because of these reasons, a Web browser is also an excellent client for hosting electronic forms used in

BPM. Forms can be changed and upgraded. Users do not have to perform any maintenance.

Another significant benefit of making Web-based electronic forms for BPM is that a Web browser provides an excellent mechanism for easily connecting or disconnecting from the BPM server. The Web browser is simply pointed to a specific URL of the server. Many BPM applications and tasks require infrequent participation in the business process by a large number of users. The ability to easily connect and disconnect from the BPM server is therefore very important.

The rapid increase in the use of XML as a document standard, and its ability to describe information contained in documents, will also increase the use of the Web browser as the default client for workflow applications. XML will enable companies to develop intelligent clients operating in Web browsers or wireless devices such as PDAs that will be able to adjust dynamically to changes in the information or the preference of the user. Finally, as noted in the introduction, one of the major benefits of BPM is that it allows a company to include its customers and partners in a business process. Making electronic forms Web-based makes this practical.

Database Connectivity

Business processes deal extensively with information and databases. The purpose of a business process is either to gather business information and accumulate it into databases for subsequent use, or to enable participants to view information in databases in order to make effective decisions that can be routed to others. Providing robust database connectivity is one of the most important challenges of electronic forms used in BPM.

A database is an excellent repository of large amounts of structured data. An automated business process is an excellent method of routing data as a part of a process. However, the proper way of routing data is not by extracting it from the database and then using a BPM solution as a container to route it. Instead, provide a mechanism for entering and displaying data in electronic forms used with business processes, then route a pointer to the database to the next step in the business process where it can be extracted and displayed using the electronic form for that step. This technique leverages the best features of a database as well as the BPM solution.

Providing a robust database is a major challenge for workflow software vendors. While vendors might want to limit their product offerings to their core competency that is the routing of data, they cannot avoid the need for becoming powerful database front-ends. Some vendors take a simple approach of not providing any electronic forms capabilities. Instead they leave it to customers to develop custom forms using third-party tools in which they can embed their own database connectivity solutions. Others provide robust electronic forms capabilities but leave database connectivity to custom scripts and actions. And yet others provide electronic forms with very robust database connectivity features and the ability to extend the forms for further enhancement using third-party plug-ins.

Document Attachments

Just as databases are good for saving structured data, the use of documents and an electronic document management system (EDMS) is an excellent mechanism for saving unstructured information. A BPM solution must be able to route unstructured information in the form of documents, images, voice and video clips as a part of a business process. This is best done by providing a document attachment control in the electronic forms used with the business process. A document attachment control enables a workflow user to attach documents to a business process and route it as a part of the process. Likewise, at subsequent steps in the business process, participants have the ability to view and modify documents attached by others as long as they have appropriate security access rights.

Document attachment can work in two ways. A document can be physically attached to the form, or a pointer to the document can be attached to the form. When a document is attached, a physical copy of the document is appended to the form and routed with the process. This is similar to how most e-mail systems handle attached documents. This works but has major drawbacks. A business process may branch into many parallel steps that are performed by different users. If a document is physically attached to such a process, it will result in multiple copies of the document, one for each user in parallel steps. Further down the process may converge into one flow, especially at the end of the process. If there are multiple copies of the document, it is impossible to decide which one of the copies should be used.

Therefore, the correct method to attach a document is not to attach a physical copy of the document with the form. Instead, the attached document is saved on a server in a specified repository and given a unique identifying code or reference number. This reference number or pointer is attached to the form and routed with the process. There is always only one copy of the document on the server. Whenever a recipient uses the attachment control to open a document, the software uses the reference number to download a copy of the document from the server. In this way there is no duplication of the document. If multiple users request the same document at the same time, it is possible to either prevent that, or to allow all users other than the first to open it on a read-only basis.

Many advanced BPM solutions provide an interface with Electronic Document Management Systems (EDMS). An EDMS provide robust capabilities for saving, archiving, searching and indexing documents. They include functions such as advanced search, version control, check-in and check-out and user-based security. By combining an EDMS with a BPM solution, one can deploy solutions that provide powerful document management as well as document routing capabilities.

Digital Signatures

Business processes of all types make extensive use of signatures for attesting to the legitimacy of the information carried by the process, or the decisions made during the course of the process. Purchase orders are approved via signatures. Performance reviews and salary increases are attested with signatures. Customer orders are confirmed with signatures. Moreover, signatures have legal significance since they identify the signer and also cannot be repudiated by the signers in a court of law. Therefore, if business processes are automated, it is necessary to provide some acceptable method of signing documents.

Workflow solutions may provide two different types of *digital signature* capabilities to authenticate users: (1) password based and (2) PKI digital signatures based. These are described below.

Password-Based Signatures: This is the simplest form of digital signatures and uses passwords to authenticate the user. When a task is to be authenticated, a *signature control* is provided in the electronic forms as a required field. Upon completing the task the user is required to sign the form by activating the control. The control prompts the user for his user name and password. This information is sent to the BPM server where it is verified against a directory of user names and passwords. If the specified user name and password is correct, the BPM server responds by sending a message to the electronic form along with the image of the company logo or stamp, or the actual image of the person's signature. This image is displayed in the electronic form in the signature control along with the name of the user. As the process moves to subsequent steps, the display of the image attests to the fact that the user has electronically signed the form.

The biggest advantage of the "password signatures" method is that it is simple to implement and has no additional cost. It only requires a directory of user names and passwords for every participant in the process. A majority of companies contemplating the use of a workflow solution already have a network in place. The network may use Microsoft Active Directory, NT Directory or an LDAP-compliant directory such as Novell eDirectory or Netscape iPlanet Directory Service for authenticating users for sign-on to the network. It is ideal for a BPM solution to use these existing directories since users will have the same user name and password for participating in business as they have for signing on to their network. Many companies have deployed Human Resource solutions such as PeopleSoft for managing information about their employees. These directories also have user name and passwords that can be used by the workflow system. Some vendors provide their own directory of user name and passwords for each user to log on to the BPM solution. This is the least desirable method because the company has to maintain yet another directory and users have to remember multiple user names and passwords.

The drawback of password signatures is that it provides weak authentication and security. Passwords are not legally binding in a court of law, and there is no independent authority that vouches for the validity of passwords. They can be leaked, and individuals inside the organization, such as network administrators, may have access to user names and passwords for all employees. Furthermore, the use of passwords is not practical when multiple companies are involved in business processes that span organizations, since each organization has its own directory of user names and passwords that are not synchronized with others.

PKI Digital Signatures: Digital signatures using Public Key Infrastructure (PKI) are beginning to be used for e-commerce. Under this scheme a trusted Certificate Authority such as a VeriSign issues a digital signature to every participant. The Certificate Authority ensures that all digital signatures assigned are legitimate and accredited after periodic intervals. A Certificate Authority can also be established by a company for the use of its employees and trading partners. The digital certificate provides each user a unique public key that is a long number which is disclosed to everyone, and a private key which each user keeps privately. The user can now use the digital signature certificate to sign electronic documents, including workflow tasks that he is required to perform. As the process proceeds, users at subsequent steps can view the digital signatures and validate its authenticity through the Certificate Authority.

In addition to using digital signatures for authentication and verification, a BPM solution may also use it for "hashing" the data that the user has signed. Hashing basically involves creating a unique number called the *hash* by combining the data and the signature of the individual using a mathematical formula that is also kept confidential. If the data is hashed, any modification of the data will result in the hash not computing properly, thereby invalidating the digital signature. This powerful technique ensures that a BPM solution can detect if data has been tampered with as it is being transmitted from one participant to another.

There are numerous benefits of using PKI digital signatures. They are legally binding and accepted by the court system in the United States and many other countries. They can be used to facilitate the participation of users inside and outside the organization who share a common and trusted Certificate Authority. The authenticity of digital signatures can be readily verified. And finally, digital signatures can be used to protect the integrity of data by using sophisticated hashing techniques. The major drawback of PKI digital signatures is that it requires a Certificate Authority infrastructure. This has considerable product and administrative costs, and most companies do not have the infrastructure in place. However, large companies are now beginning to deploy the infrastructure: the rapid increase in e-commerce is bound to accelerate the process, while at the same time reduce the cost.

A detailed description of digital signatures is beyond the scope of this book. However there are numerous books and articles on this subject [7].

Memos

In many situations it is useful for a user to attach a comment or *sticky note* to a file folder or form on an ad hoc basis. The sticky note is neither required nor expected; the user attaches it simply to provide some more elaboration or clarification for subsequent participants in the process. A BPM solution can also provide memo capabilities with electronic forms that enable the user to attach addition information on a discretionary basis. This memo is routed as a part of the business process and available for subsequent users to view. These users can also add their own comments or memos. The goal is to make the BPM solution whole and complete.

Form Object Libraries

Electronic forms used by organizations should have a consistent look and feel just like the paper forms of a company should look identical. For example, they may have the same layout for the name, address, social security, and birth date fields. They also must have the same company logo. To design consistent looking forms, a company has to duplicate effort by designing a large number of forms that use the same look and feel, and in many cases the same logic.

A "form object library" allows a company to reuse components when designing forms. It allows a process designer to take one or more controls in a form and declare that as a reusable object. This object can then be used in multiple forms and the forms designer does not have to start from scratch. Furthermore, if the company decides to change the look and feel of the object, they can change it only at one place, and this change is propagated to all other instances where the object is use. For example, the company can create one layout for logo, date and summary fields used in a form. These three objects can be declared and named as a single object and save it in the form object library. Other form designers can simply insert this object in the forms that they are designing. The design is reused and the form has a consistent look and feel. One day the company decides to change the color of its logo. It does not have to change all the forms; it can simply change the logo once in the object library. This change is then propagated to all the forms in all the processes where it is being used. Form object libraries, therefore, ensures consistency, reusability and maintainability of electronic forms.

General Requirements of Process Maps

Aside from the features and capabilities required for steps in a process map, business processes also have requirements that apply to the entire process. These process level requirements and their benefits are as follows:

1. Process Documentation: A business process is a valuable asset of an organization since it encapsulates the business rules, roles and actions of a business process. Business processes are not static. They continue to evolve with the passage of time as the organization grows and changes its business practices. Furthermore, the individuals who designed the business process may move on to new roles and responsibilities. After a business process has been designed it is desirable for the BPM solution to be able to produce some form of documentation that can be used for maintaining and updating the process.

While there are no hard and fast rules about what information concerning the business process should be included in the documentation, as a general rule the more that can be included the better it is for maintenance.

Since this may result in voluminous documentation that may not be appropriate for all readers, a useful enhancement is to allow the user to customize documentation by creating templates that can be used for various types of documents. Some of the information that is useful for inclusion in documentation includes the process name, version, description, graphical process map, step names, step description, recipients, completion time, and business rules associated with each step.

2. Process Description: A process map requires a description of the overall business process it is designed to automate. This description is a property of the process map and is used primarily for creating the documentation for the business process as described above.

3. Incident Completion Time: This property establishes a time limit for the completion of the task. If this time limit is exceeded the task is escalated to ensure that overall process is completed on time. "Process completion time" is a property of the business process that establishes a time limit for the completion of an entire incident of a business process. This is designed to ensure that the process is completed on a timely basis, regardless of the time taken by individual steps. If the process completion time is exceeded, the BPM server will typically send an e-mail notification to the process owner or the participants of the business. Alternatively, it could be used to trigger a recalculation of the individual step time limits or the priority of the incident with the goal of expediting its completion.

Like step time limits, the process completion time property can be either an absolute or a relative value. An absolute value allows the process designer to design the process so that the customer or owner of the process can specify his expectations about when the incident should be completed. For example, when a loan application for a specific customer is initiated, the initiator or loan officer can specify that the customer expects completion by 28th of June. This date becomes the "incident completion time" for the specific incident. If the incident is not completed by June 28th, the loan officer would receive an e-mail notification, or the incident could be escalated.

"Relative incident completion time" allows the process designer to specify a relative time in which any incident must be completed. The time is generally specified by the business manager who owns the process and is based on expectations of how the organization is supposed to perform and what the customer expects. When an incident is initiated, the BPM solution calculates the completion time by adding the incident completion time value to the time the incident was initiated. Any delay beyond that time would trigger notifications or escalations.

4. Customized, Context-Aware E-Mail Notifications: A BPM solution provides e-mail notification to participants when special events occur that impact the role the participants have to play for the successful completion of the business process. Events that trigger e-mail notifications include any new task, late task, urgent task, reassigned task, and aborted task, etc.

Notification messages should be customizable and context aware. Customization allows a process designer to generate messages that are appropriate to the business needs, or the specific needs of each business process. Context-awareness allows the process designer to define messages that are capable of incorporating incident-specific process information in the notification. This is conveniently accomplished by allowing process variables to be incorporated in the subject and body of the message. Based upon the values of the process variables, which are in turn determined by the current state of the incident, the e-mail message contains real-time process data that makes it more meaningful to the recipient. Instead of simply sending a message to a user that "You have a new task," the BPM solution can send a message such as "You have a <u>Purchase Order</u> for <u>New Computer for John</u> that must be purchased by <u>June 28th</u>." In this example the underlined values are the actual values of variables for Process Name, Summary and Due Date of a business process.

BPM Meets the Real World

BPM deals with the how people work and how organizations conduct their business. People work in very complex ways that are always changing. Even those business processes that appear simple on the surface become complex as soon as they are deployed for use by a larger number of people. This is because the more people that are involved, the more exceptions and special conditions will surface and have to be handled. These exceptions and special conditions are what make business process automation complex. The other reason for complexity is that in every organization most of the business processes have evolved over time in response to needs. Very few processes were engineered. Companies have been using these processes for a long time, and it is often against their instinct to change these processes because of the introduction of a new technology. Changing business processes means changing the way people work, and that is sometimes emotional, often political, and always an economic consequence. When companies adopt BPM they want to adapt it to their existing business processes with all their legacies and quirks rather than change their business processes. This *need to adapt* to the current way of doing business demands a lot of flexibility from BPM solutions.

A number of requirements must be satisfied if a BPM solution is to satisfy real-world requirements. These requirements are general in nature and not specific to any particular component of a BPM solution. They are an integral part of the type of exception-handling issues that arise when companies decide to automate their business processes. These general requirements are described below.

Proactive Notifications

Business process automation is proactive by definition. Its goal is to ensure that tasks are being completed and work is moving forward on a timely basis. However, many BPM solutions now use Web browsers as their preferred client interface. The World Wide Web is a passive medium. You have to point your Web browser to a Web site and only then will you become aware that some new information is available. A user must visit a Web site before learning that a new workflow task has been assigned. This is reactive rather than proactive. To overcome the reactive nature of the Web, BPM solutions use proactive notifications of new tasks or other events, primarily via e-mail. These e-mail notifications can contain pointers to the BPM Web site and other information necessary for users to the respond to the event. With the growing popularity of Internet Messaging, future BPM solutions will start using that as a means of notification.

Assigning Tasks

It is common for people to be unavailable for work. A workflow participant can be away from work either because it was planned or because of an unexpected situation. In either case, a BPM solution must provide means of handling participant unavailability or else a business process workflow would come to a standstill simply because one or more users were unavailable to perform their tasks. In another common situation, users who are busy with other projects may want to assign one or more of their tasks to colleagues or subordinates.

BPM solutions must provide different methods of allowing users to assign tasks to others:

1. A user can assign some or all of their current or future tasks to another user.
2. A user can assign tasks until a specific date, then take back tasks after that date.

3. The supervisor of the user may do any of the above on behalf of the user. This allows handling of situations when the user does not come to work because of an emergency or unexpected event.
4. A central workflow administrator may do any of the above.

Non-Assignable Tasks

The ability to assign tasks to another user is one of the most useful capabilities of a BPM solution for handling absence or the need for delegating tasks to colleagues or subordinates. However, once a user is given this flexibility it opens up the possibility that a user may accidentally or intentionally assign important tasks to someone else not authorized to perform them. Declaring a step as non-assignable prevents a task from being reassigned and ensures that only the recipient performs it. This is an example of the need to handle exceptions to exceptions.

Escalations

Time limits can be used to trigger notifications to the recipients of tasks to warn them of the delay. They can also be used to trigger escalations. If a step is late beyond specified limits, a BPM solution provides the means of escalation based on business rules for the process and the specific context of the incident. Escalation of tasks is generally accomplished through the "event condition" tables or through other similar mechanisms.

Rollback

Process rollback is another real life requirement encountered when automating business processes. It calls for a process incident that is still in progress to be rolled-back to a new state when certain events occur, then continue from there cognizant of the new events and associated information. Consider the common business process of handling incoming orders. A company receives an order and then starts a series of tasks to satisfy the order as a part of the order process. These tasks may include acknowledging receipt of the order, entering the order in the manufacturing system, ensuring the customer information is correct, checking for credit, creating an invoice, and many others. After the company has started processing the order, but before it is shipped and completed, the customer calls back and changes some aspect of the order. This change might involve some of the tasks to be undone or repeated, and other tasks may not be affected at all. Instead of canceling the previous order process, which would cause some amount of energy and time to be wasted, process rollback allows the incident to be rolled-back to a new state and proceed from there.

"Process rollback" is an advanced feature offered by some BPM solutions. It allows any completed task in a business process to be re-submitted with new information. A process designer can use an event condition table associated with the resubmitted event to determine the state of the incident and the value of the process variables. Based upon this information the process designer can specify the state to which the incident will be rolled-back. After the rollback, the incident continues from the new state. Notice that the BPM solution does not dictate what happens when rollback occurs. It leaves it to the process designer, who is most intimately familiar with the business requirements, to determine what to do based upon the context.

Confer

In many cases a user may want to consult with another colleague about the specifics of a particular task before completing it. A BPM solution accommodates this requirement by providing the ability to *confer* about a task with another user. When a task is conferred, it is sent to the other user to review the information about the task and enter information and comments, but the other user cannot complete the task. When the user submits the task, it is returned to the owner who can review the comments of the conferee, then make his or her own decision about how to complete it.

Work Calendar

A BPM solution enables process designers to specify time limits of individual steps and the overall process. These time limits are used for notifications and escalations. However, a company may have specific work schedules that exclude weekends and holidays. If a task has a completion time of two days, the common assumption is that it is two business days. Weekends and holidays do not count. Likewise, a BPM solution is capable of capturing process metrics in order to optimize the process. In order to capture the time consumed for completing a task, it has to exclude weekends and holidays.

A BPM solution, therefore, must be aware of the work calendar of an organization that specifies working hours, holidays and weekends. Some products provide one calendar for the entire organization, while others can be specific to departments, work groups and individuals.

Private Tasks

A robust BPM solution allows a supervisor to view the tasks of subordinates. This capability allows the management of users and their tasks to be distributed in the organization by allowing each person to manage his or her tasks, as well as the tasks of subordinates. However, there may be certain tasks relating to salary or medical information that a supervisor must not be able to access. The ability to declare a step private allows this flexibility. A supervisor can only view non-private tasks of subordinates.

Archiving

Many business processes require that critical information be archived after a case is completed. Auditors or regulators often review archived information going back several months, or even years. Some BPM solutions provide this capability as part of the product. A BPM solution may also archive the electronic forms and the associated data for review by individuals who have archive access rights.

Conclusion

A business process map is an electronic rendition of the sequence of tasks, events, actions, rules and interfaces that represent a business process. While they are generally associated with graphical flowcharts, they contain information about how processes will be executed and the rules governing their execution. Business processes look simple on the surface, but are complex inside because they have to cater to a large number of exceptions that are present in every organization, and because people work together in complex ways.

Chapter 6
Smart Ways of Routing Work

The essence of business process automation is the ability to route the right information to the right individuals or computer applications at the right time so that the latter can make decisions or take actions. Human beings work together in complex ways. Even when there are rules that prescribe the proper way of conducting business, many actions and decisions are made on an ad hoc basis for the purpose of expediting or handling new or special conditions that arise frequently. Business processes reflect the complex nature these interactions. The complexity of business processes increases in proportion to the size of the organization. Changing business processes is even more difficult because it often involves politics, economics, prestige and egos. However, there is enormous internal and external pressure on the modern organization to be able to accommodate change in order to be competitive. BPM software for the automation of business processes must provide powerful and flexible means of routing work to accommodate the complexity and the ever-changing variety of these interactions.

A number of methods for routing work are necessary for the flexibility required to automate complex processes. The constructs and mechanisms offered by modern BPM software can be adopted for different methods of routing work, and BPM software is evolving to offer even more sophisticated and intelligent options. When a business process is designed, a *recipient* is specified for each step. Because the specified recipient determines the routing of a business process, it is important to understand the various *types* of recipients and the flexibility that each offers.

Name-Based Routing

Name-based routing is the simplest method of assigning and routing work. Each task in a business process is assigned to a specific, named individual. For example, a company has a rule that Jane Doe must review all change orders, as shown in Figure 6.1. When an incident of the process occurs, the Review step is simply routed to Jane Doe.

Although simple, this approach is practical for only the smallest organizations and relatively small processes. If Jane Doe is promoted, leaves the company, or otherwise changes job responsibilities, the process will no longer work since the task will no longer be Jane Doe's responsibility. The business process therefore has to be redesigned, and Jane Doe's successor has to be named as the recipient of the Review step. A solution that requires changing a business process simply because of changes in job responsibilities is not viable. Name-based routing is therefore suitable for the simplest business processes in small organizations.

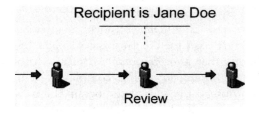

Figure 6.1. Name-Based Routing

Role-Based Routing

Role-based routing addresses the limitations of name-based routing. Instead of assigning a task to a specific, named individual, assign it to a job function or *role* that is responsible for performing the task. This requires the definition and maintenance of roles that can be accomplished through a roles table.

For the Change Order process example discussed earlier, the Review step is assigned to the job function called "Configurator," as shown in Figure 6.2.

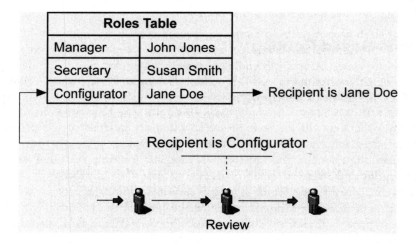

Figure 6.2. Role-Based Routing

Currently Jane Doe is the Configurator for the company as shown in the associated roles table. When an incident of the process reaches the Review step, the BPM server will use the roles table to determine that Jane Doe currently play the role of Configurator. The Review step will therefore be assigned to Jane Doe. If Jane Doe leaves the company or is promoted, the roles table is changed and John Doe is named the Configurator. From then on, new incidents of the Change Order process will automatically go to John Doe. The business process does not need to be redefined. It changes dynamically as soon as the roles table is changed and adjusts itself to the new role.

Role-based routing makes business processes independent of individuals by assigning tasks to job functions. While the job functions and the structure of a company's organization chart are also not static, the rate and magnitude of change is generally less than the change in employees. Role-based routing, therefore, makes it easier to implement and manage business processes in an organization.

Advanced BPM software provides comprehensive organization chart capabilities that are closely tied to the network or human resource directories maintained by companies. An organization chart enables a company to identify all the roles and the people who perform the roles, making it easier to implement role-based routing.

Relationship-Based Routing

Numerous business processes require routing of tasks based upon reporting relationships. For example, the employee's supervisor must approve an expense report submitted by an employee. The employee's department manager must approve a purchase requisition initiated by the employee. Role-based routing is not able to handle this requirement because there are many employees with different supervisors and managers.

Relationship-based routing allows a task to be assigned to a job function that has a specific relationship with another job function. Since relationships between job functions are dictated by the company's organization chart, relationship-based routing necessitates the definition of an organization chart. Furthermore, relationship-based routing requires the specification of two pieces of information: (1) what is the relationship, and (2) with respect to whom, or the *seed*. There are four typical types of relationship-based recipients:

1. *Supervisor of Initiator:* The recipient is the *supervisor* of the person who initiated the workflow incident.
2. *Supervisor of Previous Step:* The recipient is the *supervisor* of the person who completed the previous step in the business process.
3. *Manager of Initiator:* The recipient is the *manager* of the person who initiated the workflow incident.
4. *Manager of Previous Step:* The recipient is the *manager* (the relationship) of the person who completed the previous step in the business process (the seed).

This can be generalized as follows to accommodate any combination of relationship and seed with respect to which the relationship is established:

Recipient = Relationship (Recipient who completed Step N)

Figure 6.3 illustrates a Purchase Requisition process in which the Approval step is assigned to "Supervisor of Initiator." This means that the Approval step will be performed by the person who is the supervisor of the person who initiated the purchase requisition. Anyone can initiate a purchase requisition and the Approval step will always go to his or her supervisor. Similarly, in the same business process the Capital Approval step is assigned to the manager of the previous step and the step is conditional and activated only if the total amount is greater than $1,000.

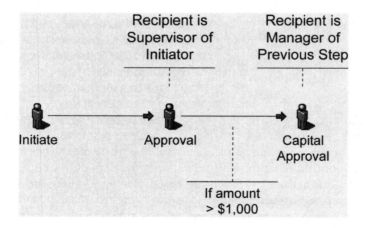

Figure 6.3. Relationship-Based Routing

The recipient of this step is determined by several factors:

1. Who initiated the purchase requisition?
2. The answer to the first question determines the recipient of the second step: who is the supervisor of the initiator?
3. The answer to the second question determines the recipient of the Capital Approval step: who is the manager of the person who completed the previous step? However, this step is invoked only if the total amount is greater than $1,000.

Some form of an organization chart that defines relationships and is accessible to the BPM software is necessary for relationship-based routing.

Groups

In many business processes a task must be performed by a group of individuals instead of an individual. This generally happens when the collective opinion or input of more than one individual is required. For example, a sales forecasting process may require all regional managers to provide their forecasts; or a manufacturing control process may require the input of all quality managers. In both cases the recipient is a *group*.

A business analyst can design a workflow process that uses multiple steps in parallel to obtain feedback from a group of individuals. For example, the analyst could design a sales forecast process as shown in Figure 6.4 that has five steps in parallel that are labeled "Forecast 1" to "Forecast 5." Each step is assigned to one regional sales manager. This approach will work, but has significant drawbacks:

1. The process is unnecessarily complex. An identical activity performed by five different individuals is represented by five different steps. All five steps have to be designed and maintained. It is easy to imagine what the process map would look like if the company had 20 regional sales mangers.
2. If the number of regional sales managers increases or decreases, the business process will have to be redesigned.

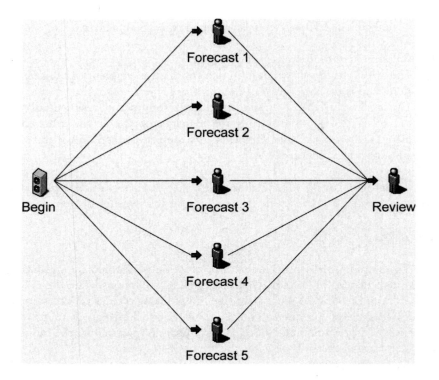

Figure 6.4. Routing to Members of a "Group"

Group-based routing provides an excellent method for addressing these drawbacks. If a group is named as the recipient of a step, all the members of the group are assigned the task in parallel. Coming back to the sales forecast example, the process map using group-based routing is illustrated in Figure 6.5.

There is only one "Forecast" step. The recipient of this step is the group named "Regional Sales Managers." When the "Forecast" step is invoked, each member of the group will receive the task, and the workflow will not proceed until all of them have completed the step.

Group-based routing effectively addresses the two limitations listed above. Regardless of whether the number of the regional sales managers increases or decreases, the business process does not have to be redefined. Only the members of the "Regional Sales Managers" group have to be changed. Moreover, the process map is clean and uncluttered without redundant steps. Even if the number of regional sales managers increases to 50 as the company grows, the process map will contain only one step for the activity of entering the sales forecast. Furthermore, since the members of the group are determined at run-time, any change to the list of members is reflected in new incidents as soon as they are made.

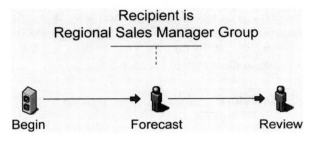

Figure 6.5. Group-Based Routing

For some business processes it is desirable to assign a step to a group, but then proceed with the workflow as soon as a subset of group members have completed their tasks. For example, a process may require any three out of the six quality managers of the company to provide their input before it can continue. Adding a "minimum response" feature can enhance the group-based routing. The step is assigned to all members of the group. However, if the minimum response property is set to 3, the workflow will proceed to the next step as soon as the first three members of the group have completed their tasks.

Sequential Groups

Many business processes require that a document be reviewed, signed or approved by any one member of a group that has a specific authority level in the organization. For example, a company may have a rule that any one director must approve every new job requisition greater than $50,000. Therefore, the requirement is to find one of the directors who is available and has the time to review the job requisition. If the director is not available, then the search must begin to find another director who can perform the task.

If this business process is automated, it is necessary to automate the task of looking around, or *hunting*. One convenient technique is to declare the recipient of the step to be a sequential group, then assign a group to that step. A time limit is also specified for the step and the members of the group can be ordered in an appropriate sequence. The BPM system will send the task to the first member of the group. It will then wait for the specified time limit. If the first recipient performs the task in the specified time limit, the workflow moves on to the next step. If, however, the first recipient does not perform the task in the specified time limit because he or she is busy (or perhaps not even at his or her desk), the task is removed from the first recipient and assigned to the second. Using this technique the BPM server essentially *hunts* to find the person from the list in the group who can do the task, as illustrated in Figure 6.6.

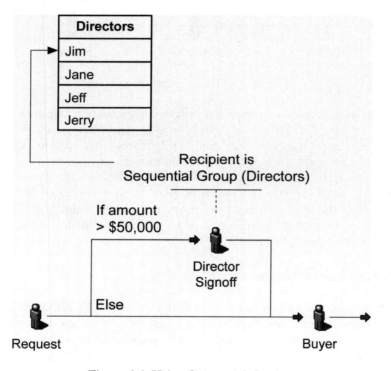

Figure 6.6. Using Sequential Groups

In this example, the Director Signoff step is invoked if the purchase request is more than $50,000. This step is assigned to a sequential group called Directors. This group includes Jim, Jane, Jeff and Jerry. If the step is invoked, it is first assigned to Jim. If Jim does not complete the step in a specified time, it is removed from Jim and assigned to Jane. This continues until one of the directors completes the step.

Queues

In many business processes a task has to be performed by any one member of a group. However, at any given time, it is not known which member is available and with what other tasks the member is preoccupied. If a task is assigned to one of the members, he or she may not be able to perform it in the required time while another member may be free and available. Therefore, the common practice is to assign the task to a shared in-basket or *shared inbox*. Any member of a group who is available and free can pick up the next task from the queue.

BPM software makes this type of routing possible via queue-based routing. The recipient of a step can be a queue, which is a shared electronic inbox. Each queue is associated with a group. Any member of the group can pick the next task from the queue.

As an example, a company may have four buyers. Any buyer can process an approved purchase requisition and place the order with a vendor. Instead of assigning the Buyer step to a specific buyer, it is assigned to a queue and the group called "Buyers" is named as the recipient of the queue, as illustrated in Figure 6.7.

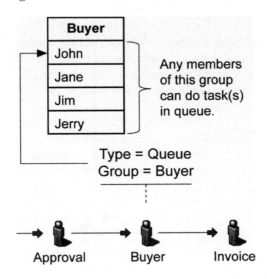

Figure 6.7. Routing to a Queue

As with other features, there are exceptions that always surface when queue are used in real-life situations. BPM software that offers queue-based routing are faced with the need to handle the following exceptions related to the use of queues:

1. Queues can be blind or selective. In a blind queue, a group member is given the next task in the queue based upon priority or first-in, first-out criteria. The user does not have a choice. In a selective queue, the user is given the choice to look at the list of tasks in the queue and select the one he or she wishes to perform. Since organizations have their own preferences, BPM software has to provide both types of queues.
2. After the user has selected a task from the queue in order to perform it, the task is removed from the queue so that no one else can download it and duplicate effort. The user may then decide that he or she does not want to do it after all. For this eventuality BPM software has to provide a method of allowing the user to place the task back into the queue.
3. A user may be involved in multiple queues. When a user requests or selects a task from the queue, the BPM software must determine all the queues that the user belongs to, then create a combined list of tasks from all the queues.

Relative Role-Based Routing

Role-based routing enables tasks to be assigned based upon roles instead of individuals. Role-based routing, however, is not sufficient for effectively handling many real-life business process routing requirements of larger organizations. Figure 6.8 illustrates this point.

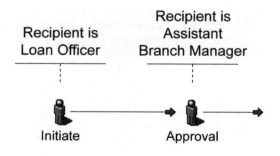

Figure 6.8. Routing to a Job Functions

In this Loan Approval process, the loan application is initiated by the loan officer and must be approved by the assistant branch manager. This is easily accomplished by assigning the Initiate step to the job function "Loan Officer" and the Approval step to the "Assistant Branch Manager." This will work well as long as the bank has only one branch.

However, the bank grows and acquires two new branches so that it now consists of Branch A, Branch B and Branch C. Each branch has a different assistant branch manager. To distinguish between the three different branches the job functions are named "Branch A/Assistant Branch Manager," "Branch B/Assistant Branch Manager," and "Branch C/Assistant Branch Manager." In this larger company, if a loan officer in Branch A initiates a new loan application, it must logically be routed to "Branch A/Assistant Branch Manager" and not to any of the other two assistant branch managers. Therefore, the resulting business process becomes more complex, as depicted in Figure 6.9. This uses three Approval steps, one for each of the assistant branch managers. Conditional routing, based upon which loan officer completed the first step, is used to activate one of the three Approval steps.

This approach will work, but simply by adding two new branches to the process map has become more complex as additional steps and conditions are added. If the bank continues to grow and add hundreds of branches (as is not atypical for large banks), it is clear that pretty soon the business process will have a large number of steps just to take into account all the branches it owns. Designing a business process like this is not practical. There are many other real-life business processes that face the same problem as the organization grows, or if BPM is deployed across departments and divisions of large companies.

Relative role-based routing offers an excellent solution for this type of routing requirement. In relative role-based routing, a "relative job function" is specified along with a *seed*. The "relative job function" consists of only the base job function without any departmental or divisional qualifiers, and an indication that it is to be applied relative to the part of the organization to which the seed belongs. The seed can either be the person who initiated the business process, the person who completed the previous step, or some other workflow participant. Applied to the example used above as shown in Figure 6.10, the relative job function would be "...\Assistant Branch Manager" and the seed would be the initiator of the business process. In this case, the BPM software will first determine who the initiator is, then determine the department the initiator belongs to, and finally, route the Approval step to the assistant branch manager of that department.

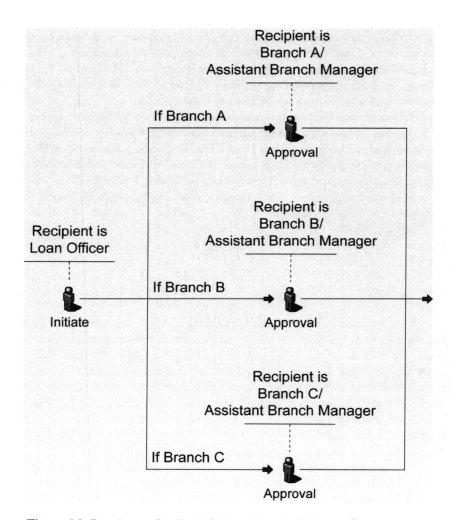

Figure 6.9. Routing to Similar Job Functions in Different Departments

As can be seen from Figure 6.10, the multiple steps in Figure 6.9 are replaced by a single step. Even if the bank has a large number of branches, only one step is required.

Relative role-based routing therefore enables the design of sophisticated business processes that can be applied to many departments within organizations, without having to change the basic design or making it unnecessarily complex.

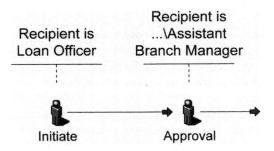

Figure 6.10. Relative Role-Based Routing Simplifies Process Designing

Dynamic Routing

In many business process automation applications it is not possible to determine the recipients of process steps when the business process is being designed. Instead, it is only possible to determine the recipients of steps at run-time after a process incident is activated, and based upon information gathered by the business process. The following two cases illustrate the need for dynamic routing:

1. A general-purpose document-routing business process is used to route documents to various individuals in an organization for their review and feedback. A document can be routed in series or in parallel. For this workflow application, the recipients of the workflow steps are known only when a user initiates a new incident of the process and decides and selects the other individuals who will participate in the review. In this example the recipients of the review steps are selected by the initiator of a workflow incident, and not by the person who designed the business process.

2. A purchase requisition process is designed to enforce a rule that a requisition must be charged to a particular account, and that the account owner for the selected account must also approve the requisition. A company may have many accounts with different owners. In this case a person wishing to buy something will charge it to a specific account. A database table consisting of account numbers and their owners is used as a directory to determine who the owner of the account is. The approval step is then routed to the account owner. In this case, the recipient of the approval step is not known when the process is designed; it is determined dynamically when an incident of the process is executed.

The dynamic recipient feature of some BPM systems allows a process variable to be assigned as the recipient of a step, and the variable specifies the name of a user, job function or group who will be the recipient. The variable can be populated at run-time by other workflow participants selecting names in electronic forms, by database lookup based on specific criteria, or by any other means (such as input from external scripts of applications). This latter feature enables external scripts or applications to specify recipients dynamically, and is a very powerful method of extending the logic of BPM engines to handle any unique or customized routing method.

An example of the use of dynamic recipient using the second example listed above is illustrated in Figure 6.11.

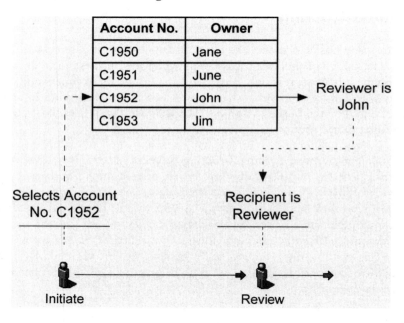

Figure 6.11. Dynamic Routing

The recipient of the second Review step is the variable "Reviewer." At the first step of this workflow process, the user completes a purchase requisition form and selects an account number from a list of account numbers in a database. Behind the scenes, the workflow logic extracts the name of the account owner from a database table that corresponds to the selected account. This account number is assigned to the variable called "Reviewer." Therefore, as soon as the Review step is invoked, it is automatically assigned to the owner of the account selected in the first step. Since this can be done for all steps in a workflow process, the recipients of all steps can be determined at run-time by the information present in the data handled by the process. Furthermore, by invoking scripts and third-party applications that can return names of recipients to variables, a process can activate external applications or logic to determine the rules for routing the business process.

If the variable used for dynamic recipients is an array (a group of variables), then this feature enables the implementation of dynamic groups. This powerful feature allows a group of recipients to be determined dynamically at run-time instead of at design time as shown in Figure 6.12.

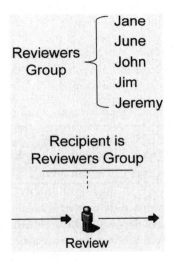

Figure 6.12. Dynamic Groups

Skills-Based Routing

Skills-based routing enables a process step to be routed to a different individual based upon the complexity or importance of the task to be performed. The complexity or importance is determined at run-time based upon an evaluation of the process data for a particular incident. The following examples illustrate the need for skills-based routing:

1. A Credit Approval process may stipulate that the Approval step be performed by different appraisers based upon the amount of credit sought.

2. A Software Problem Resolution process is designed to route a problem report to different developers based upon the complexity of the problem. Simple cosmetic problems may be routed to junior programmers, whereas highly complex issues that cause product instability or loss of user data have to be routed to senior programmers.

Without skills-based routing, the business process would be complicated as shown in Figure 6.13 (on page 119), since the process map and conditions will be used to route the task to different recipients depending on their skills. If there were a large number of skills or gradations of various skill levels, the process map would become proportionally complex.

Skills-based routing is easily implemented by providing "conditional recipient" capabilities. The recipient of a step changes based on one or more conditions that the process designer specifies. The process diagram in Figure 6.14 (on page 120) illustrates how this can be used to provide skills-based routing, while at the same time simplifying the design of the business process. In this example, the recipient of the Approval step is based on the following conditions:

Recipient	= Credit Appraiser A if credit limit < $5,000
	= Credit Appraiser B if credit limit ☐ $5,000 and < $25,000
	= Credit Appraiser C if credit limit ☐ $25,000

Note that in this solution only one step is required. However, the task is assigned to different users depending on the complexity or skills required. Furthermore, while the example involves a simple condition, it is very easy to expand the approach for situations where a complex set of conditions can be used to determine the skill levels and the recipient who has the required skills.

Routing for Workload Balancing

At times it is useful to distribute tasks to various members in a group based upon their workload, how much work they have already completed, or some other quota. For example, in a claims processing workflow it may be useful to distribute new claims to claims processors who have the least number of tasks to do. This requires BPM software to provide a means of assigning recipients based upon some workload-balancing algorithm.

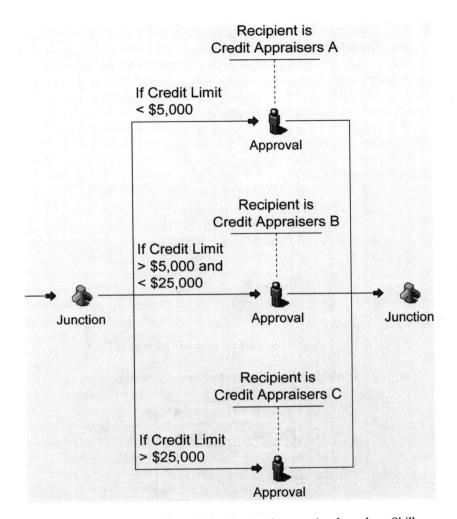

Figure 6.13. Process Map for implementing routing based on Skills

A weighted group is an example of a simple load-balancing technique. In this technique a group is assigned as the recipient of a process step. Each member of the group is assigned a *weight* that dictates the distribution of tasks among members of the group. When a new task is generated, the BPM server will calculate the ratio of tasks already performed or assigned to the members of the group, compare this with the ratio of the weights assigned to each member, and then assign the new task such that the ratio of tasks assigned is the closest to the ratio of weights. A supervisor or manager can change the weights at any time with the resulting change in the distribution of the tasks. If the weights of all the group members are equal, the tasks are distributed in a round-robin fashion.

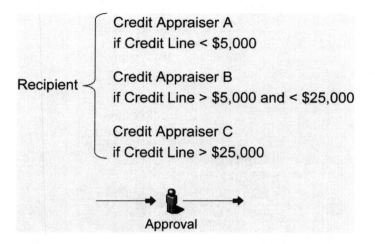

Figure 6.14. Skills-Based Routing Simplifies Process Designing

The example in Figure 6.15 illustrates how this works.

Claims Processors	
Member	**Weight**
A	2
B	2
C	4

Recipient is
Claims Processors

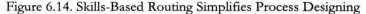

Figure 6.15. Workload Balancing

A group called "Claim Processors" is assigned to the Review step. There are three members of the group (named A, B and C) and their assigned weights are 2, 2 and 4 respectively. Assuming that the business process is starting from day one, new claims as they come in will be assigned to A, B and C, as shown in Table 6.1.

Table 6.1. Task Assignment Using Weighted Groups

Incident	Assigned To	Total Number of Incidents Assigned		
		A (Weight=2)	B (Weight=2)	C (Weight=4)
1	C	0	0	1
2	C	0	0	2
3	A	1	0	2
4	B	1	1	2
5	C	1	1	3
6	C	1	1	4
7	A	2	1	4
8	B	2	2	4
9	C	2	2	5
10	C	2	2	6
11	A	3	2	6
12	B	3	3	6

While this is a simple method of distributing tasks based on workload, it may not be suitable for all situations. There are many other sophisticated algorithms that can be used for load balancing of tasks assigned to users. Two examples follow.

1. BPM software can measure the average task time for all tasks and keep a database of average times. These statistics can be updated periodically using metrics from real processes. When a new task is to be assigned, it can determine the number and type of tasks in a user's inbox, apply the average time to each, and determine how long it will take the user before she can work on the new task. By calculating this for all users, the software can assign the task to the user who is most likely to get to it the earliest.
2. BPM software can determine the number of tasks performed by all users and compare it against a weekly quota established for the users.

It can then assign the task to the user who is available and also is the furthest from achieving his or her quota.

Every organization has its own concept of load balancing and what is equitable in terms of assigning tasks and measuring the performance of individuals. It is therefore not a good practice for BPM software to dictate one algorithm for workload balancing. BPM software must provide the flexibility of defining organization-specific algorithms that cater to the unique requirements of each organization (and indeed, each individual).

The *dynamic recipient* concept provides an excellent mechanism for implementing organization or application-specific workload balancing as depicted in Figure 6.16.

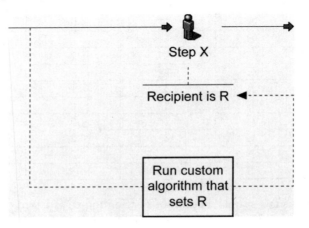

Figure 6.16. Custom Workload Balancing

A process variable is assigned as the recipient of the step that has to be performed by a group of individuals using a customized workload-balancing algorithm. Before the step is invoked, an external script is executed that implements the custom algorithm. The script can be used to perform any algorithm or calculation for workload balancing suitable for the unique needs of the organization. It can use a number of criteria to determine the recipient for the step such as:

- Availability of workers
- Past distribution of work among the workers
- Current backlog of work for the workers

- Performance goals or quota of the workers
- A combination of the above

The algorithm returns the name of a worker in the process variable. This name then becomes the recipient of the step.

Presence Aware Routing

Instant messaging (IM) started as a consumer phenomenon rooted in the success of AOL Instant Messenger, MSN Messenger, ICQ and other similar services. In addition to allowing consumers to easily and inexpensively *chat* with their colleagues, friends or buddies, instant messaging has another significant benefit that it provides *presence awareness*. IM users know when their buddies are online so that they can chat with them. Internet messaging is fast becoming an enterprise-class product that can facilitate real-time collaboration between members of an organization, their customers and partners. It has the same appeal in the enterprise as in the consumer market: namely ease-of-use, low cost and presence awareness.

Business process automation can benefit from presence awareness in several ways:

1. A BPM system can provide a "presence aware recipient" type for steps in a business process. A group of users capable of performing the task can also be associated with a step. The software can use IM functionality to determine which members of the group are available at any given time. Instead of assigning a task to a user who may not be available, it can use the presence awareness feature of the IM platform to assign the task only to the user who is available. As instant messaging becomes more sophisticated, a BPM system will be able to determine not only who is available, but also what type of task the user is currently interested in performing.

2. The sequential group recipient type is designed to *hunt* for a person within a group who is available to perform a task. This hunting mechanism is slow since it happens sequentially. With instant messaging, a BPM system can send a message to all the members of the group and inquire who is available to perform the task. It can then assign the task to the first person who replies in the affirmative. This approach is proactive and much more efficient.

These and other reasons will give momentum to the use of instant messaging in conjunction with BPM software in the future. The industry has to overcome the hurdle that instant messaging is still considered a consumer phenomenon and companies are only beginning to deploy IM infrastructure. Furthermore, there are still a number of competing instant messaging standards and issues regarding authentication and security.

Routing and EAI

In addition to routing as it applies to people-centric workflow, routing is also an issue in EAI where information is moved from one application to another as a part of a business process. However, the routing challenges are simpler and easier to handle in an EAI solution for a number of reasons:

1. A business process dealing with enterprise applications has only a limited number of applications that can be recipients of a task or information. Companies having hundreds or even thousands of employees do not have a large number of enterprise applications. Typically there may be a dozen or two enterprise applications and those that are involved in a specific business process may only be a handful.
2. Applications play well-defined roles that are fixed. There is no need for role-based, relative or skill-based routings.
3. Workload balancing is not a major issue with applications. Most applications support some form of *message queue* that enables messages or tasks to be queued for processing when the needed application becomes available. Generally, the processing time for application tasks is very fast. With proper process modeling, a business process can be designed to ensure that there is no unacceptable backlog.

Conclusion

Task routing is a major goal and challenge for BPM systems, especially those dealing with people-centric business processes. Since organizations are complex and dynamic, BPM systems must provide means of handling change without redefining business processes or relying on hard-wired code that define the routing of work. As the use of BPM systems grows in a company, one of the most significant capabilities will be how well the systems cope with dynamically routing work in response to the constant flux in the organization and its ecosystem.

Chapter 7

BPM Solution Architectures

A BPM solution consists of a number of applications that work together to facilitate the design, development, testing, deployment, administration and continuous improvement of business processes. The BPM system must provide robust tools necessary to manage a business process through its life cycle. Multiple software modules are needed to cover all the stages in the life cycle of a typical business process. These software modules make up the overall architecture of a modern BPM solution.

The Business Process Life Cycle

A business process goes through a well-defined life cycle with distinct stages as shown in Figure 7.1.

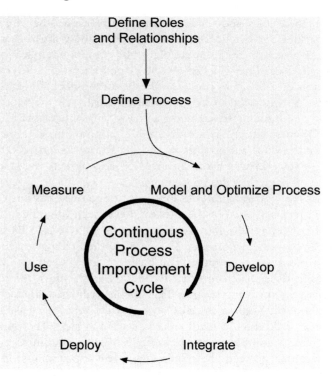

Figure 7.1. Detailed View of Business Process Lifecycle

The stages are as follows:

1. *Definition of Roles and Relationships:* The first stage in the business process life cycle is to define the roles and relationships of the participants in the process. This is an activity that is done by default in most companies, even before the use of any process. Roles are created for each employee as he or she joins the company, and employees's relationships with others are defined. In some small companies, the definitions of roles and relationships may be informal, but they do exist. Large companies usually have formal definitions in their organization charts and the roles of their employees. Roles and relationships are generally not tied to a particular business process and once a role has been defined, it can be associated with multiple processes. In any case, the availability of people, their roles and their relationships to each other are necessary prerequisites for business processes, even if they are not automated. For EAI processes the roles are played by computer applications.

2. *Defining Business Processes:* The second stage in a process life cycle is the definition of a business process. The definition generally evolves from the need to automate an existing manual process or the need to implement a new process based upon a change in the strategy of the company. Business processes are defined by business process owners who perceive the value for process innovation or improvement. This is a *paper design* stage in which the business process and its requirements are defined on paper in a design document.

3. *Modeling and Optimizing Business Processes:* After a need has been identified and the requirements of the process have been identified, a business analyst converts these into a series of tasks that have to be performed in order to satisfy the need. This is a detailed design of the process from a business perspective. The business analyst can also model the process in order to ensure that the design will achieve the results and benefits that are being sought. This entails making a series of assumptions about the volume of tasks, cost of each step, the availability of resources and the time it takes to complete each step. The purpose here is to create a complete process definition from a business perspective to ensure that it meets the requirements and expectations of the process owner.

4. *Developing Business Processes:* In this stage the business process definition created in the previous stage is converted into a practical solution that can be deployed. This activity is best performed by skilled IT professionals who understand the BPM tools and the technologies that work

in conjunction with them. These technologies may include databases, messaging, electronic document management systems, desktop applications, enterprise applications and user interfaces (among others). Testing is an integral part of the development stage. Because a BPM solution is a distributed application involving a large number of users, it is not practical to test it after it is deployed. This will inconvenience all the users and is also very difficult logistically. The use of simulation, much like aircraft designers use simulation for their new designs, can help accomplish much of the needed testing and reduce the burden on the users of the BPM system. A BPM tool with integrated simulation capabilities enables designers and quality assurance engineers to role-play and test the functionality and usability of the solution.

5. *Integration with Other Applications:* Once a process has been developed, it is necessary to integrate it with a variety of other desktop or back office computer applications. This activity is typically performed by software developers who use tools such as software development kits (SDKs), scripts, XML and Web Services to integrate the BPM solution with other computer applications. In many cases, BPM solutions provide *application agents* to integrate with specific applications, or use EAI *connectors* to enable the BPM system to communicate with other applications.

6. *Deployment and Administration:* After a business process has been developed, tested and integrated, it is ready for deployment. This stage requires some form of version control, migration from one platform to another, and the ability to configure and manage the BPM system and its various components.

7. *Active Processes:* This stage begins when the business process has been deployed and is live. Workflow participants can start using and benefiting from the BPM system. Users participate in a business process through user interfaces to the system that enable them to perform a variety of functions and manage their tasks.

8. *Reports:* BPM systems can capture valuable feedback on the efficiency and productivity of overall business processes and the performance of the individual participants. During this stage BPM systems use their reporting capabilities to capture process metrics that can be analyzed to optimize business processes or reallocate resources to improve performance.

9. *Optimization:* At the end of each cycle, business metrics generated through the reporting tool are used as feedback to the business process definition stage. The business process is refined to meet the realities discovered by reports generated by the BPM system. The refined

business process is re-developed and re-deployed as a new version, thus starting a new cycle of improvement and optimization.

As just explained, a BPM solution goes through iterative cycles of definition, development, deployment, use, measurement and optimization. Each stage of the life cycle involves different types of participants, including process owners, analysts, IT designers, developers, administrators and ultimately business users. The process life cycle is itself a business, a process of improvement that spans these many participants. Modern BPM software provides appropriate tools to support the various participants at each stage in the life cycle. These tools must be optimized for each type of participant that touches the business process. Table 7.1 lists the stages, the users involved in each stage and the tools used in that stage of the cycle. Taken together, these tools make up the overall BPM solution architecture.

Table 7.1. BPM Lifecycle Stages, Tools and Roles

BPM Lifecycle Stage	BPM Tool	Used By
Define Roles & Relationships	BPM Organization Chart	Process Owners
Define Process	BPM Modeler	Process Owners
Model & Optimize	BPM Modeler	Business Analyst
Develop	BPM Developer	IT Developer
Integrate	BPM Developer	Programmers
Deploy	BPM Administrator	IT Administrators
Use	Workflow Client	All Process Participants
Measure	BPM Reports	Business Analyst

Typical BPM Solution Architecture

The architecture of a contemporary BPM solution is illustrated in Figure 7.2. It shows the tools that are used in the various stages of the process life cycle, and the relationship of these tools to each other. The architecture is a classic, three-tier architecture that separates the information, the logic and the presentation or user interface into each separate layer. The information tier consists of the databases that are used in the business processes and to define and control these processes. The logic tier consists of the BPM server that interprets the business definitions, the roles and the rules to control and manage the processes. The presentation tier is the BPM client or user interface that enables users to interact with the BPM system and participate as players in the business processes.

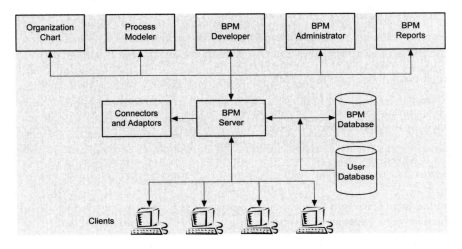

Figure 7.2. Typical BPM System Architecture

The organization chart is a tool used to define roles and relationships in an organization. Some BPM solutions provide a simple roles table or scripting capability to define roles and relationships. These roles tables can be cumbersome to work with, and thus are often maintained by IT staff who do not control these roles and relationships. The IT staff works at the behest of others, such as the human resources staff. Some BPM solutions, on the other hand, provide full-fledged, graphical organization chart tools that can be used by non-technical staff in the HR departments or other business units where the decisions about roles and relationships ultimately belong. Such advanced tools facilitate separating the business and technological aspects from each other, giving business units the ability to directly maintain their own definitions of roles and relationships.

The process modeler is used to design, document and model business processes. This tool is therefore used in the first stage of the business process life cycle by business process owners to define and document processes. It is important to understand that processes are *owned* by business units. BPM systems, however, are managed and maintained by IT departments that own the IT infrastructure on top of which the BPM solution operates. In other words, the IT staff does not *own* the business processes that run under the control of the BPM system. The process modeler is the tool that brides the gap between those who own business processes and those who own the technology infrastructure that enables the automation of these business processes.

The BPM developer is a software tool that enables IT professionals to convert business processes created using the process modeler into executable process software that automates the process. Every business process deals with databases, electronic forms, documents, business rules and variables. The execution of operational business processes relies on the facilities provided by application servers, Web sites, portals, authentication, security and data integrity software. All of these are technology issues that are outside the domain of typical business process owners who are the consumers, rather than providers, of technology. The combination of the process modeler and BPM developer enables process owners and IT professionals to excel in their areas of expertise without being burdened by the technologies or concepts from areas that are outside their primary focus and expertise.

Connectors and adaptors are software components provided by BPM systems that enable processes to integrate with desktop and enterprise applications.

The administrator consists of the tools needed to deploy and administer business processes. Common functions of such tools include installing new processes, upgrading existing processes by installing new versions, controlling access rights and privileges of participants, handling exceptions by reassigning tasks to other users, and the overall maintenance and management of the BPM server.

The BPM server is a *black box* whose function is to control and process live business processes and related tasks such as notifications and alerts. Since it is black-box software, it has no direct user interface except for the administrator. The BPM server is event triggered; it waits for specific events generated by the actions of process participants, including human actions and those of computer applications involved in the process. When an event occurs, the BPM server uses the process definition, the current state of the process saved in the BPM database, the nature of the events, and the user data to make decisions about the actions that are to be executed next. The BPM server then activates other steps, aborts steps or performs other activities to support the progress of the business process until it reaches completion.

The BPM database is used to store information necessary to manage and control the operational business processes. It is the *memory* of the BPM server and contains information such as the definition of every business process, as well as the rules and roles, the state of each instance of a process, the list of all tasks assigned to each user or application, and the metrics associated with each step. The BPM server uses this information to make decisions and take actions to proactively push for the completion of each process instance. The structure and content of the BPM database (called the *schema* by IT people), is established by the BPM software vendors since it is designed primarily for the benefit of the BPM server. However, many BPM system providers expose the schema to enable business analysts to gain access to the metrics and state information in the BPM database to generate performance-related reports. On the other hand, writing to the BPM database could be very dangerous since it may cause the integrity of processes to become corrupted. Therefore, some BPM systems provide read-only access to the BPM database.

The user database is any other database that is used in the business process. One of the main benefits of BPM systems is that they collect information for subsequent use. Such information can be disseminated to make decisions and take actions based on those decisions. A properly-designed BPM solution integrates user databases to facilitate seamless interaction between the live business process and corporate information. The user database is owned by a business unit. Therefore, its schema is controlled by the business unit and not by the BPM system. A BPM solution must provide a seamless method for the business process to interface with the user database without interfering with its schema. Furthermore, it is important to provide access with appropriate security mechanisms so that only those who have access rights can view or change specific types of data.

The client is a software component that allows users to participate in active business processes. It is essentially an electronic *inbox* that lists the tasks the user has to perform, as well as the status of tasks and other functions that make it easy for users to participate in the business process.

The reports module allows business managers and analysts to generate metrics reports for measuring the efficiency of the overall process, its steps or participants. This data can then be used to adjust resources or optimize the process.

Conclusion

BPM systems must provide scalability in ways extending beyond the traditional definition that uses transactional volume as the sole measure of scalability. A business process has a lifecycle during which many different categories of individuals interact with the process. These individuals have different skill sets, and therefore require different software tools that a BPM system must provide in order to scale for enterprise-wide use. Ease of developing modeling, automating, integrating, using, administering, measuring and optimizing business processes are also important factors that will dictate the wider adoption, or scalability, of the solution. By combining workflow and EAI, and by providing a means of extending business processes to employees, customers and partners, BPM systems will continue to require robust transaction volumes.

Chapter 8

Business Process Modeling and Analysis

The life cycle of a business process begins when it is conceived and sketched, models and scenarios are created, and its behavior is analyzed to optimize its performance. These three steps are collectively referred to as Business Process Modeling and Analysis (BPMA) and should take place before incurring the cost of developing and deploying a given solution. BPMA is vitally important for the success of BPM initiatives, but the work involved is often underestimated in the rush to deploy solutions. Business process modeling and analysis can be useful even if there are no plans to automate a business process, because this activity develops a clear definition and understanding of the process, often leading to improvements and optimization.

The first step in BPMA is to discover process requirements and graph a flow. This involves constructing a map of the business process along with detailed documentation of the requirements it must satisfy. Many BPM projects fail because not enough time is spent up-front to understand and prioritize user requirements. Business process owners play a key role in this first stage since they own the business requirements and the resources available. After the process has been designed it is in some cases important to model it in order to statistically predict how it will behave in real-life. The goal of modeling is to verify that the design will behave as expected, and to produce results that are consistent with the requirements of the business owners as well as the expectations of the customers who will be served by the process. Modeling is the domain of business analysts who use their judgment about the resources available to perform the tasks, the time it takes to complete each task, and the probabilities of various events that might occur in the course of the process. Information gathered by modeling can be used by business process owners to refine and optimize the model. This is the last step in BPMA.

This chapter first discusses the tools and capabilities required for building business process maps, and the roles of the individuals involved in this activity. This is followed by a discussion of modeling business processes in order to optimize their performance before they are developed and deployed. After the process has been modeled and refined, the next stage is to actually build it into an automated solution that can be deployed and used. This is a development activity that is best performed by skilled IT professionals and is discussed in Chapter 10, "BPM Process Development."

Why BPMA?

The best way to understand the importance of BPMA is by analogy. Building a new aircraft is a very expensive proposition. If a newly designed aircraft is built for the first time and fails its flight tests, the consequences are very bad and the cost of fixing the problem and rebuilding could be prohibitive. To avoid these consequences, aircraft manufacturers first generate requirements, and then develop a design on paper. Once this design has been finalized, they build a small-scale model at a fraction of the cost of the real thing, and test it in a wind tunnel to verify its performance. If the model fails in the wind tunnel, the aircraft is redesigned and another model is built and tested. This iterative process, which may be called "Aircraft Modeling and Analysis," continues until the design is perfected and the performance optimized. Only then does the aircraft manufacturer commit to producing a full-scale version. Furthermore, the team involved in designing and modeling in the wind tunnel is different from the one that builds the full-scale version. Other large-scale projects, such as building new cars, skyscrapers, ships and bridges, also use this methodology of gathering requirements, designing on paper, and building models to verify performance before full scale construction.

Business processes also have the same initial life cycle requirements for design, modeling and analysis for a number of reasons:

1. Business processes are often complex. It is important to fully understand and document user requirements before development. Failure to do so is often the reason why BPM initiatives are not successful.
2. Developing and testing a BPM application is an expensive undertaking for mission-critical or high value-add processes. Companies cannot afford the economic and political cost of failure caused by deploying poorly designed or un-optimized business processes. The effective use of BPMA minimizes the risk of failure and enables flaws to be detected and corrected before an automated process is developed and deployed.

Business processes are owned by business managers who are generally not IT savvy and do not own the IT infrastructure. On the other hand, automated business processes are developed and deployed by IT people who have the expertise for the development and control of the IT infrastructure that is used for hosting and enabling automated business processes. BPMA tools bridge the gap between the business process owner and

IT. They do this by enabling the former to design, document and optimize processes, and the latter to take the process design and convert it into deployable IT solutions. Without BPMA, the interaction between business owners and IT can be much more challenging and complex, resulting in a costly mismatch of expectations.

BPMA and Six Sigma

Six Sigma process improvement initiatives are becoming popular in corporations seeking to reduce business costs and improve customer satisfaction. As companies explore opportunities for improvement they discover that somewhere in the range of 60% to 70% of their projects are transactional business processes as opposed to design or manufacturing activities. During Six Sigma projects the role of the Six Sigma expert, the Black Belt, is to map the process, determine root causes of process problems and determine breakthroughs in performance. Black Belts use the Define, Measure, Analyze, Improve and Control (DMAIC) methodology as their road map for improvement.

Table 8.1 shows the relationship of Six Sigma DMAIC and BPMA activities as they apply to business process modeling and optimization.

Table 8.1. Relationships Between Six Sigma DMAIC and BPMA

Six Sigma	Activity	BPMA
Define	High level process map	Design process map
	Detailed process map	
Measure	Gather empirical process data	Model the process
	Determine process capability	
Analyze	Analysis of data	Analysis of data
	Determine root cause	Identify improvements
Improve	Determine "should be process"	Improve the process
	Eliminate, simplify, automate	Automate workflow
	Determine risks	Model all improvements
	Pilot & validate improvements	Validate improvements
Control	Determine controls	Document process
	Complete documentation	Determine savings
	Compute benefits	

As the table shows, BPMA is a natural extension of Six Sigma, particularly when the project is heavily weighted toward transactional activities.

Because modern BPMA software tools are simple to learn and use and provide an organized method for process mapping and analysis, they are ideal additions to the Six Sigma toolkit. In fact, the core competency for Black Belts and Master Black Belts includes the ability to use BPMA tools for process mapping, modeling, analysis and improvement and as the front-end for complete process automation.

BPMA and ISO 9000

The essence of ISO 9000 quality initiatives is "Say what you do, and do what you say." ISO 9000 requires organizations to understand and document their processes, then train their employees to ensure that the processes are properly executed as documented. The goal is to improve the quality of the organization by ensuring that the processes are repeated consistently. Performance improvements can be implemented only after a process can be measured and repeated consistently.

BPMA provides a methodology to understand and document business processes. Therefore, it provides a mechanism for organizations to codify their processes to benefit from quality improvement initiatives such as ISO 9000. Conversely, if organizations have achieved ISO 9000 certification and documented their processes, they can leverage this effort to use these documented processes as the first step to business process management.

Business Process Design

The first stage in business process management is the creation of a business model, or map, of the process to be automated, and the discovery and documentation of its key requirements. Modeling means building the conceptual design of the process from a business perspective and defining its various steps. This stage should be clearly differentiated from the technical development and implementation of the process. During this phase key decisions are made about many aspects of the business process:

1. What events trigger the initiation of new incidents?
2. What are the tasks that must be performed during the course of the process from beginning to end? What is the sequence and granularity of these tasks?
3. Who will perform tasks at each step?
4. What are the important pieces of information that must be provided at each step? What are the actions that individuals or applications performing these tasks must take? What are the outputs or results that

have to be obtained from each step?

5. What are the rules that govern the activation of each step?
6. What are the special conditions or exceptions that must be handled by the process?
7. What are the expected completion times for each task and the overall process, and the actions that must be taken if these expectations are not met?
8. What interfaces have to be provided with external systems for receiving or submitting information that is used or produced by the process?
9. How are special conditions and exceptions to be handled? For example, what must happen if a user of a particular task returns the step for lack of information? What happens if new information is received about the case while it is already in progress?

Business process owners responsible for managing the delivery of information, goods or services are in the best position to provide answers to these questions. Business process owners must match the overall strategy of the company, the resources available to them, and the requirements of the customers served by the business process. They decide on the sequence of activities that must be performed, and are also aware of the exceptions or special conditions that must be handled in specific ways. However, business process owners are generally not skilled IT professionals, and neither should they be involved in detailed development and implementation of automated solutions. Their role is the definition of the model and the business rules that govern its execution, and not the conversion of the process model into deployable solutions. For these reasons, the software tools used for modeling should be simple so that non-technical process owners can be comfortable in their use. In many ways, BPMA software serves as *electronic paper*. Instead of using paper and pencil, business owners use the software to electronically sketch out the process and take notes about key requirement, exceptions and special conditions.

A *process designer* is a software tool for BPMA that can be used by non-technical business process owners to model business processes. A key component of the process designer is the map designer that allows the user to graphically layout the sequence of steps involved in a business process from initiation to completion. Chapter 5, "Inside Business Processes," outlines the components that make up a process map and the flexibility that must be embedded into processes in order to create robust solutions. A process designer must be able to provide this flexibility. The following are some basic requirements.

1. A process designer must allow the graphical insertion of various types of steps into a map.
2. A process designer must link steps in the sequence they must be executed.
3. A process designer must allow the insertion of labels to annotate the map with useful and descriptive information.
4. A process designer must be able to add anchors in the map, so as to route links as straight lines or to bypass other objects in the map.

After a process map has been developed, the BPMA tool enables the user to add properties to the map and each step of the process. These properties include descriptions of activities, recipients and special events and conditions that impact the process. It is important to note that in the design and definition stage the primary focus is on the description of the process and its components, and not the actual implementation.

After a business process has been designed and the key requirements, exceptions and special conditions documented, it is often necessary to render the design into an electronic document that can be reviewed and shared with others. The purpose of this documentation is two-fold. First, it is the means of educating other participants or beneficiaries about the purpose and requirements of the process. Second, it is the means for transferring the requirements and knowledge of the business process owners to the IT team responsible for developing and deploying the solution. Modern BPMA tools also provide the capability to take the process map and produce an electronic document that describes the process, its components and requirements.

Modeling Business Processes

Developing and deploying process automation solutions are often complex and expensive IT projects. Therefore, it behooves a business organization to try to predict the behavior of a process after designing and documenting it, but before incurring the cost of development and deployment. This is analogous to the design of new airplanes whose development is very expensive. Aerospace engineers first build a model of a new airplane and test it in a wind tunnel. If it does not behave as expected or desired, it is time to go back to the drawing board to change and improve the model and test it again. Only after they are satisfied that the model behaves according to design objectives do they commit to its development and production.

The purpose of process modeling is to assess the behavior of a business process before it is actually developed and deployed. If the model behaves as expected, the project can proceed with development and deployment. Otherwise, the project team has three choices. First, they can change the process model to eliminate the bottlenecks or other factors that do not measure up to expectations. Second, they can add more resources to improve the performance or eliminate bottlenecks. Third, they can reset the expectations of the customers served by the process so that the expectations are consistent with what the model predicts. All three of these choices are acceptable as long as they are accepted and understood before the automated process is put into production. Doing so afterwards causes frustration and disenchantment with the overall BPM solution.

BPMA software can perform workload and throughput analysis on a process prior to the development of a deployable solution. This capability enables business analysts to use the process developed by the process owner and provide estimates about resource availability and completion times for each step. BPMA software can then run a large number of process incidents through the model and produce statistical data indicating lag time, elapsed time and bottlenecks in the process. The results of modeling can be used by process owners and business analysts to change the process, or the resources used by the process, with the goal of optimizing its performance. Modeling enables business owners and analysts to predict the behavior of a process well before it is actually developed, deployed and used. By knowing this behavior, business owners can understand the benefits and the constraints of the solution. An example of how modeling can help in optimizing a business process is provided later in this chapter.

Statistical modeling for optimization is not necessary for all business processes. It is generally useful only for processes that have high volumes and resource constraints, such as claims processing, order processing and call centers. For these types of processes it is necessary to optimize the process design and the allocation of resources in order to ensure that it is efficient and cost-effective. On the other hand, processes that are not resource constrained, or involve creativity by knowledge workers, cannot be optimized using statistical modeling. Creativity should not be constrained by strict time restrictions, and the creative process has its own dynamics that may not follow pre-defined paths and assumptions. Trying to optimize such a process through modeling will most likely be counterproductive. Likewise, many administrative processes that are not resource constrained will not benefit from statistical modeling techniques. For example, employee performance review processes are prevalent in every organization and are excellent candidates for process automation. A manager may perform ten performance reviews a year. The manager is not performing reviews all the time. If a review becomes due, the manager will have to find the time in his or her schedule to conduct the review. It generally does not make sense to use modeling to optimize such a process. And the company will most likely not hire another manager simply because a particular manager could not do reviews in time. The organization's policies and procedures, and not the results of modeling, will determine how performance reviews are performed.

Modeling enables the business process owner or analyst to ask questions such as:

1. How many incidents of the business process can be completed in a week?
2. If new cases are coming in at the rate of 100 per day, how many new people should be added to various steps in order to ensure that every case gets processed in three days?
3. What is the cost of performing a particular step in a process?
4. If the number of claim appraisers is reduced to half, how long will it take to process a typical claim?
5. How long does it take the bank to process a loan? How much more will it cost to reduce the time by 50%?
6. What is the minimum amount of time a person will have to spend to perform a particular step in a business process without creating a bottleneck?
7. How much time and money can we save by automating a particular step in a process? Does that automation allow us to adjust resource loads elsewhere and still meet our goals?

Modeling Scenarios

Modeling is the domain of business analysts. They use their experience to define scenarios that approximate real-life conditions. A scenario is a set of assumptions about the resources used in a business process and the probabilities of various events that might occur during the course of a process. Some of the assumptions are about the process overall and reflect the business rules of the company that may influence the process. Other assumptions are about the resources and time used at various steps in the process. Finally, there is a set of assumptions relating to the probabilities of various events that might happen at specific points in the process. Each set of assumptions constitutes a scenario.

Process-Level Assumptions

Process-level assumptions are assumptions that are made about the business process as a whole. They include the following:

1. Rate: A business process starts because of some event, such as the receipt of a new order, hiring of a new employee, or submission of a new claim. These events trigger an incident of a business process designed to respond to the event. The rates at which these events occur determine the number and frequency of the incidents. This will dictate the resources required to handle the work generated by these incidents.

2. Incident Count: The purpose of modeling is to run a number of incidents of a process in order to gather statistical data that predicts how the process will behave under a given set of assumptions. Some business processes are not resource constrained and will achieve steady state behaviors after only a few incidents. Others might be more complex and achieve steady state behavior after many incidents. And yet other may never reach steady state. The Incident Count setting in a scenario specifies the number of incidents that must be run through the model in order to provide enough data that is statistically significant.

3. Pre-Load Incidents: The goal of modeling is to measure and optimize the performance of a business process when it is in the midst of operations. When a process starts, there is nothing in the *pipeline.* The first few incidents that go through the system are processed relatively quickly because people or applications are waiting to perform tasks and have nothing else to do. The true measure of the response time and efficiency of a model is when the pipeline is full. The "pre-load incident" parameter in BPMA tools allows the analyst to specify the number of incidents that are run before it begins to capture data for modeling. These incidents fill up the pipeline in order to provide a more realistic estimate of the responsiveness of the model. If the incident count is set to 100 and the pre-load is set to 10, the scenario requires that 10 incidents to be started and processed, but the data from these incidents is not used. The 11th to 110th incidents are used to gather the data for statistically determining the behavior of 100 incidents.

4. Day Calendar: Modeling involves mimicking the behavior of individuals as they go about completing process tasks assigned to them. Companies have pre-defined work hours and break times scheduled for their employees. A scenario should include a specification of the work hours of the individuals involved in the process, and the break times during which they are not working. Specification of a working day calendar makes the model realistic. The day calendar has to span one day only, and not be concerned with weekends or holidays. This is because the model will replicate behavior over a specific number of business or working days only, and discounts weekends and holidays.

5. Task Priority: When a user selects a task from the task list, the user can prioritize the tasks in two different ways. First, the user may simply decide to perform the first task that is in his or her inbox regardless of any other factor. This is the first-in, first-out (FIFO) approach. Second, the user may decide to do the task belonging to the incident that was started the earliest under the assumptions that the incidents should be prioritized in the order they were initiated. This approach is called "incident priority". The selection of one of these methods of prioritizing tasks can significantly impact the model, especially if the business process is not a simple linear flow. Incident priority should therefore be included in the scenario.

6. Method of Generating Random Time Durations: BPMA software allows the business analyst to specify expected times for completing various activities performed by users or applications. In the real world it is unrealistic to expect any activity to always take a precise time. To make modeling realistic, the BPMA software must enable the analyst to specify how to generate a random time for each activity within some range. This is accomplished by allowing the analyst to select either a "uniform distribution" or a "normal distribution" as part of the process level assumptions.

If a uniform distribution is selected, the analyst has to specify a minimum and maximum value for the time duration of each activity. When the software generates the time for an activity, it uses a random number generator to generate a number between, and inclusive of, the maximum and minimum specified. In this way the software ensures that the probability of generating the time is evenly distributed between the minimum and maximum values. The likelihood of the time being at the "minimum" or the "maximum" is the same as every other intermediate value. This is illustrated in Figure 8.1. A uniform distribution is easier to understand and implement, but is not realistic. In most cases the time estimated for any activity will be closer to some average or mid-point between the maximum and minimum. It is easier to estimate the mean average. Furthermore, a uniform distribution implies that the chance of getting any value within the range is equal to any other value. However, for any value outside the range the chance suddenly drops to zero, which is not realistic.

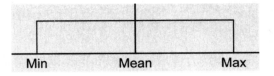

Figure 8.1. Uniform Distribution

A normal or Gaussian distribution can be used to make time estimation more realistic. If this method is selected, the analyst has to specify an estimated mean and a standard deviation (also called sigma or σ). In a normal distribution the probability of randomly generating the time is the highest near the mean, and decreases further away from the mean, as illustrated in Figure 8.2. Furthermore, a normal distribution guarantees the probability of generating a time value in certain ranges measured around the mean.

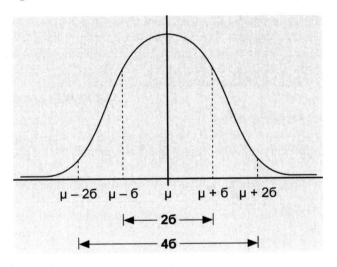

Figure 8.2. Normal Distribution

These probabilities and ranges are shown in Table 8.2. Thus, if the mean is 10 and the standard deviation is 2, the probabilities of generating values in various ranges are as follows:

68.27% of the values will be between 8 and 12
95.45% of the values will be between 6 and 14

99.7% of the values will be between 4 and 16
99.99% of the values will be between 2 and 18

Table 8.2. Probabilities for Various Sigma Values in Normal Distribution

Sigma (σ)	Probability Value is between (Mean- σ) and (Mean+ σ)
1	68.27%
2	95.45%
3	99.73%
4	99.99%

From this explanation it is easy to see that most of the values will fall around the mean. The chance of a value being very far from the mean decreases, but it is always possible. The standard deviation is a measure of how close the values are likely to be in relationship to the mean. A small standard deviation implies that most of the values will be closer to the mean, whereas if standard deviation is large the values will be spread out. By using a normal distribution, the analyst can specify the mean or expected value, and also the variation about the mean.

Step-Level Assumptions

A scenario also contains assumptions about each step. These assumptions are related to the time it takes to perform tasks at the step:

1. Task Time: This is an estimate of the amount of time it takes to perform the task for a step.

2. Lag Time: This is an estimate of the minimum dead (or *away* time) between tasks. It is based on the assumption that when a person completes a task, he or she does not immediately start working on the next task. This is especially true if the assigned task is not the primary responsibility of the person; this individual might have other duties to perform that have nothing to do with this business process. On the other hand, if a person is totally dedicated to performing this task and has no other responsibilities, the "lag time" property can be specified as "0." In this case, the person will start a new task as soon as the previous task is completed. However, if the lag time property is not set as "0," it is assumed that the person will spend a minimum time equal to the lag time after the completion of the task: performing other duties before starting the next task. The emphasis is on the word minimum, because after this time has elapsed the person can start the next task only if there is a new task in his or her inbox. If there is no new task in the inbox when the lag time has expired, the next task will start as soon as it arrives in the inbox.

3. Number of Resources: More than one individual may be assigned to perform a particular task in the business process. Therefore, for each step, the number of people assigned to the step must be specified. If a step involves computer applications or machinery instead of people, then this parameter is used to specify the number of applications or machinery available to perform the task at that step.

4. Task Rate: This is the burden or overhead rate of the users assigned to completing the task for the step. By multiplying the overhead rate with the task time, the software can calculate the cost of performing the step.

5. Percent (%) Returned: A certain number of tasks for a step may be returned for lack of information or some other factors. The "percent returned" variable in a scenario can be used to specify the probability of a task being returned.

6. Percent (%) Resubmitted and Resubmit Time: After a task has been completed, it is sometimes necessary to open and resubmit the same task again because of the availability of new information or some other external event. For example, if a customer places an order it may trigger a business process when the order entry clerk enters the order form. However, at some point after the order has been placed, the customer may change his or her mind about some aspects of the order (such as the quantity to be purchased). Instead of canceling the entire incident, the order entry clerk may simply resubmit the order with the new quantity. This ensures that tasks that are not impacted by the change are not affected, whereas those that are impacted can be performed again. A scenario, therefore, should provide a "percent resubmitted" setting that allows the analyst to estimate the probability that a task may be resubmitted. Furthermore, if a task is resubmitted, there is another variable called "resubmit time" that allows the analyst to specify an estimated time duration after which the step may be resubmitted.

Event Conditions and Probabilities

Each step in the process map may have event conditions and actions associated with it (as discussed in Chapter 5, "Inside Business Processes.") These event conditions and actions allow the process map to incorporate business rules that change the flow of the process when events occur under specific conditions. While modeling a process and defining a scenario, the business analyst has to make assumptions about the probability of a particular action being taken. For example, a business process may have a rule that the department manager must approve a purchase order if the amount of the order is more than $1,000, or if the item being purchased is hazardous material. In real life, the business process will be driven by the actual value of the order or the type of the item being purchased. However, while modeling the behavior of the process, the business analyst must make assumptions about the probability of occurrence for these events. BPMA software allows the business analyst to enter probabilities for conditional events in the model. These probabilities become an integral part of the scenario and impact the routing and performance of the incidents during modeling.

When constructing process models and defining scenarios, it is often necessary to link or associate one event with the occurrence of another, as shown in Figure 8.3.

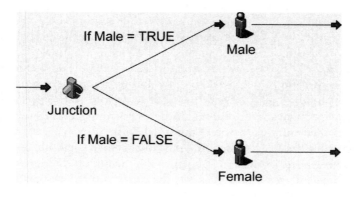

Figure 8.3. Linking Probabilities of Events

The Male step is to be invoked only if the candidate is a male, and the Female step is invoked if the candidate is female. The candidate can be one or the other. If the chances of the candidate being male are 49%, the business analyst cannot simply assign a probability of 49% to the Male step and 51% to the Female step. This is because they are two independent, random numbers. It is therefore entirely possible that the first number results in the determination that the candidate is male, and the second number results in the determination that the candidate is female. This situation will result in both steps being activated. What is needed is a mechanism to tie these steps together so that if a random determination is made that the candidate is a male then it is inferred that it cannot be a female. This is accomplished by using a variable, then setting the value of the variable based on the random number. In our example, a variable called "Male" could be defined like so:

Male = TRUE if Random Number □ 49 Else FALSE

Then a condition could be assigned for the Male step as "activate" if Male=TRUE; for the Female step, "activate" if Male=FALSE. There are many other similar situations where variables are necessary for linking conditions.

Executing a Model

The modeling of a process starts after the business analyst has created a scenario. During the course of modeling, the BPMA software uses the information about the model and the scenarios to run a large number of imaginary incidents through completion in order to capture statistical data reflecting the performance of the process under the given scenario. The BPM software does so by playing three different roles:

- It plays the role of the individuals or applications performing tasks at each step of the process. The scenario assumptions pertaining to each step provide information about the lag time and task time. The software uses this information to determine when and how fast each step is performed.
- The software plays the role of the engine or BPM server. It uses the process map to decide the sequence in which the steps are executed, and the conditional event probabilities in the step scenarios to determine those that are to be executed on a conditional basis.
- The software plays the role of *time*. It maintains an *internal modeling clock* in lieu of real time. It advances the internal modeling clock as soon as an activity is completed so that the model can be completed much faster than it would be in real life. Furthermore, it uses a random number generator to determine probabilities for various events and the time taken for each activity.

By playing these different roles, the BPMA software can run a specific number of incidents through the process and mimic how each incident would be processed in real life. During the course of modeling, it captures data about how long it takes to complete each step, the overall process and the bottlenecks encountered during execution. This data is then used to generate reports or the data is exported to third-party applications for statistical analysis.

There are two primary methods of implementing statistical modeling:

time-driven and event-driven. In time-driven statistical modeling, the software maintains an *internal modeling clock* (IMC) and increments the IMC by a specified constant value. After each increment, the software evaluates the process map, the tasks for each *worker* and the task time and lag time for each activity. It then takes all the actions that need to be taken at that given time. The IMC is incremented, and decisions are made and actions taken for the new time. This cycle is repeated until the number of incidents specified by the "incident count" setting is completed. Figure 8.4 represents a flow chart for time-driven statistical modeling.

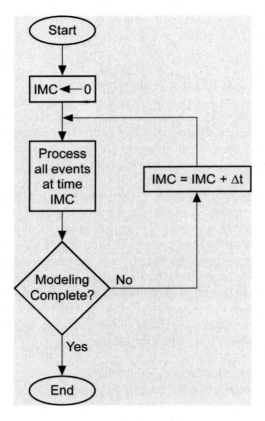

Figure 8.4. Flowchart for Time-Driven Modeling

Time-driven modeling is easier to understand since most events in life are driven by time. However, it is inefficient because the IMC increments have nothing to do with how fast events are happening in the model. Time-driven modeling, therefore, results in a large number of redundant cycles where precious time is wasted because no events are occurring. Furthermore, it requires the analyst to select the time increment. If the increment is too small, the modeling will go through a large number of unnecessary cycles and simply waste time. If it is too large, it is possible that modeling may produce incorrect results because critical events that fall within the increments may not be accounted for in a timely manner.

Event-driven modeling is more complex. However, it is very efficient since it only involves as many cycles as are absolutely necessary to produce accurate results. In this technique the software begins by determining all known events that have to take place next for every step in the model, and the time when each event will take place. The internal modeling clock is set to the time at which the next event will take place. All decisions and actions at that time are taken and any new resulting events are determined and included in the list of events. The IMC is set to the next earliest event time, and the cycle is repeated. A flow chart for event-driven statistical modeling is shown in Figure 8.5. Since the IMC is incremented to the time at which the next event will occur, it involves only as many cycles as there are events from the start to the end of modeling. Furthermore, the analyst does not have to judge the size of the increment. The software determines the increment itself and adjusts it dynamically based upon what is called for in the model and the scenario.

Results of Modeling

Modeling is capable of producing a variety of statistical results that enable business analysts to analyze and optimize the performance of a process. Some examples of relevant reports include:

1. Incident Elapsed Time: This report provides statistical information about the total time it takes to complete a business process. It enables business owners to set realistic customer expectations about how long it will take the organization to process a loan, a claim or some other request. Or it can be used to measure the overall performance or throughput of the process as compared to the expectations of customers. It provides a histogram of the number of incidents that were completed in various time durations. The mean value indicates the typical time it takes to complete a process incident. The standard deviation provides a measure of the consistency of performance. If the standard deviation is small, it implies that the process is

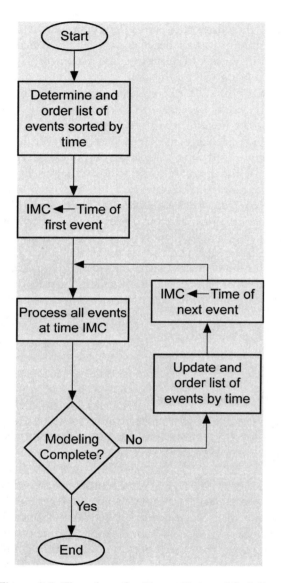

Figure 8.5. Flowchart for Event-Driven Modeling

controlled and can consistently complete incidents close to the mean time. On the other hand, a high standard deviation means that there are large fluctuations in performance. This report is most commonly used to determine whether the process is being completed in the time desired. If the rates are substantially higher or lower than desired, or the deviation is high, then additional resources or more automation may be required to achieve desired time results.

2. Incident Cost: This report provides statistical information about the cost of processing an incident. It allows business owners to assess the benefits of the process versus its overall cost. The cost can be either provided as a single number for the entire process, or can be broken down by each step in the process. This allows business managers to determine the task or activities that contribute most to the overall cost of the process. By analyzing these costs, business managers may be able to redesign or modify the process with the goal of reducing the overall cost. For example, if the incident cost report indicates that a significant percentage of cost is incurred by tasks that have to be performed by a senior executive, perhaps the process could be redesigned so that fewer tasks are assigned to senior executives.

3. Step Task Time: This report provides statistical information about the time it takes to complete a particular step in a business process. Since the task time for each step is one of the assumptions in the scenario, the step task report will closely match the step task time specified in the scenario with variability introduced only by randomness.

4. Step Lag Time: This report provides information about the lag or dead time for any step in the business process. The lag time is a combination of the lag time specified in the scenario plus the unproductive time a user spends waiting for new tasks. The latter becomes the major factor in the lag time if the business process is not balanced. To be *not balanced* means that the process is designed such that some steps have a high workload so that the participants cannot keep up, while others have too little work and they are waiting for tasks.

5. Step Elapsed Time: This report provides information about the total time consumed by each step in the business process. It is a measure of how long on the average it takes a task to be completed from the moment it reaches a particular step in the business process. The elapsed time is a combination of the task time and the lag time of the step. It measures the throughput of the step.

6. Step Cost: This report calculates the cost of a step in the business process. It is calculated by multiplying the task time with the rate cost for each step. It can be used to determine how much each step contributes to the cost of the entire process. This enables the business analyst to assess the cost of each activity in a process and weigh it against the benefit of the activity to the success of the overall process.

7. Step Utilization: This report displays the distribution of the time for a step that was consumed in performing the task (task time), waiting for tasks (wait time), or spent in other activities not related to the task (lag time). It provides insight in to how time is being consumed. If the wait time is very high, it is an indication that there are too many resources being used at the step, and these resources are not being effectively utilized. On the other hand, if the task time is very high and the wait time is negligible, there is too much work for the amount of resources. To address this, the analyst has to either add more resources, or decrease the lag time so that more time is available for this particular step.

8. Process Utilization: This report is similar to the step capacity utilization, but shows how time is utilized across all steps in the process. It provides an overview of how time is being utilized by all the resources used at every step. Again, if the wait time is high and task time is low, resources are being under-utilized and are waiting for new tasks to be processed. On the other hand, if the task time is high and the wait time is negligible, resources are being effectively utilized. In this case there is the risk that if the rate of incoming incidents increase, bottlenecks may develop in the process.

9. Under Utilization Report: This report displays a pie chart of the wait time for all the steps in a process. This allows the analyst to graphically determine which steps in the process have the most under-utilized resources. The analyst can then zero in on these steps in order to reduce the wait time.

10. Balance Report: This report simply plots the incident number versus the total elapsed time for the incident. This provides a graphical view of the change in the total elapsed time to complete each successive incident of the process. It provides a good mechanism for determining if the process is stable and its resources are balanced. If the graph is flat and each value varies about some mean value, it means that the resources are balanced and the elapsed time of all incidents is not systemically increasing. If, on the other hand, the curve continues to increase it means that the process is not balanced and the elapsed time will continue to increase because there are not enough resources to perform the tasks. Work is backing up. When optimizing a business process, the first step is to make sure that it is balanced. Once the process has been balanced, then the business analyst can try to optimize cost or reduce the elapsed time while ensuring that it does not become imbalanced.

Conclusion

Business process modeling and analysis is an important part of BPM that enables organizations to understand, document and optimize their business processes. It can add value and improve organizational productivity even if the business processes are not automated. BPMA tools enable organizations to identify opportunities for reducing time, decreasing cost, and managing the workloads of individuals involved in business processes. If processes are automated using a BPM system, BPMA allow actual process metrics to be used for continuous improvement of business processes.

A free copy of a BPMA tool has been provided to demonstrate the use of modern BPMA software for modeling, documenting and optimizing business processes. Interested readers can download this software tool from *www.practicalbpm.com* by using the Access Code CQN1952. A sample process and a document describing how to use the software for process optimization can also be downloaded.

Chapter 9

BPM Server and Administration

A BPM server is at the heart of a BPM system. It is a "black box" whose purpose is to control the execution of business processes and ensure that process incidents continue to move towards completion. If a BPM system is the central nervous system of an organization, the BPM server is the cerebral cortex that provides the logic and memory interfaces to control the overall system. This chapter will first discuss the requirements and technologies used for modern BPM servers. This is followed by an in-depth discussion of two important tools that are needed to support the BPM server. The first is the BPM administrator, which is the user interface of the BPM server and is used to manage it. The second is a "roles manager" or organization chart that enables the BPM server to be aware of the human resources available in order to involve people in business processes using the routing techniques discussed in Chapter 6, "Smart Ways of Routing Work."

The BPM Server

The BPM server is the brain of a BPM system. In most cases, the BPM server has very little or no user interface. Instead it is a service running on a back office server that monitors and controls business processes. The BPM administrator provides all the configuration and management facilities of the BPM server. The key requirements of a BPM server are:

1. *Reliability:* The BPM server must have a very high uptime. Any downtime results in the business processes of the company coming to a standstill. While reliability is important by itself, its importance increases as the volume or the mission-critical nature of processes increases.

2. *Scalability:* The BPM server must enable companies to expand the number of users and the tasks they are performing. BPM is initially adopted in companies as relatively small departmental initiatives with a handful of processes. Once the benefits of the solution have been verified, its use is expanded to other departments and a larger number of processes. Thus, the BPM server, and indeed the rest of the BPM solution, must be able to scale in terms of the number of users and the number of transactions that it can support.

3. *Error Detection and Recovery:* The BPM server must provide some mechanism for detecting errors in a business process or in the operating environment, and a method of gracefully recovering from these errors.

Scalability and Speed

A BPM server must be able to respond quickly to events. When a user initiates a new process incident, the BPM server must determine the next steps, activate those steps, and in the case of steps performed by people, send out an e-mail notification to the recipient of the those steps. When a user completes a step the BPM server must again respond rapidly to the action and decide whether to execute subsequent steps. As the number of users, the number of automated business processes, and the number of incidents for each process increase, so does the need for speed as more and more demands will be placed on the BPM server. BPM solutions that cater to application-to-application or EAI processes have much higher speed requirements than people-centric processes. This is obvious because application-centric processes move data among enterprise applications that can operate at much faster speeds than people.

The speed of the BPM server depends on a number of factors:

1. *The performance of the computer hardware used to host the BPM server.* In general modern systems require high-speed multi-processor computers, a large amount of memory, and fast disk drives with ample space. The price of hardware is constantly declining. Upgrading hardware is one of the most cost-effective ways of improving overall system speed and performance. Moreover, the configuration of the computers on which the BPM server is deployed also contributes immensely to overall performance.

2. *The design of the BPM server software and its architecture.* Once a BPM system has been selected, its architecture cannot be changed. Therefore, it is important for potential buyers to investigate the architecture of the BPM server before they purchase in order to verify that it uses modern technologies that will not create performance bottlenecks.

3. *The size of the business process.* The larger and more complex a business process, the longer it will take to interpret it in real-time and make decisions about subsequent steps when a particular step is completed. Large complex business processes typically need more resources that impact performance.

4. *The complexity of business logic.* Whenever a process step is completed, the BPM server has to make decisions about the next steps to be activated. If a step has associated condition tables, this evaluation takes longer. The more complex the condition tables the longer it take to perform the evaluation.

A high performance BPM server provides a scalable architecture that maintains its performance and responsiveness as more and more users are added to the system and is required to perform an increasing number of transactions. This is achieved by object-oriented design and the use of network and object load balancing techniques offered by modern operating systems. While a detailed description of these operating systems is beyond the scope of this book and covered in excellent references [8], a basic understanding of how this is accomplished is provided in the section on architecture below.

Reliability

Many users participate in business processes automated by a BPM server. If the BPM server breaks down, business process will come to a standstill and will have a very negative impact on productivity. A BPM server must provide excellent reliability and uptime. This is best accomplished by using an architecture that supports fail-over redundancy. If one server fails, there is always one or more back-up servers that can kick-in and continue processing with negligible impact on the participants or throughput of processes. How this can be achieved will be discussed later in this chapter. However, reliability of a BPM solution does not depend on the reliability of the BPM server alone. It also depends on a number of other infrastructure resources that are necessary for the operation of the BPM systems. These include network connectivity and reliability, databases and their reliability, and the reliability of other systems involved in BPM. These include e-mail, document management, directory services, Web servers, and others. When planning the reliability of a BPM system, it is important to analyze and improve the reliability of all other systems used with the BPM system.

Fault Detection and Recovery

A business process can come to a standstill even when there is no failure in the operating system or the hardware used to host the server. This happens when a process incident stalls due to poor or incorrect process design. When an incident stalls, no task is active for any user and no one is aware that the incident has stalled unless someone is constantly monitoring the incident. This, of course, is impractical. Furthermore, if one incident stalls, it is likely that many others will also stall in due course. Therefore, a BPM server must provide a mechanism of detecting stalled incidents and notifying appropriate process owners, who then can take corrective actions to resolve the root cause of the stall. There are two mechanisms that a BPM server can use to detect and handle stalled processes:

1. *Periodic Housekeeping:* This is an independent software service that operates as a part of the BPM server. It is designed to run at periodic intervals. During these periodic intervals it performs a number of housekeeping tasks to ensure the integrity of the system. These tasks may include checking for stalled incidents, monitoring the availability of system resources such as memory, disk space and database connections, and finding out if tasks are late. If the housekeeping service determines that one or more incidents have stalled, it can generate e-mail or system alerts so that corrective actions should be taken.

2. *Incident Completion Time:* Some BPM systems provide an "incident completion time" property as a part of the process definition. This is the time allowed for the incident to complete after it has been initiated. If a process stalls, the incident completion time will eventually expire, triggering a notification event. This feature may also be used to alert the BPM administrator that the incident time has been exceeded. However, this is not as good a solution as the first, since it waits until the incident completion time has expired instead of taking corrective action as soon as the incident stalls. Furthermore, the incident completion time may expire for reasons other than the incident stalling, such as a user who fails to perform his task in the allotted time.

Architecture of a BPM Server

Key attributes of the architecture of a BPM server include speed, scalability and high availability. The architecture is based on modern object technologies supported by various versions of Microsoft Windows servers such as COM, COM+ and .NET. Similar distributed object technologies are provided by UNIX/LINUX platforms in the form of CORBA or J2EE.

A modern BPM server has fundamentally the same architecture as any other n-tier enterprise application designed for scalability. These applications use Distributed Object Models (COM, COM+, CORBA or J2EE). A detailed description of these technologies is beyond the scope of this book and there are several excellent references that cover them in detail [9],[10],[11]. However, a discussion of the core concepts of these technologies is provided to offer an understanding of how they can be used to offer scalability, reliability and redundancy.

The easiest way to understand an "object" is to think of it as a self-contained piece of software that can be called by other applications to perform a specific service or task. When an object is called upon to perform a function, a copy of the object is created in the server's memory. This object persists for only as long as it is needed to perform the functions. During this time it consumes resources such as memory and database connections to perform the functions. Once the function is completed, the object "dies" and frees up the resources it was using so that they can be used by other objects. This is illustrated in Figure 9.1. A client application wants the server to perform a specific function. It therefore sends a request to the server. The server creates an object capable of performing that function. The object then performs the function; once the object completes that function, it sends the response back the client, and then dies.

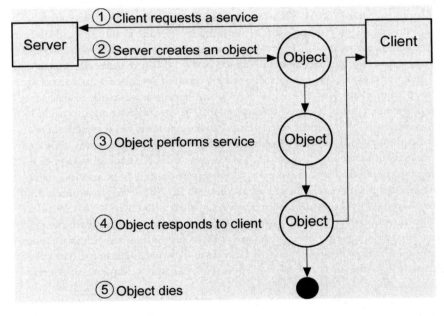

Figure 9.1. Using Objects to Handle Client Requests

One of the most significant things about objects is that their design needs to be concerned about supporting one client. They are "single user and single function," and therefore much easier to develop than a program that performs a function for many clients simultaneously. If more than one client asks for the same function, the server simply creates another copy of the object to handle that request. Thus, objects are created to handle a specific request then die when the request is completed. Many objects can live simultaneously on the server to handle multiple requests concurrently.

Modern server operating systems provide an environment for the creation and management of objects. These environments have different marketing names, but for the sake of generalizing they can be called Transaction Processing Environments (TPEs). The TPE provides an environment and services that allow for the creation and termination of objects and the allocation of resources for the objects.

In addition, the TPE also provides two other very powerful capabilities. The first is "transactional integrity." If an object is created and performs a part of its function, but then a non-recoverable failure occurs (such as a hardware crash or connection failure), the TPE "rolls back" the partly completed transactions. This means that the task an object was created to perform is either fully performed or not performed at all. TPE, therefore, ensures transactional integrity. Second, the TPE provides scalability that ensures that the performance of the system does not degrade as the number of users increases. System performance degrades because as more and more users require services from the server, the server creates the necessary objects to satisfy the request. As more objects are created they contend for resources such as memory and database connections. This eventually leads to bottlenecks and severe degradation of performance. Modern TPEs provides a feature called "object load balancing." This basically means that instead of deploying a singe server, the application can be installed on multiple hardware servers running in a cluster. In Windows 2000 Server, the number of servers in a cluster can be as high as 64. In a clustered server environment, the TPE can distribute the creation of the objects on different servers in the cluster based on which server has the most resources available. Since this object load balancing happens dynamically, the performance of the server can be maintained by simply adding more servers to the cluster.

This discussion has focused on objects and how they are created in response to requests by clients to perform a specific function. The second area where a server has to provide scalability is how clients connect to the server. The method of connection can be divided into two broad categories of applications:

1. *Client/Server Applications:* In a client/server application, the clients and the server are located on the same physical local area network (LAN), generally behind the firewall of the company. In these applications the

client communicates with the server through technologies such as DCOM (Distributed COM) in Microsoft environments and CORBA in UNIX environments. In this case the connection from the client to the server is over the company's LAN. LANs generally have high bandwidth and do not pose scalability issues except in extreme situations of very large or complex applications.

2. *Web Applications:* In a Web application the Web browser is the client. It communicates with the server via HTTP over the TCP/IP protocol. For these applications, the application server typically also includes a Web server. The Web server has a URL as a unique address and all HTTP requests for service are directed to this Web server where they are mapped to an object that performs the service.

For Web applications all the requests go to the same Web server. This is a point where bottlenecks are likely to occur as the number of users increases and the Web server will not be able to respond to all the requests simultaneously. Network load balancing is the technique used to overcome this bottleneck. In network load balancing, multiple Web servers are used as the front end. Network load balancing ensures that all incoming HTTP requests to a specific URL are routed to one of the Web servers that has the maximum resources available and can respond the quickest. Since this determination is made dynamically for each request, network load balancing ensures that load balancing is dynamic and adjusts with the condition and status of the service.

Object load balancing and network load balancing also provide another significant benefit that is inherent in the design: redundancy. If multiple servers are used in a cluster to support object load balancing, failure of any one server in the cluster means simply that the work is dynamically redistributed to the other servers in the cluster. Advanced operating systems such as the Microsoft Windows 2000 Application Center Server also provide fail over redundancy. This requires specially configured hardware for a primary server and a secondary (or "fail over") server. In case the primary server fails, all running objects are transferred to the secondary server.

A typical architecture of a BPM server is shown in Figure 9.2. It consists of the following components:

1. *BPM objects and object layer:* The BPM objects provide the business logic layer. These objects make decisions about actions based on the state of a process incident and other context information.
2. *The BPM server database:* This database contains information about the

state of all process incidents and user tasks. It is used by the BPM
server to make decisions, and is also updated following the actions
taken by the BPM object.

3. *The external database:* These are databases external to the BPM system
    and contain business information that is used, processed or acquired by
    the BPM system.
4. The Web server layer.
5. Clients.

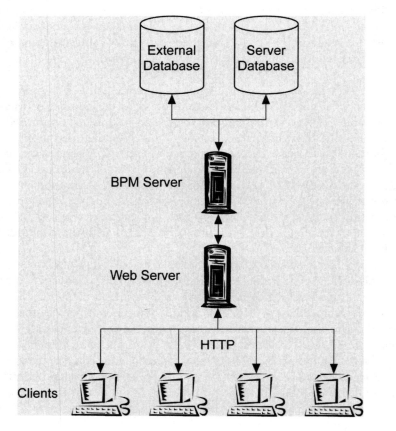

Figure 9.2. Typical BPM Server Architecture

Having discussed the various aspects of a BPM server, it is also important to understand how such installations might be deployed for different
levels of scalability. That is discussed next.

Small or Pilot Installation

Figure 9.3 illustrates a small installation recommended for a demo or pilot installation of a BPM solution. In this configuration, all components of the solution are installed on the same server. These include the database, BPM objects, Web server and other related services. Since everything is running on the same hardware, high performance from such as system cannot be expected.

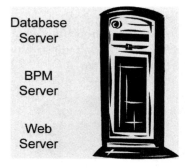

Database
Server

BPM
Server

Web
Server

Figure 9.3. Small BPM Installation

Medium Installation

A medium-sized installation is illustrated in Figure 9.4.

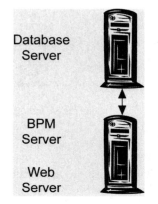

Database
Server

BPM
Server

Web
Server

Figure 9.4. Medium BPM Installation

In this configuration a separate database server is dedicated for the databases, including the BPM server and the external databases. Most companies already have dedicated servers for their databases and it is generally recommended that databases be hosted and maintained on their own servers for security and maintenance. This frees up more resources for BPM objects and provides more scalability.

Larger Installation

In a large installation a separate server is dedicated for the databases, BPM server and the Web server (as shown in Figure 9.5). By separating the Web server from the BPM server, this configuration provides faster Web response as well as increased resources for the BPM objects to perform their functions.

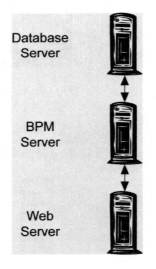

Figure 9.5. Large BPM Installation

Very Large Installations

For very large installations the recommended configuration is shown in Figure 9.6 and uses clustered servers. The servers are clustered in two tiers. The first tier, the Web tier, provides network load balancing. Incoming service requests over HTTP are routed to the Web server that is able to respond the fastest. The Web server then causes the creation of a BPM object on a server in the object tier that has the fastest response time at that instant. This ensures dynamic network load balancing, object load balancing, as well as redundancy. If any one of the servers is out of commission the HTTP request or the creation of the BPM object is dynamically distributed to the other servers.

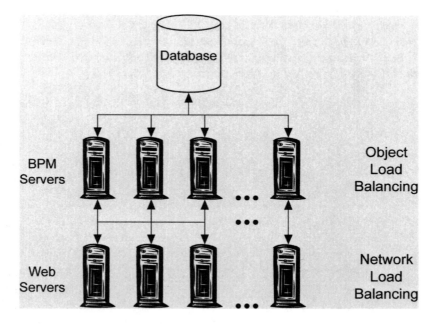

Figure 9.6. Very Large BPM Installation

Distributed Server Architecture

For large organizations scalability requires the support of multiple, distributed servers. In large organizations it is routine to find teams of people working together on specific business processes in different geographic locations spread out across the globe. Business processes span these locations. This brings up the challenge of providing a means for users or applications in satellite locations to participate with full fidelity in business processes. Using the Internet application model, it is possible to allow these remote uses to connect to a central server over the Internet and participate in business processes with the same capabilities they would have if they were local. This topology is illustrated in Figure 9.7.

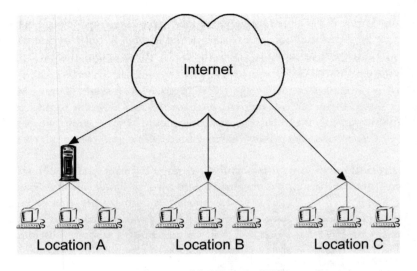

Figure 9.7. BPM Server with Users in Different Locations

For a number of reasons, it is not practical or advisable to deploy a BPM solution in the configuration shown in Figure 9.7. First, the connection between the remote location and the BPM server over the public network may not be fast. This will degrade the performance of users at remote locations. Second, the connection may be intermittent, which means that users may unexpectedly lose the work they are doing. And finally, if an organization is very large with many users leveraging many different business processes, it may not be advisable to use one very large server to manage the business processes of the entire organization.

The preferred architecture for handling these requirements is to use a federated BPM server architecture as shown in Figure 9.8. In this architecture, each location has a BPM server that is independent of all other servers. However, these BPM servers are loosely connected in a "federation" over a Virtual Private Network (VPN). The term "loosely connected" refers to the fact that the connection between the servers does not have to be available all the time, or available at the high speed. BPM servers use modern message queuing technologies to ensure that when they communicate with another BPM server, their messages are guaranteed to be delivered to the remote BPM server whenever the connection is available.

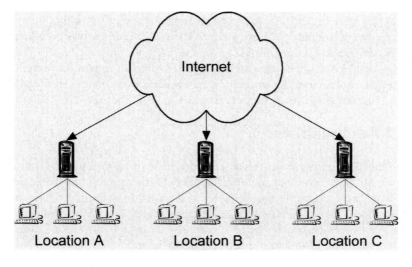

Figure 9.8. Federated Server Architecture

In this federated server architecture, a business process may be local or global. If a business process is local, it is available only to users in the domain of the BPM server it is installed on. However, if a business process is global, some steps in the business process may be designated for users who are not in the host domain of the BPM server it is installed on. Instead, these users may be located in any of the other domains. The host BPM server manages the execution of the process. When a step(s) has to be performed by remote users, the host server communicates with the remote server and sends a packet of information identifying the tasks to be performed and the user who must perform the task. It is then up to the remote server to ensure that the task is performed. At the completion of the task, the remote server communicated the results back to the host.

There are many significant implications of the federated server architecture:

1. The management of business processes is distributed. One server does not have to control the execution of processes for the entire organization.

2. A server can communicate with remote servers over a loose connection. This allows remote users to perform without being constrained by network speed or downtime. Whenever a connection is available, the remote server can transfer all the tasks and information to each other

so that users at each location can then perform them at will.

3. The overall architecture is transparent to the user or business process owners.

4. As laptops become more robust, the use of small federated servers will enable mobile users to participate in business processes even when they are disconnected from the server.

BPM Administrator

The BPM administrator is an application used to manage and administer a BPM server. In most high performance BPM systems the BPM server is a "black box" that controls business processes. It is optimized for speed and has none, or only a very limited, user interface. The BPM administrator is the user interface for the BPM server. It performs a number of tasks for management and administration that typically include the following:

1. Installing new business processes on the server
2. Installing new versions of existing processes with version control
3. Uninstalling business processes that are no longer used
4. Disabling processes temporarily for maintenance or some other reason
5. Facilitating migration of processes from one environment to another
6. Monitor the status of process incidents
7. Administer user tasks, and provide the ability to reassign tasks from one user to another in case of absence
8. Handling exceptions and special conditions
9. Control user access rights and privileges
10. Manage configuration settings of the BPM server

These capabilities are discussed below.

Installation and Version Control

An automated business process has to be installed on different platforms during its life cycle. The preferred methodology for business process automation is to design and develop an automated process in a design environment. Once the design is completed, the process is installed in a test environment where it can be tested. After testing, the automated process is installed on the production system where it "goes live" and is available for the participants to use. This is illustrated in Figure 9.9 that also shows the main activities that are performed at each stage.

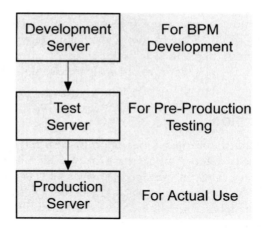

Figure 9.9. BPM Servers for Different Environments

The BPM administrator is used to install an automated business process in an environment. Since each environment may have different resources, the installation process must include integrity checks to verify that the resources available in the environment match those required by the process. A business process uses resources such as databases, third-party applications, organization charts and entities in the charts, external scripts and DLLs, etc. For the business process to function successfully, these resources must be available in all the platforms it is to be installed upon, or suitable alternatives must be identified.

In addition to integrity checking, the BPM administrator must determine if a previous version of the business process has already been installed in the target platform. If there is no previous version, the process is installed as version 1. However, if a previous version already exists, the process has to be installed as a new version. In this case there is a further complication if there are incidents that are already in progress. When a new version of a process is installed, the process designer may want to upgrade all running incidents to the new version. This has the advantage that if the new process version contains modifications to the business rules or user interface, all running incidents can be upgraded and the new business rules will apply to them on the fly. On the other hand, if a new version of the process contains new steps, variables or some other changes, and if these are applied to running incidents that were created using the old definition(s), it may cause unpredictable problems and situations under which the incidents could stall. The BPM administrator, therefore, has to provide a choice when installing new versions of processes. It should allow upgrading incidents of older versions to be upgraded to the new version. However, the process designer must exercise this option with great caution after carefully analyzing the changes in the new version and their impact on the incidents that are in progress.

Process Migration

A BPM administrator must also support process migration. This capability facilitates the transfer of a business process from one platform to another. When an automated business process is installed to a new target platform, the BPM administrator determines the external resources needed by the process and matches it to the resources in the target platform. If the resources do not match, the BPM administrator must identify a list of one or more mismatched resources and allow the process designer either to redesign the business process, or identify substitute resources that are available in the target platform. It can then proceed with the installation of the process. It can also save the list of re-assigned resources so that if the process is installed again, the system already knows the alternate resources.

Status Monitoring and Managing Exceptions

A BPM administrator provides means of monitoring the status of any process incident from a centralized location. Advanced systems provide a graphical as well as a tabular view of the status of any incident. This capability enables a workflow manager (an individual who monitors the BPM administrator) to check the status of a specific incident to see if there are any abnormalities. It also permits handling exceptions or emergency situations. For example, if a process incident comes to a standstill because a user has an emergency and cannot complete a task, the workflow manager can select the task and re-assign it to someone else.

For large BPM installations the number of incidents that are live and in-process at any particular instant may run into the thousands. For these installations it is impractical for a workflow manager to select a specific incident from such a large list. To make this selection easier, high-end systems provide a method for defining filters. A filter is basically a database query that the workflow manager can define in the BPM administrator that can be used to narrow down the list of incidents to search through. The query may use parameters such as the name of the process, the date the incident was started or completed, the person who initiated the incident, the priority of the incident, incident summary, or the name of the individual who initiated the incident. Once the workflow manager has defined one or more filters, they can be used to narrow down a large list of in-process incidents to a manageable number that can be used to select the incident to be monitored.

Status monitoring of incidents may also be used for other administrative purposes:

- In some instances process incidents stall because of a logic error that causes all the paths of the process to be blocked. This occurs typically when the business process has not been rigorously tested for all possible scenarios and data values. In these situations of stalled incidents, the status monitoring capabilities may be used to examine the value of variables for specific incidents, change the errant variables, and enable the incident to proceed.
- Sometimes process incidents stall because external applications used by automation agents fail or are unavailable for some reason. Once the problem is rectified, the status monitoring feature may be used to re-submit the task to the automation agent so that it can process it and continue with the incident. Alternatively, the administrator may wish to simply bypass the automation agent step in order to enable the incident to proceed.

Workload Management

Incident status monitoring allows a workflow manager to monitor the status of a specific incident. This provides visibility not only about the status of each incident, but also the participants who have completed the various steps of the incident or have active task. This shows the workflow from the perspective of an incident. However, the workflow manager may want to determine the status of business processes in general from the perspective of a specific participant. Workload management capabilities in a BPM administrator allow the workflow manager to select a specific user and observe three different categories of tasks that the user has to perform:

1. *Active Tasks:* These are tasks that the user has to perform and are currently active in the user's inbox.
2. *Active Tasks Assigned to Others:* These are active tasks that are "owned" by the user, but have been assigned to others. The user continues to be the owner and responsible for the tasks.
3. *Future Tasks:* These are all the tasks the user may be called upon to perform in the future. Basically this is a list of all the process steps of all

installed processes for which the user has been named a recipient.

The BPM administrator empowers workflow managers to select one or more tasks for a specific user and reassign these tasks to some other user indefinitely or for specific time duration. These capabilities are necessary for handling exceptions and absence.

Managing Stalled Incidents

Workflow incidents sometimes come to a standstill, or "stall." They cannot progress forward because of some design inconsistencies or changes in the system that prevents the BPM server from determining how to proceed. Two examples of how this could happen are:

1. A business process is developed using a job function recipient called "Application Engineer" for a step in the business process. However, after the process is running, a user in the HR department uses the organization chart to change the organization's internal structure and delete the job function called "Application Engineer." The next time an incident of the business process reaches the step whose recipient is "Application Engineer," the BPM server will not be able to find the recipient, and, therefore, the process comes to a stall.
2. A business process branches into two paths, as shown in Figure 9.10. Each path is taken based on specific conditions. However, under some situations the actual values may be such that both conditions evaluate as false. In this example, if the amount is less than $5,000 the BPM server will be unable to determine which path to take, and the incident will stall.

A BPM administrator must provide a mechanism of specifying three things in order to handle stalled incidents. First, a "system user" account should be created that is assigned all tasks that are causing incident to stall. Whenever a task cannot be assigned to a specific user, job function or recipient, it is assigned to the "system user." Second, the BPM administrator should be configured to notify the workflow manager when an incident stalls. And lastly, a housekeeping interval and service should be enabled that periodically checks for stalled incidents.

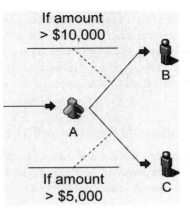

Figure 9.10. Example of a Stalled Process

Access Rights and Customized Views

Many users participate in business processes. These include a large number of people who only participate as recipients of workflow tasks. Others use BPM reports to determine the status of processes or capture metric information to measure the performance of the organization or their specific departments. Some are involved in designing and testing business processes. And yet others may be involved in maintaining the organization chart or using the BPM administrator to manage the BPM server. Therefore, it is essential for a BPM system to provide a mechanism for controlling access rights of all participants. Without tight control of access rights, it is likely that inadvertent or malicious access to the BPM system could produce severe repercussions.

The BPM administrator provides a mechanism of controlling access rights and privileges for all users of BPM systems. This provides a centralized location from where access rights of all participants may be established, reviewed, saved or changed. Access rights may be assigned to an individual or a group.

In addition to access rights, it may be necessary to control the "view" for each user in the Workflow client (the module that provides the user interface for people participating in automated business processes). A company may have power users who participate in business processes, or non-technical users who are only beginning to get familiar with computers and software applications. Each user needs different user interfaces and capabilities in the Workflow client they use to participate in business processes.

Powerful BPM systems allow a workflow manager to create customized views for each user or group. This allows the workflow manager to specify the folders the user can view, the content of each folder, the look and feel of the client and a number of other configuration settings that allow the client to be tailored to the skills of the intended use or the needs of the organization.

System Configuration

A BPM server may also have a number of parameters that need to be changed based on the requirements of the specific target platform, related systems, or for optimization. These parameters may include security settings, pointers to data sources, directories, supporting external applications or scripts, and many others. The workflow manager provides the user interface for viewing and changing these parameters.

The Organization Chart

Business processes deal with people, job functions, reporting relationships and groups. Employees initiate claims and expense reports. Their supervisors approve them. If the amount exceeds certain limits, the department managers must also approve them. Once the approvals have been secured, the claims processors act upon them to disburse funds. Thus, even in this simple every-day example, we have encountered people (the employees), job functions (department managers), reporting relationships (supervisors) and groups (claims processors). Knowledge of the participants, their roles, relationships and group membership is essential for the successful implementation of BPM solutions. As discussed in Chapter 6, "Smart Ways of Routing Work," there are many ways that a BPM system can benefit from organizational information to determine recipients of tasks. An organization chart application allows a BPM system to capture this organizational information so that it is available for use by BPM systems.

Some BPM systems allow users to define roles and relationships by using a simple "roles table," while others provide rudimentary scripting capability so that custom scripts can be used to determine the recipient of workflow steps, thus alleviating the need of an organization chart application. These scripts rely upon the existence of network directories or employee database tables to determine information needed for selecting recipients. However, roles tables and scripts become difficult to manage and maintain as the size of the organization increases. For large deployments it is ideal to have a way to graphically define a company's organization chart using an organization chart application.

An organization chart application allows a company to graphically define its organizational structure. This includes specifying the departmental structures, job functions, users who perform the job functions, and the definition of groups within the organization. A typical example of an organization chart is shown in Figure 9.11.

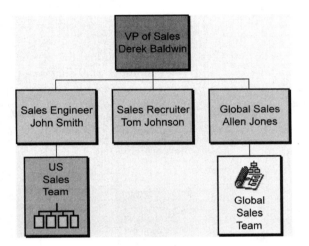

Figure 9.11. An Organization Chart Used for BPM

It consists of three distinct object types, which are described below.

Job Functions

These objects represent distinct job functions and the individuals who perform these functions. Since the organization chart is created as a hierarchy, the relationship of the job functions also explicitly specifies the relationship of the individuals who are assigned to these job functions. For example, in the chart displayed in Figure 9.11, John Smith is the Sales Engineer and Derek Baldwin is the VP of Sales. Derek Baldwin is also the supervisor of John Smith.

In every organization there are individuals who have more than one job function. In our example chart, Derek Baldwin is the VP of Sales and VP of Marketing. Therefore, his name appears in both job function boxes. An organization chart application must support this feature. However, if a person can have multiple job functions, his name will appear in multiple locations in the chart. In this situation it will be impossible to determine who the supervisor is of such people, since each job function he or she occupies could report to a different individual. To avoid this confusion, the organization chart application must provide the capability of specifying a "primary job function." An individual can have one primary job function and multiple secondary job functions.

Job Function Groups

It is common to have several individuals perform the same type of job in an organization. Thus, a company may have five Buyers, three Application Engineers and four Clerks. To accommodate this it is always possible to design an organization chart with multiple job function objects. For example, Figure 9.12 shows a part of an organization chart showing the five Buyers in the company. Since the job function names must be unique, they are called Buyer 1, Buyer 2, Buyer 3, Buyer 4 and Buyer 5. This is acceptable, except that it makes the organization chart unnecessarily large without adding any additional value. If the company had 15 buyers the chart would become even more unwieldy.

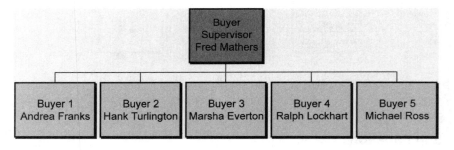

Figure 9.12. Multiple Users with Similar Job Functions

Job function groups are designed for this purpose. A job function group is physically represented as one object in the organization chart. However, it can include any number of individuals. Figure 9.13 shows a job function group that represents all the buyers. Each buyer is represented internally in the group by assigning it a name ("Buyer 1" through "Buyer 5"). Even if there were 20 buyers, they could all be represented by one job function group.

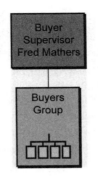

Figure 9.13. Job Function Groups

Sub-Charts

It is not practical or advisable to represent an entire company with a large number of employees in a single organization chart. Not only would this be practically impossible, it will be very difficult to manage and find job functions and people in one large chart. The organization chart must provide a "sub-chart" object that can be used to represent divisions, departments, sections, sub-sections or other entities of an organization. Each sub-chart can embed an organization chart of its own to represent the entity. By allowing charts to embed sub-charts, and sub-charts to embed other sub-charts, complex organization charts can be defined in a modular building block fashion. Furthermore, by providing means to control edit privileges to individual charts, an organization chart application can offer a means of distributing the management of these charts to individuals within each chart, or to those who have the say in the structure of the organization.

Groups

While groups are not represented in an organization chart, they are used widely in organizations to define cross-functional teams created and assigned to perform a specific task. Since these tasks often end up becoming a part of a business process, it is important for a BPM system to provide a method of defining and maintaining groups. This again is the role of the organization chart application. The organization chart application may allow companies to define groups with the following attributes:

1. *Groups with individuals:* In this case the members of the group are static. If one member leaves the company the group has to be redefined.

2. *Groups with job functions:* Instead of defining a group using individual names, it is defined by creating a list of job functions. This has the advantage that if a person leaves the company or changes job responsibility, the job function belonging to the person is assigned to the new person. The new person then automatically becomes a member of the group. The definition of the group is therefore dynamic as long as the organization chart is maintained.

3. *Groups consisting of other groups:* A group may be composed of other groups. In this case, the definition of the group is dynamic and depends on the definition of its constituent groups.

4. *Groups consisting of charts:* A group may consist of all the members of a chart. This again is a dynamic definition. If the chart is modified, the membership of type group changes automatically.

5. *Composite groups:* These are groups that can consist of individuals, job functions, groups and charts.

Organization Charts and Directories

Virtually every company contemplating the use of a BPM system already has a computer network installed, since a network is an essential prerequisite for the deployment of a BPM system. Networks use directories that allow network administrators to establish accounts for users, their passwords, access rights and other relevant information. This information is saved in a network directory. Users log on to the network using their assigned user name and password. In some cases the network directory may also contain information such as the job function, supervisor, e-mail address and departments of each user. This information overlaps with the information kept in the organization chart for the BPM system and raises issues about maintaining or synchronizing the organization chart information with the directory information.

The ideal solution, of course, would be to use the network directory information to build the organization chart. Companies already have invested in creating and maintaining these directories as their employees join and leave the company. Having only one repository of all organization chart information eliminates the need of maintaining two different directories or implementing elaborate synchronization techniques between the two. The BPM system could simply read organizational information from the directory and determine the names of users, their job functions, departments, group memberships, e-mail addresses, reporting relationships, and also authenticate the users at login using the directory. There are, however, several problems with this approach:

1. Network directories were designed by network developers for use by network administrators to manage complex networks. They were optimized for this purpose and their scope was also limited. Network directories were never developed for business process management that have some similar, but many different, requirements. Some of the obvious requirements of business process management that cannot be satisfied by current day network directories include the following:

    a. Network directories were designed with a user being the primary node of information. The directory consists of a list of users. These users are assigned properties such as the groups they have access rights to, e-mail addresses, and job functions. On the other hand, an organization chart for business process management has job functions as the primary node of information. A company creates job functions, and then assigns people to these job functions. The job functions have a relationship to each other. This difference between these two requirements causes many issues when trying to use network directories as a substitute for organization charts.

    b. Business process management requires a person to have multiple job functions for reasons already noted. Network directories only provide one job function per user.

    c. While most network directories support the concept of groups, none of them support the concept of job function groups described above that is very useful in business process automation.

    d. Most network directories contain only very rudimentary information about each user: such as their user name, passwords and simple relationship information. Organization charts used for BPM must provide many other pieces of data: such as availability, salary, phone numbers, supervisor's name, department name, buying authority and others.

2. Network directories were designed for network administrators. Thus, the user interface for most directories is fairly complex and suitable for only skilled IT administrators. However, the organization chart used in business process management contains employee information that is best managed by HR staff or business managers for whom the user interface of most network directories is fairly difficult to use.

3. The IT department of a company controls network directories. Since it controls access to the corporate IT resources, the IT department is very reluctant to relinquish control about the management of directories to

anyone other than a select group of network administrators, and rightly so. However, the organization chart of a company is determined by the business managers. They must have access to the tools used to maintain the organization chart for business process management and other purposes.

4. Every network directory has its own proprietary information schema and interface for accessing information in the directory. This means that a BPM system will have to interface with a variety of different directories using different schemas.

Over the last several years the Lightweight Directory Access Protocol (LDAP) has emerged as a widely acceptable standard for interfacing with directories. Directory vendors can internally store information in any format or schema. However, if they are LDAP-compliant, they use the LDAP protocol, which ensures that external applications can work with the directory's information. Furthermore, current versions of LDAP allow external applications to modify and extend the schema of the directory. Therefore, even if the vendors of the directory did not include a particular property, a third-party application can extend the schema and include the property. Thus, LDAP provides a standard interface to directories and the flexibility necessary to extend it for business process management. All leading vendors of directories, including Novell, Microsoft, Sun, and Netscape, have adopted LDAP. However, because of the enormous size and complexity of directories that are already are in place, migration to LDAP is gradual. A detailed discussion of LDAP is beyond the scope of this book, but there are several excellent references devoted to the subject [12],[13].

Microsoft NT Directory

Microsoft NT Directory is the most widely used directory in the world today because of the popularity of Windows operating systems. However, it is also the weakest in terms of its usefulness as a directory for a BPM system. There are several reasons for this:

1. NT was designed as a departmental server. Thus, the NT Directory was conceived for the needs of a department. BPM on the other hand cuts across departments and spans the enterprise and beyond. For example, NT Directory enforces unique user names within one domain (roughly equivalent to a department). It has no way of enforcing unique user names across domains. An enterprise-wide solution such as a BPM system needs to have unique user names across the enterprise.

2. NT Directory only contains minimal information about user names, passwords, job function, etc. It does not contain information needed by a BPM system such as e-mail addresses, multiple job functions for each users, job function groups, etc.
3. The schema for NT Directory is not extensible. Therefore, it is not possible to save any information in NT Directory beyond what is already included in it.
4. NT Directory does not support LDAP.

These reasons make it difficult to use NT Directory as the sole directory for robust BPM systems. Therefore, most vendors resort to one of two approaches:

1. Use NT Directory in conjunction with a vendor-specific directory. In this case, NT Directory is used for logon and authentication. However, a separate database is used for all other information required by the organization chart. A one-to-one relationship is established between users in the organization chart and their accounts in the NT Directory. This approach allows users to browse NT Directory and populate the organization chart with names from NT Directory.
2. Create a separate directory that by-passes NT Directory. This is the approach used by ERP and HR vendors such as SAP and PeopleSoft.

There is no automated mechanism for synchronizing the two because of the limitation of NT Directory. Therefore, both these approaches suffer from higher administrative cost because of the need to maintain two separate directories. While NT Directory is the most widely used, it is being phased out due to the introduction of the Microsoft Active Directory.

Microsoft Active Directory

Microsoft Active Directory was released with Windows 2000 and is an enterprise directory that supports LDAP. With this release Microsoft has addressed the limitations of the NT Directory:

1. Since Active Directory is based on LDAP, it is easier for third-party enterprise applications such as BPM to work with it.
2. Active Directory provides a rich set of properties for each object that includes basic information such as user name and passwords, as well as many others such as phone numbers, home addresses, digital signatures, photographs, etc.

3. The schema for Active Directory is extensible. Therefore, even if a particular property required by an application is missing, the schema can be extended to include it.

Active Directory is therefore better suited for business process management systems as the repository of directory information. In this case the organization chart of the BPM system can simply become the graphical front end for Active Directory so that even non-technical HR staff can use it to maintain the organization charts of the company. If this is done, there is only one employee directory, which eliminates the need for synchronization with other directories. The administrative cost of ownership is reduced.

The major obstacles that limit the use of Active Directory as the organization chart for BPM are:

1. Active Directory is based upon user accounts as the primary node of information (instead of job function). This is contrary to the requirements of business process management, as already explained.
2. Active Directory is primarily a network management tool. It is not easy or advisable for business or HR staff to have access to the directory for reasons of security. The major problem is that IT/network management of most companies simply will not allow business or HR managers to have access to Active Directory. Therefore, in almost every case, a company ends up having two directories: one for network management that is controlled by the IT staff, and a second for business process management that is controlled by business managers of the HR department.
3. Active Directory is being adopted slowly by businesses. This is because companies have very large and complex employee directories, and it is not easy to migrate all this information to Active Directory.

Other LDAP-Compliant Directories

There are many other directories that are LDAP-compliant. These include Novell's eDirectory, Netscape iPlanet Directory and the Sun Directory Service. Since they use LDAP, these directories can also be used with BPM and other enterprise applications. The major hurdle to their adoption is the degree of compliance and efforts required to verify them. Every software vendor who uses LDAP can theoretically claim to support these directories. However, the challenge is the extensive series of tests and verifications to ensure that the integrated application will indeed perform as specified. It is wise of software vendors not to proclaim blanket support for all

LDAP directories because it is liable to cause problems unless they have tested against all of them. Instead they should select the directories most commonly used by their target customers, validate their application against these, and only support these directories.

LDAP directories also have many of the same limitations that Microsoft Active Directory does.

Organization Charts and HR Applications

As we noted earlier, many HR applications, such as those offered by PeopleSoft, SAP and Oracle, also have integrated employee directories as a part of their offerings. When companies using these HR solutions want to adopt a BPM system, an obvious requirement is the ability to integrate their current applications to the BPM system. Many such vendors have adopted LDAP for their directories. If that is the case then a BPM system that has an organization chart capable of supporting LDAP may be able to work with these directories. The caveat here is that the BPM system and HR application must adhere strictly to the LDAP standard and validate their products against each other.

If, however, the HR application or the BPM system is not LDAP compliant, then the adopting companies have two possible avenues:

1. Develop or use a sync application that periodically synchronizes the HR system database with the BPM system's organization chart. This is graphically illustrated in Figure 9.14. This may be an expensive proposition, but once deployed, eliminates the need for managing and administering two different employee databases. Some BPM systems provide this capability out-of-the-box.

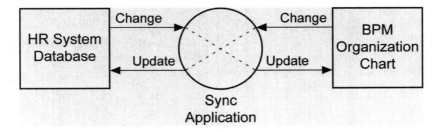

Figure 9.14. Synchronizing BPM Organization Charts with HR System Database

2. Maintain two separate employee directories. This greatly increases the cost of administration because of the need to manually synchronize both directories.

Other Requirements of Organization Charts

Organization charts have some other requirements when they are used for business process management:

1. Each person or resource in the organization chart database must be uniquely identified. This is because in a large company, it is very possible to have more than one person with the same name. The unique identifier is generally caller the "user name" or "short name," and it is used as the key to store information internally about the person.
2. While internally the BPM system uses the "user name" to identify a person, when this information is presented externally to other individuals as a part a business process, the person must be identified by their "long name" or full name. Otherwise workflow participants will not be able to distinguish or identify who a person is. For example "John Doe" may have a short name 'jdoe," and Jane Doe may have a short name of "jdoe." If a person is identified only by the short name in user interfaces and messages, it will be impossible for people who use this information to distinguish if the process is referring to John Doe or Jane Doe.
3. Since a BPM system deals with the automation of business processes, it almost always needs much more information about participants than applications such as e-mail or document management systems. For automating a business process, one might need information such as location, department, salary, phone numbers, fax numbers, digital certificates, etc. This information is provided in some HR systems and is also very useful in process automation.
4. Chapter 6, "Smart Ways of Routing Work," discussed the role of sequential groups and weighted groups as two ways of routing work. Sequential groups require members of a group to be assigned an order so that routing to the group will follow the order. Weighted groups require each member of a group to be assigned a weight that is used to determine the distribution of workload. When groups are defined in an organization chart, it is also important to be able to assign orders and weights. These are requirements of an organization chart that are not commonly provided by directories.

5. An organization chart application must provide some mechanism for searching for users or job functions. Search capability is useful in large organizations to find a person or job function.

6. An organization chart application is designed for use by HR staff or business managers. As such, it must provide chart-locking capability so that any individual chart or sub-chart may be accessed only by individuals who have been given access to the chart. This feature allows divisions and departments to manage their own organization charts.

Conclusion

A BPM server is the "brain" of a BPM system. It controls the execution of automated business processes. To perform its functions, the BPM sever needs a "memory" that is provided by a database, and an understanding of hierarchy and roles that is provided by organizational information. It also needs "senses" to be aware of what is happening in the organization. This is provided by the inputs that a BPM server receives from humans who participate in the process and systems that are integrated with it. The agility of the organization's business processes is dictated by the quality of the "brain" that governs these processes.

Chapter 10

BPM Process Development

Business processes are valuable assets of an organization, like buildings and machinery. Many would argue that they are more valuable than most other types of assets. The development and maintenance of business processes poses many of the same challenges as does the development and maintenance of other organizational assets. Some of these challenges include the need for collaborative design capabilities; tools for enabling a variety of users with different skills to participate in the development of processes; a repository for saving design knowledge so that it can be shared, maintained and reused; security; the ability to test processes before they are deployed; and the ability to publish and deploy processes. In addition, the design tools must provide a means for users to incorporate and configure many of the functions and features described in this book in a manner that make sense and is intuitive to users. All these requirements combined make the business process development application one of the most important and complex software component of a BPM system. It is safe to say that BPM systems are best measured by the ease of use and completeness of their process development tools, since these tools encapsulate the capabilities of the system to automate business processes.

This chapter discusses the general requirements for BPM process development tools. This includes the various roles involved in the development of processes, since the development tools must cater to the skills and needs of these roles. Furthermore, the requirements for a typical BPM process development tool, and how it is used for each role, are discussed. Finally, a discussion of each design tool is presented in slightly more detail, with the idea of providing a general overview without getting involved in the detailed features of specific products.

User Roles in Business Process Development

A variety of individuals with different skill sets and needs play different roles in the development of business processes. In some organizations and situations, more than one individual may share a role, while in others one individual may perform more than one role. These roles are:

1. *Managers and Other Business Process Owners:* These individuals own the business process and therefore are responsible for the overall design and specifications that dictate the behaviour of the process. These include performance requirements that the automated process is expected to achieve.

2. *Analysts:* These individuals work with the process owners to ensure the right resources are available to meet process requirement and performance expectations. Their role is also to ensure that the design of the process is optimized to achieve the performance requirements within the resource constraints of the organization.

3. *Project Managers:* These individuals supervise the development of the processes, assign tasks and make sure that the tasks are performed in the proper sequence.

4. *IT Designers:* These individuals are responsible for the design of automated processes by using design tools provided by the BPM system, without getting involved in programming.

5. *Code Developers:* These individuals develop programs and scripts that are used in conjunction with the BPM system to extend its functionality, provide custom functionality, and develop programmatic interfaces to third-party applications that do not have standardized interfaces.

6. *Database Developers:* These individuals work with the organization's databases to create new tables, views, stored procedures and other components that may be needed for business process automation.

7. *User Interface Developers:* These individuals develop electronic forms, Web pages and graphics that are used by the individuals who participate in business processes.

8. *Technical Writers:* These individuals develop the technical documentation for processes and the online help files for end users.

9. *Testers:* These individuals are responsible for testing the automated business process and its components.

A BPM process development solution has to provide tools and capabilities for all these roles. Some solutions may offer proprietary standalone or third-party tools for each role that are not integrated with each other. Others provide an integrated design environment where individuals who play these roles can work together in a collaborative environment. Of course, from a customer perspective, the latter solution is ideal and offers the most value measured by the ability to reduce process development cost. These integrated BPM process development solutions are the subject of the rest of this chapter, with the understanding that in most cases vendors will provide a sub-set of this functionality depending on the completeness of their product offering.

Integrated BPM Process Development Architecture

The architecture for an advanced, integrated BPM process development solution is shown in Figure 10.1.

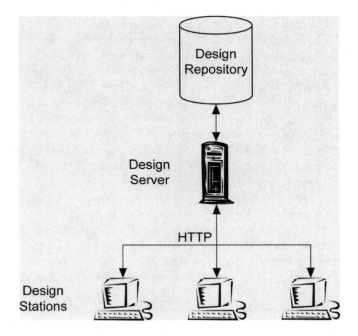

Figure 10.1. BPM Development Architecture

Like typical enterprise applications, it has a three-tier architecture that lends itself for scalability. It consists of the following components:

1. *Design Repository:* The process design repository is a database used for saving process definitions and all objects that make up the process. Advanced BPM systems decompose a process into a number of components such as forms, business rules, steps, and properties. Each of these is an "object" and is saved independently. The granularity of these objects allows users to collaborate in the development, and also share and reuse the objects in other processes. If a process is decomposed into steps, forms and business rules it is possible for different individuals to work with different objects at the same time. It is also possible to

upgrade one of the objects independently of all others. And finally, an object can be reused and shared with other processes. Thus, the use of a design repository facilitates collaboration, maintenance and reuse.

2. *Design Server:* The design server provides server-side capabilities and implements the logic and rules that are associated with the process development effort. Since the objects saved in the repository can be accessed by multiple users at the same time, the design server provides common collaboration functions that may include the following:

a. *Check in/Check out:* A user can check out an item for the purpose of working on it. When an object is checked out, other users can view it but are not able to modify it. This ensures that only one person is working on an object at any given time. When the work is finished, the users can check in the object so that others can use it.

b. *Version Control:* Every time an object is modified and checked in, a new version is created. This allows the development team to keep track of various versions of their work.

c. *Audit History:* This provides a brief history of who created new versions of an object and what modifications were made.

d. *Rollback:* If a new version of an object is created and the process designer realizes there was mistake, rollback allows the changes to be undone and revert to the previous version.

e. *Fine-Grained Security:* For smooth collaboration it is essential for the design server to provide security and access control at the smallest object level that is practical. This enables only authorized users to check out items they need to work on. Furthermore, if security is applied at the smallest object then a user can check out a component at that level, thereby enabling other users to work on other components. Advanced BPM collaboration servers provide security at the level of electronic forms, business rules, and properties of each step.

f. *Publish:* The design server enables users with access rights to publish an object to a server so that it is available for use. This provides the ability to dynamically change processes on the fly.

3. *Design Station:* A design station is the "client" for the BPM process development solution. This software is used by various individuals who collaborate in the development of processes. It provides a collection of "editors" for the various types of objects that constitute a process. It enables a user to view and check out an object to which he has access rights. When the user checks out an object, the design station invokes the associated editor that enables the user to then develop, update or modify the object. The design station also enables the user to use the

collaboration functions that are provided by the design server. Finally, advanced systems allow the user to check out one or more objects and disconnect from the repository. This provides the capability to support offline users who may not have access to the design server for some period of time, such as when they are working at home. When they return and connect back to the design server, they can simply check in the item.

One or more BPM servers may be connected to the development solution as illustrated graphically in Figure 10.2. These are the servers on to which the processes developed and tested in the development solution are "published" so that they are available for use by end users who participate in the business process. Typically, the environment will consist of a BPM server dedicated to process development, a second dedicated to test or pre-production, and a third dedicated to production that manages live running processes. Segregation of BPM servers ensures that the development and test activities do not interfere with live running processes. Such a configuration is highly recommended.

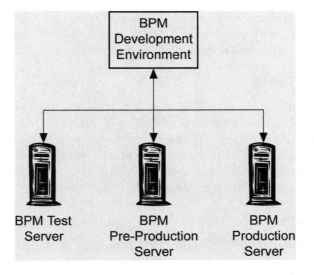

Figure 10.2. Multiple BPM Servers Connected to
Development Environment

In most cases, the BPM process development solution will also have an administration tool that is used for configuring and administering the various components of the solution, and for assigning access rights to individual users.

BPM Process Development Editors

The following sections offer a brief description of the major types of editors that are typically included in BPM process development solutions. A vendor may provide some or all of these editors, depending on the scope of their offering. This is a brief overview since this book does not discuss the specifics of individual products.

Process Design Editors

Process design editors are tools for business process owners and managers who are not IT experts. Therefore, these tools must offer easy-to-use graphical process design interfaces, and should not be burdened with advanced IT or development-related concepts and terminology. These tools are described in detail in Chapter 8, "Business Process Modeling and Analysis." The purpose of process design tools is simply to facilitate the "electronic paper" design and documentation of processes.

Modeling Tools

Modeling is typically provided as a part of the process design tool. Modeling tools enable a business analyst to model and optimize processes to ensure that they will perform as expected by the process owner and given the resources and capacity constraints of the organization. Chapter 8, "Business Process Modeling and Analysis," provides an in-depth description of modeling and how it is performed.

Map Editors

The map editor is the tool for IT professionals. It enables them to take the process definitions developed in the process designer and convert them into deployable applications. As is clear by now, business process automation is complex and involves numerous technologies such as databases, e-mails, electronic document management systems, electronic forms, digital signatures, and many others. Therefore, using the map editor to develop processes is an activity that is best performed by skilled IT professionals who are adept at these technologies. The tasks that are typically preformed in the map editor include the following:

1. Defining and creating process variables that are used to make decisions
2. Implementing business rules and conditions
3. Specifying electronic forms that will be used in the process
4. Linking electronic forms with databases
5. Configuring notification triggers and messages
6. Training automation agents for third-party applications
7. Specifying and configuring sub-processes used in the process
8. Creating subject and body of e-mail messages to be used for proactive e-mail notifications

A robust BPM process development solution enables users to create business processes with the capabilities discussed in Chapter 5, "Inside Business Processes." Since the actual functionality is very specific to each software vendor, a detailed discussion is beyond the scope of this book.

Form Design Tools

Electronic forms are the user interface of business processes that enable people to participate in these processes. Chapter 5, "Inside Business Processes," discusses the requirements of electronic forms. BPM process development solutions have to provide tools to enable the design and use of these forms. There are many electronic form technologies, and each has its own advantages and disadvantages. Some popular form technologies include HTML, ASP .NET, Adobe Acrobat, and Microsoft InfoPath. Each form type has its own design tool. A BPM process development solution should provide integrated capabilities to design such forms, either through built-in functionality or by providing the ability to plug-in third-party form design tools.

Programming Tools

No BPM system, regardless how robust it is, can handle all the requirements of every business process in every organization. This means that in many cases the capabilities of a BPM system have to be customized or augmented for the unique needs of specific customers. This is typically accomplished by writing software code or scripts, and involves the services of software developers who can program or write scripts using development tools. A BPM system, therefore, should provide a means for developers to work within the system and develop these programs that can be managed in the same repository. Since code development solutions are very complex, the ideal solution is to leverage powerful tools already provided by software companies such as Microsoft or Borland. This uses the concept of plug-in editors, whereby third-party software development tools can be incorporated into the BPM process development solution. While integration of programming tools is beneficial, it is important to emphasize that advanced BPM systems minimize the need for programming by providing a full set of functionality out-of-the box as well as standardized tools for integration such as Web Services, automation agents and robust database connectivity. This is because every resort to programming reduces agility and increases the cost of ownership.

Testing Tools

After a business process has been designed, optimized, developed and integrated with other applications, the last major hurdle is to test it before it can be deployed. Testing an automated business process poses a unique challenge, since the process typically involves many users and several third-party applications. It is not practical to test the automated process by installing it in a live environment and checking out all possible scenarios. It would simply be too disruptive for all involved participants and third-party applications. To provide a means of testing, advanced BPM process development solutions provide a simulation capability to test an automated business process. By using simulation, a QA engineer can role-play and test the entire functionality of the automated business process on one computer. This includes testing the flow, user interface, business rules and exceptions that are configured to be handled automatically by the process. In advanced BPM systems, the QA engineer also has access to workflow variable values so that testing can be performed in the context of the data handled by the process and the impact of changes in data can be evaluated. Simulation is a prerequisite for more extensive testing in a test environment before the solution is taken to the pilot stage.

Documentation Tools

Documentation is essential for the development and maintenance of business processes. Three types of documentation are necessary:

1. *Process Design Specification:* This documentation is owned by the business process owner or analyst, and describes the requirements of the process

from a business perspective. It is best produced in the process design tool used by business process owners. Its purpose is to ensure that the intent of the business process owner is properly understood, so that the resulting automated process does indeed reflect its intent as much as possible. The simple act of creating and writing process design specifications before starting the development improves the process design by pointing out issues and possible solutions upfront. It forces business process owners to think of how the process needs to work, and ensures that the requirements of the business as well as all end users are given due consideration. Indeed, one of the most common reasons for the failures of business process automation is incomplete or incorrect design specification.

2. *Technical Documentation:* This describes the implementation of the business process from a technical perspective. It includes descriptions of key variables, roles, database connections and other resources. The purpose of technical documentation is to ensure that the automated business process can be maintained and updated. With the passage of time the individuals who originally developed the process will no longer be involved with it. As new developers start working on enhancements and improvements to make new versions of the process, it is important that they have access to the technical documentation to understand how the process was initially automated.

3. *User Help:* This documentation provides help to users who participate in the process at various stages. It must be available online for users, and explain how to use electronic forms and its functions at each step in the process.

Since documentation is an important part of the process automation activity, it is important for a BPM process development solution to provide tools to easily create and maintain documentation. This is best accomplished by providing third-party plug-in editors for applications such as Microsoft Word and HTML development tools. This allows the writer to use best-of-breed tools, and the output of these tools can be managed in the repository with full check in/check out and version control features.

Conclusion

BPM process development tools are aimed at enabling a number of individuals with different technical skills to play different roles in the development of automated business processes. These include business process owners who define and own processes; business analysts who optimize processes and recommend resource allocation; IT designers who use graphical tools for power users to convert business requirements into deployable applications; developers who develop custom integrations and functional enhancements not supported by the BPM system out-if-the-box; and form designers who create the user interfaces for the participants. In addition, business processes are often very large and complex, making it difficult for one person to develop them alone. For these reasons, a collaborative design environment is essential for the development of automated business processes.

Chapter 11

Workflow Client:
The End-User Experience

A workflow client is the software and user interface that enables users to participate in business processes. The easiest way to describe a workflow client is to compare it with an e-mail inbox that everyone is familiar with. Like an e-mail inbox, the workflow client receives and presents users with a list of tasks related to business processes, and the means of completing them. A workflow client, however, has to be much more sophisticated than the typical e-mail inbox. Since business processes could involve a large number of people with different skills and requirements, a workflow client has to be highly flexible and configurable. This chapter discusses the role and functions of workflow clients, and provides some insight into the evolution of next-generation workflow clients.

The Role of a Workflow Client

Business processes can involve a large number of end-users, both inside and outside the organization. The fundamental purpose of a workflow client is to enable all users to easily perform all their roles in an automated business process. Depending on the role played, a user will require different features and capabilities from a workflow client. These range from completing tasks and monitoring status, to advanced features such as managing subordinates and their tasks. The four major categories of end-users in business processes that might use a workflow client are:

1. Initiators are employees-at-large, customers and vendors who initiate business processes that require actions or decisions by workers (described below). A workflow client must enable initiators to start new process incidents and check the status of these incidents. They generally do not participate in intermediate steps of the business process.
2. Workers are employees who participate in intermediate steps of the process to make decisions or take actions. Workers need to be notified of new tasks, warned if tasks are late, allowed to complete tasks and check the status of process incidents.
3. Supervisors need to manage the workload of workers and handle exceptions (such as the absence of a worker). They need the ability to check the status of incidents handled by their subordinates, as well as the ability perform, monitor and assign tasks to others.
4. Managers own the business processes and are interested in their performance metrics and optimization. They need the ability to capture metrics for optimizing processes and determining the resources needed

to comply with demand.

This diversity of requirements results in the need to configure the workflow client user interface to the unique needs of different organizations, group, and workers.

The five major capabilities of the workflow client are discussed in the following sections.

Work Inbox

The primary role of the workflow client is to be the work inbox for the user. This is the application that users use to perform tasks related to business processes. While the e-mail inbox is a place for the user to receive and send e-mails, the workflow client is the place to perform a variety of different tasks that may include purchase order approvals, document reviews, claims processing, and submitting performance reviews. As the number of automated business processes installed by an organization increases, so will the variety of tasks that a user will have to perform in his workflow inbox. Users must have the ability to configure the workflow client to their specific work needs, which will differ for different processes and different roles.

There are two primary models for distributing tasks to users. The "push model" is like e-mail. Tasks are pushed to the user's inbox and appear in the task list. The user can select any task and perform it. This model is suitable if tasks are assigned to a specific user. The second model is the "pull model" which uses the concept of queues, or shared inboxes. In this model tasks are placed in a queue and not sent to a specific individual. Any member of a group associated with a queue can "pull" a task from a queue and perform it. This model is suitable when tasks are assigned to a group and anyone in the group can perform it. Since each model is appropriate in different situations, a modern workflow client has to provide support for both.

Management of Subordinates

E-mail is personal. It is point-to-point communication between one user to another user, and nobody else needs to be involved in this communication. If other individuals do need to be involved, the sender makes a conscious decision to include them in the distribution list. Workflow, on the other hand, generally deals with the business of the organization. If an employee receives a task, it is important for management to know about the task and its status. If the task is not performed in the expected time frame, it is again important to have the ability to reassign the task to someone else in order to expedite it. This is where the management of subordinates and their work becomes important. It is possible to manage the workload of individual employees from a central application, such as the BPM administrator as discussed in Chapter 9, "BPM Server and Administration." However, this is feasible only in small organizations where the workflow manager may be aware of all users, their availability and work responsibilities. In medium and large organizations it is impractical to expect a workflow manager to be able to manage the workload of all employees and reassign tasks in case of absence or delays. The only practical way is to distribute the management of employees throughout the organization, and let every manager or supervisor manage the workload of their subordinates using the hierarchy dictated by the organization chart of the company. A supervisor is the best person to be aware of workload of team members, their availability and priorities.

The workflow client is the logical application for managing the workload of all participants. Modern workflow clients enable supervisors to not only work with their own tasks, but also with the tasks of their subordinates. This means the ability of viewing and performing these tasks, checking their status and assigning them to others. Every supervisor needs the flexibility to handle tasks of subordinates just as if they were his or her own tasks.

Centralized Client Configuration

An organization may have a very large number of workflow participants. These could include partners and customers in addition to employees. The computer skills of these participants will vary. Moreover, the nature of the tasks they perform as a part of the workflow will also be significantly different. Some may be involved in a variety of different general-purpose processes, while others may be involved primarily in one or two high-volume processes that are very specific to the business of the company. A single user interface may not be sufficient to handle this diversity. A workflow client requires a centralized mechanism for tailoring the user interface for individuals (or groups of individuals) that makes the client more suitable for the type of work preformed, or for the skill levels of the participants. With this capability the user interface can be controlled and modified from a central location, thereby making it easier to manage users and reduce the cost of ownership.

Database Connectivity

Another major difference between an e-mail inbox and a workflow client is the need for database connectivity. E-mail messages do not need or provide any connections with databases. However, almost every business process deals with information that the process either collects or distributes in order to make effective decisions. A workflow client must provide a mechanism for connecting to corporate databases with speed and security. This sounds easy, but it is fairly complex because in most cases workflow clients are used remotely from the database and BPM servers, and the connections with these servers are infrequent but data intensive.

Security

Finally, providing security is one of the major roles of the workflow client. Business processes often deal with mission-critical information that is proprietary to the business. If an automated business process is deployed over the public Internet, the issue of security takes on even more importance. The workflow client must provide security in several different ways:

1. *Authentication of Users:* The workflow client must ensure that users who log on are authenticated. If this is not the case, the information handled by the business processes will be compromised.
2. *Authentication of signatures:* The workflow client must ensure that users who sign documents or electronic forms are who they say they are. This is because a user may be away from his desktop after he has logged on successfully into the workflow client. During his absence someone else may be able to approve and sign items using his computer unless there is proper authentication of signatures the instant an electronic document or form is signed.
3. *Data Transmission Security:* The information that is transmitted from the BPM server to the workflow client must be secure and not vulnerable to interception.

E-Mail Client versus Workflow Client

The first reaction of individuals newly introduced to business process management is that the workflow client and the e-mail client should be one and the same application. This is natural, since e-mail is ubiquitous and e-mail clients provide a simple interface for users to receive, view, send and manage their messages. Modern e-mail clients such as Microsoft Outlook and Qualcomm Eudora provide many features and functions that make working with e-mail easy. All users would like to see their workflow tasks presented in their e-mail clients so that they can manage everything they have to do from the same interface.

While the desire for a unified client is natural, it is not practical because business process requirements are a super-set of e-mail requirements, and not a subset. Business processes require a lot of capabilities and features that are not required by e-mail. Therefore, the desire to make a workflow client a part of the e-mail client will greatly restrict the functionality provided by modern workflow clients. Some of the major differences between the requirements of an e-mail client and a workflow client are listed in Table 11.1.

Table 11.1. E-Mail Client versus Workflow Client

E-Mail Client	Workflow Client
Deals with text and attachments, but not data. Has no need for database connectivity.	Deals with text, attachments and data. Database connectivity is essential.
Deals with e-mails of only one individual.	Deals with workflow tasks of an individual and subordinates in order to facilitate workload management of subordinates.
E-mail is a one-step process. It goes from one person to another or a group. Generally there is no provision to monitor the status other than determining if the recipient has received the message.	Workflow can be a complex multi-step process. It requires the sophisticated reporting of status.
E-Mails are ad hoc with few rules.	Business process tasks are structured with many rules.

These differences make it very difficult for a workflow client to function within the constraints present in current generation e-mail clients. The optimal solution is to use an e-mail client in conjunction with the workflow client. The e-mail client can receive messages, informing the user that they have new tasks. The workflow client uses its functionalities to allow users to actually perform those tasks, and the variety of other capabilities required for BPM. As BPM moves in to the mainstream and client applications become increasingly more sophisticated, it is likely that e-mail and workflow clients will converge into a single application. Even today, some BPM systems try to provide a unified inbox by using Microsoft Outlook or a portal.

Functions of a Workflow Client

A workflow client provides a variety of functions in order to support the roles outlined in the previous section.

Work Inbox

The function of being users' work inbox for business processes they participate in is the most important feature of a workflow client. To do this it has to provide a number of capabilities:

1. *Task List:* A display of all the tasks that have to be performed by the user.
2. *Views or Folders:* The ability to segregate tasks into different categories so that the user can easily organize and complete them. Categories may include "Current," "Overdue," "Completed," "New" and others.
3. *Status Reporting:* The ability to display the status of a particular task in the process. This is generally accomplished by displaying a tabular list of all the steps, their recipients, and the current status of the tasks at each step. Advanced systems also provide a graphical view of the process map and the colour-coded status of each step.
4. *Assign Tasks:* A user may want to assign one or more tasks to some other user in case he is busy, or feels that the other person is better able to handle the task.
5. *Assigning Future Tasks:* A user preparing to be absent for a specific length of time may wish to assign tasks to another user. Such assignments may be time-based: that is, a user may specify that a particular task be assigned to another user until a specific date.
6. *Confer:* A user may wish to confer with another user. In this case the user can send the task to the other user. The recipient can review the task and enter comments, but cannot complete the task. The ownership of the task continues to rest with the original user. When the conferee completes the task, it returns to the original user who can then review the comments and complete it.

Configuration of Client Views

The use of folders to manage e-mails of different categories is a useful feature in popular e-mail programs. This helps reduce clutter and improve user productivity. For the same reason, managing tasks in a workflow client also benefits from the ability to create and use folders. There are many other reasons to customize the workflow client:

1. Business processes manage the work that people have to do. Work falls into many different categories that the user needs to be aware of, such as completed, overdue, urgent, belonging to a specific process, belonging to a specific person, or belonging to a specific step in the process. All of these are ways in which a user may want to categorize tasks by using intelligent folders.
2. Workflow participants have a variety of skill levels. Some users may require advanced features while others may prefer simplicity and the ability to quickly get the job done. This requires the ability to configure the features or options available in each folder.
3. Every company has different terminology for identifying work. When presenting a task list to users, it is important to be able to configure the client to use the terminology used by the company. Instead of relying on generic terms such as process name, task name, due date, or summary, a company may wish to configure the client to identify tasks by "Account Number," "Part Number," "Client Name" or some other specific terminology. This is not simply a matter of changing the names of columns in the task list, but actually presenting customer- or process-specific columns as names in the task list.
4. As noted above, a workflow client should allow a user to view and manage his own tasks as well as those of subordinates. Only by providing this capability is it possible to distribute the management of the workload of all users to their supervisors in the organization.

One convenient method of providing these capabilities is to allow users to define customized folder views. A folder displays a collection of tasks in a format that is unique to the folder. Since the format is associated with each folder, the user interface changes when the user switches to another folder. The types of information that could be changed in the folder include the following:

1. *Change the number of columns and their order in the task list:* In this way the

columns only display the information suitable for selecting tasks of a particular category.

2. *Allow users to add their own custom-defined columns in the task list:* This enables users to view and select tasks based on the terminology used in the organization, or specific to the task.

3. *Associate a filter with each folder:* The filter will allow the user to display only those tasks that match certain criteria. This could allow the display of tasks that meet a combination of the following criteria:

   a. Belong to specific processes
   b. Belong to a specific step
   c. Due within a specific time period, or a specific time
   d. Have a specific status such as "current," "overdue" or "urgent"
   e. Belong a specific subordinate or a group of subordinates
   f. Have data values that match some criteria (for example "Total amount greater than $1,000")
   g. Belong to a certain priority

   This provides a good mechanism to filter down and only show those tasks that belong to a particular category, making it easier for users to find and complete their tasks.

4. *Change the functions and buttons that appear in the view:* By eliminating all unnecessary buttons the view can be simplified for novice users.

Customizing views enable the workflow client to be configured to the skill levels of specific users or the tasks they have to perform. Advanced BPM systems go one step further: they enable a workflow manager to define views for a user or a group from a centralized application such as the BPM administrator. This powerful feature ensures that when workflow participants use the workflow client, they will only see the views that have been configured for them. This capability eases administration of the workflow client and reduces the cost of ownership.

Head-Up/Heads-Down Modes

The task list in a workflow client can display the tasks that a user has to perform in a variety of ways. Once the user selects a task, the workflow client displays the information or electronic form belonging to the task and allows the user to read or enter data, review attachments and make decisions. This is generally accomplished by presenting an electronic form associated with the step. There are two ways in which forms may be presented to the user and are suitable for different work environments:

1. *Heads-up Mode:* In this mode the user selects a task from the task list and the associated electronic forms are displayed. When the user completes the form and submits it for processing, the form is closed and the user interface reverts back to the task list. This allows the user to select a different task. This "heads up" mode works very well when the user is working with different tasks with different forms, and using the client on an occasional basis.

2. *Heads-down Mode:* In this mode the user selects a task and the form is displayed. After the user completes the associated electronic form and submits it, the form does not close. Instead, the next task that uses the same form but with different data for the next incident is displayed. The significance of this is that the user does not have to go back to the task list and select the next task; the next task is displayed automatically. Furthermore, time is saved because the client user interface, as well as the form, does not have to be displayed again. This speeds up task processing. Heads-down mode is very useful if the user is performing the same task over and over again for different incidents. Examples for such use include claims processing or invoice processing applications.

Working with Queues

BPM systems use push and pull methods (discussed previously in this chapter) for proactively ensuring that work gets done. Placing tasks in the task list of a user is the "push" method; tasks automatically appear in the task list. The "pull" method requires the use of queues. Any step can be associated with a queue, and a group of users assigned to each step. When the BPM server sends a task to the queue, it actually goes into a common inbox that is shared by the group. Any user can select the next task from the queue, and the task is assigned to that user to perform.

The method described above is a blind queue. The user is not aware of which task in the queue will be received. The tasks are prioritized based on the time they entered the queue and their priority. The user simply gets the next task. An alternative method is to allow a user to view all the tasks in a queue, and then select the one they wish to work on. Modern BPM systems support both types of queues.

Online Help

Providing online help is a basic requirement for all modern software applications. A user may be using a workflow client to perform different tasks belonging to different processes. For each of these tasks the user may need two different types of help:

1. *Task Specific:* This online help provides users with instructions that are specific for the proper completion of a particular task. It explains the meaning of the information presented with the task, what the user has to do, and how.
2. *Process Specific:* This provides information about the business process to which the task belongs. It explains why the user is performing the task and how it is related to other tasks in the process.

Since business processes and tasks are unique to each organization, it is not possible for these online help documents to be a part of the BPM system. The BPM system can provide generic help about the use and functionalities of the workflow client. The organization deploying the BPM solution has to create the help documents that are specific to the organization's business processes. The role of the workflow client is to provide a mechanism to easily associate help files for specific business processes and steps within the process. Furthermore, since the Web browser has become ubiquitous, it make sense to offer help documents in HTML format so that it can be viewed from anywhere and managed centrally.

Client Technologies

BPM vendors use many different technologies to develop workflow client applications. Each has its own benefits and drawbacks. These are discussed below.

Client/Server

The first generation BPM systems were based on client/server technology. The workflow clients they offered were traditional "fat" clients. These were stand-alone applications that had to be installed on each user's desktop and connected with the server via the network. They offered high speed since the workflow client was tightly connected with the server. However, they were expensive and difficult to manage because the client software had to be installed and configured on each desktop. When the software was updated, each desktop had to be reinstalled.

Client/server BPM systems are an excellent solution for very high volume process applications that are used within departments for applications such as claims processing or call centers. Fat clients continue to be used for these types of applications where speed is paramount and deployments are confined to departments.

E-Mail Clients

With the advent of e-mail in the early 1990s, some vendors started using e-mail as the workflow backbone and the e-mail client as the workflow inbox. The major advantage is that the e-mail client is ubiquitous; there is no need to install proprietary clients just to support business process automation. E-mail messages could be used to send process information from the server to the client, and vice versa. In addition, e-mail can be used inside and outside the organization, making it easier for external participants to engage in business processes.

BPM systems using e-mail clients were limited to simple workflow applications that were not mission critical because of the limitations of e-mail:

1. E-mail does not provide a means of database connectivity. Only the very simplest workflow processes do not require database connectivity. Therefore, workflow systems that use e-mail clients are limited to very basic and simple workflow applications.
2. E-mail is not the recommended medium for secure, mission critical information. E-mail messages go through many gateways and the chances of losing attachments or interception are high. This limits such solutions to very simple workflow processes that may have to do with simple notifications.
3. As discussed in the previous section, requirements of an e-mail client are very different from those of a workflow client. If anything, a workflow client is a super-set of an e-mail client. Trying to force-fit a workflow client within the constraints of an e-mail client will limit the flexibility of the former.

Browser Clients

The advent of the World Wide Web in the mid-1990s resulted in the development of Web browsers as workflow clients for BPM systems. Using the Web browser as a workflow client has many advantages:

1. The Web browser is ubiquitous like e-mail. Almost every desktop already has a Web browser, and a very large number of people are already familiar with its use.
2. Web browsers provide a quick mechanism for connecting to a server. A

user can be anywhere and can connect to a server simply by selecting a URL.

3. Web browsers use HTTP to connect to the server. This is a mature and reliable technology. Furthermore, the HTTP/S protocol provides 128-bit encryption and is very good for most secure commercial communications between the browser and server.

4. For database connectivity and other functions that require rapid access to the server, a Web browser can use the HTTP protocol that is already available and used by the browser.

Browser-based clients that use pure HTML are referred to as "thin clients." They can be used on many operating systems thanks to the HTML standard. They are, by definition, cross-platform clients. However cross-platform support is achieved at a cost:

1. HTML only supports basic user interface objects such as check boxes, edit fields and combo boxes. HTML does not offer any advanced controls such as calendars, data-bound grids and others that are common in the user interface of client/server applications. Therefore, the user interface of pure thin clients is not as powerful as that provided by client/server applications.

2. A Web browser is not connected to the server. A connection is made only when the user submits a browser page. This causes the server to run a script to process the information, and if necessary, regenerate a new HTML page that is refreshed in the browser. Thus, a thin client requires pages to be refreshed in order to update information. This consumes time and is sometimes irritating or confusing to users. It also reduces the speed at which tasks can be performed.

3. To provide advanced functions and capabilities, and overcome some of the limitations of HTML, thin clients make extensive use of VisualBasic or JavaScript. This causes three problems. First, the code becomes complex. Second, since scripts are compiled at run-time, the speed of execution starts to degenerate. Finally, scripts are sensitive to the platform they are running on. The use of scripts may cause inconsistent behaviour on different platforms or even in different Web browsers. The development of new technologies such as ASP and .NET (that used pre-compiled code) will reduce these limitations over time.

Thin clients are very good solutions for BPM applications that have medium complexity and medium database connectivity requirements. A thin client is also an excellent workflow client for the increasing number of mobile Personal Digital Assistants and Tablet PCs. As technology improves with the related improvement in performance, thin clients are likely to become the preferred means of participating in business processes because of their cross-platform support.

Active Browser Clients

To overcome the current limitations of thin clients and pure HTML, some BPM vendors offer active browser clients. These workflow clients use the Web browser, but enhance it by using active controls to supplement the functionality of HTML. There are two types: workflow clients that use Dynamic HTML (DHTML) with Microsoft ActiveX controls, and those that use DHTM and JavaBeans. As one might expect, the former works only in Microsoft Internet Explorer on the Windows platform, whereas the latter functions in Web browsers that support specific versions of Java.

While "active browser" clients do have the limitation that they will work only on specific Web browsers, they have many advantages:

a. Active controls are much more capable and feature-rich. They can be programmed to provide virtually the same functionality as traditional clients in client/server applications.

b. Active controls are precompiled. Therefore, the performance is much better than thin clients.

c. Active controls can perform operations in the background and can dynamically update their values. They do not require screens to be refreshed as is the case with thin clients. This gives users the perception that they are working in a client/server environment.

In many ways active browser clients are a cross between client/server systems and pure thin forms. They are lighter than the traditional fat clients, but heavier than thin clients. They provide performance like a client/server application, yet are browser based. And finally, they do not require configuration on each user desktop, but are limited to specific platforms. Since they involve downloading active code components, the first time they are used on computers in certain highly secure IT environments, their use could be problematic. Some companies simply prohibit their use, which is not really warranted in an intranet environment. New technologies such as the Microsoft .NET Framework and Web Services are enabling the development of thin clients that provide dynamic behavior in a Web browser environment.

The Future of Workflow Clients

As BPM matures in to a mainstream business application, the role and capabilities of workflow clients will continue to expand. This section discusses four major trends that are ongoing in the development of workflow clients.

Lightweight Clients for Portable Devices

Wireless-based handheld devices such as Personal Digital Assistants and Tablet PCs are poised for rapid growth. Many BPM vendors are offering thin client based solutions for such devices that leverage their native HTML browser capabilities. Currently these solutions are designed for desktop computers, and they can work on handheld devices with some limitations. They are not optimized for handheld devices because of their smaller screen sizes and processing capacities. However, as the popularity of these devices grows, vendors will start developing pure HTML based workflow clients specially targeted at the handheld market. New features that these next generation workflow clients need to support are:

1. The ability to adjust the user interface to the screen display and form factor of the handheld device.
2. The ability to provide a high degree of functionality despite limited memory, processing and other resources offered by the handheld device.
3. The ability to optimize the performance of the workflow client by judiciously leveraging the resources of the server, but at the same time downloading the necessary information and functionality to the client that will enable it to respond quickly to user actions.

Disconnected Workflow Clients

As the workforce becomes mobile and the use of wireless and handheld devices increases, more and more users will find themselves in situations where they are unable to connect to their server. To handle these situations, workflow clients will need to develop a means of allowing users to perform tasks while disconnected from the server. This is easy for applications such as e-mail that do not offer database connectivity. However, as pointed out previously, even the most basic BPM solution requires some form of database connectivity. When a user is disconnected from the server, it is not possible for the workflow client to connect to databases that are located on the server. Neither is it practical to download a chunk of data from server-side databases into client computers since it is impossible to determine in advance which data and how much storage will be needed. Supporting disconnected workflow clients is therefore a difficult problem to solve.

Disconnected user support will initially rely on allowing users to perform workflow tasks that do not require database access, such as approvals and review of information that is static and not bound to database tables. As the storage capacity of handheld devices increase, workflow clients will start implementing smart synchronizing schemes that will take a snapshot of the business data for local storage that can be used when disconnected from the server.

Ability to connect to Multiple Servers

In current generation BPM deployments, a workflow client typically connects to a single BPM server and can view the tasks and processes managed by that server. However, a user may be responsible for participation in business processes that are managed by different BPM servers. If the user points to a different server, the tasks and processes switch over to those that are managed by the new server. There is no unified inbox that gives a total view of all the tasks that a person has to perform regardless of the servers. As BPM becomes more widely adopted, organizations will start deploying multiple BPM servers managing different processes. Furthermore, partners and suppliers will also start deploying BPM servers that employees may be required to participate in. Next generation workflow clients will provide a unified inbox for each user. The inbox will show all the tasks the user has to perform, regardless of the number of BPM servers that are managing these tasks. If a person is participating in two internal processes, one process for a customer and one process for partners, the task list for the user will collect all tasks from the three different servers and provide a consolidated view of all the tasks.

Web Services and XML-Based Clients

The next generation of BPM servers will rely on Web Services. Web Services use the XML-based Simplified Object Access Protocol (SOAP) to enable clients' software to communicate with servers. XML and SOAP are neutral protocols and fit equally well in Microsoft-centric or UNIX/Java-centric environments. By developing XML-based workflow clients that use

Web Services, BPM vendors will be able to provide a rich client experience in Web browsers that are cross-platform and do not have the baggage associated with active browser clients. Furthermore, Web Services enable a browser to be "active." Users will benefit from the experience and performance of client/server applications that are able to dynamically update screens with new information as they are going about performing their tasks.

Conclusion

A workflow client provides a rich inbox for human participants in an automated business process to perform their tasks. While in some ways it is similar to an e-mail client, a workflow client needs features that exceed the requirements of the former. These features are driven by the flexibility people need when they are working. As BPM evolves into a widely-used enterprise solution, the features and flexibility of the workflow client will continue to increase.

Chapter 12

BPM Reporting
and Monitoring

A BPM system controls business processes. A prerequisite for control is the ability of a BPM system to be aware of the status of each task, incident, participant or application that is involved in the process. This required ability enables a BPM system to monitor and measure the performance of the processes, the participants and the organization as a whole. The ability to capture process metrics is one of the most valuable by-products of business process management that has tremendous potential for improving the performances of organizations and the ability of management to respond to inefficiencies or changes in internal or external demand for goods and services. There are many possibilities for the types of metrics a BPM system can generate, and the use of these metrics will vary from industry to industry and, indeed, from organization to organization. This chapter discusses the two major categories of process metric reports. It then covers the variety of report types in each category and explains how these reports can be used by process owners and managers to improve the performance of the organization.

BPM Report Categories

Business Activity Monitoring (BAM) is a term often used by the analyst community and some vendors in the BPM market for metric reports and the capability to monitor the performance of business processes. The acronym BAM is not used in this book for two reasons. First, BAM is an extension of business intelligence and enables proactive reporting of all types of business information, some of which may be derived from BPM systems, while others might be produced by enterprise solutions such as ERP, CRM and financial. Thus, BAM encompasses a very broad super-set of reports. What is of concern in this chapter is reporting that is specific to measuring and monitoring business processes automated by a BPM system. Second, BPM reporting is more than simply monitoring mechanisms. They can provide a wealth of statistics and other information to measure the performance of the organization's computer and applications as they participate in end-to-end business processes. Such performance measurements extend beyond just monitoring, allowing users and managers to determine the status of processes.

BPM reporting can be grouped into two broad categories depending on how the reports are generated:

1. *Process Metrics Reports:* These reports are generated on demand at the

request of business users who need to determine some particular set of metrics. They are passive in the sense that the reports are only generated when a user requests them.

2. *Process Notifications:* These reports are generated by the BPM system itself on a periodic basis, or when certain performance thresholds are exceeded. Process notifications are active in the sense that they are generated automatically by the BPM system and sent to various business users. They are used to notify process owners or managers about conditions relating to performance or volume that may require intervention by management.

Process Metric Reporting

Process metric reporting enables users to generate metric information about business processes on an ad hoc basis. These reports measure the volume, time and cost of business processes on an overall basis, or broken down by individual steps, users or groups of users. This information can also be used to measure the performance of processes, departments or individuals, and the distribution of work among users. Process metrics can be used by business owners and analysts to improve the business process, or to optimize the use of resources. Since these reports provide statistical data about the actual time and cost of tasks in the business process, the output of Process metric reporting can be used as input to business process modeling tools discussed in Chapter 8, "Business Process Modeling and Analysis." Process metric reporting, therefore, "closes the loop" for continuous process improvement by measuring process metrics from live processes, and then feeding this information back into the model that was used initially to build and optimize the process. This continuous improvement cycle is illustrated in Figure 7.1, "Detailed View of Business Process Lifecycle."

There are many types of process metric reports that can be generated by a BPM system. Some of these are generalized and are beneficial to many different processes across organizations. Others are very specific to individual businesses and are best customized to the requirements of the organization or their specific business processes. The next section discusses some of the generic reports and describes how customized reports may be defined and used.

Incident Volume Reporting

Incident volume reporting provides information about a particular process' volume of incidents that are in various stages of completion in a BPM system. These reports enable their users to find answers to the following types of questions:

1. *How many incidents of the process are currently active?* This measures the current level of business activity related to the process, and is useful in managing the resources needed to handle the activity.
2. *How many incidents are overdue by a specific amount of time?* This report provides an indication of how the organization is performing with respect to its goals or customer expectations.
3. *How many new incidents started in a specific time interval?* The number of incidents started in a specific time interval allows managers to determine the resources needed to handle the workload.
4. *How many new incidents were completed in a specific time interval?* The number of incidents completed provides a measure of the capacity of workload the organization can handle.
5. *What is the average number of incidents that are active at any given time?* This can provide a measure of the cyclical variations of workload experienced by the organization and can also be useful in planning resources.

For example, a business manager may want to know the number of customer orders currently being processed as well as the number that are overdue, completed or aborted in a specific time frame. By understanding the volume of incidents, the business manager can plan the resources required in order to manage the workload without compromising delivery times or causing excessive dead time. Furthermore, if incident volume reporting can be obtained with trend information, it can be used to predict future volume during various days of the week or month, or seasonal variations. These BPM reports may be extended through the use of business intelligence tools to generate information about order volumes by region, by product category, and the like.

Incident Cost Reporting

Incident cost reporting provides information about the cost of process incidents on an individual basis, or a statistical basis, for a group of incidents. They are useful for measuring the cost-effectiveness of a business process and to determine if the cost is consistent with the value provided by the process. Today, most businesses are not aware of the cost of their processes. Therefore, they are unable to make sound decisions about improving, changing or discarding business processes by comparing the cost against the benefits provided. Incident cost reporting enables business managers to answer questions such as:

1. What is the cost of processing a customer order?
2. How much does it cost the company, on the average, to conduct a performance review? Is the cost too high, and if so, how can it be reduced?
3. What is the cost of responding to a Web inquiry, and is this cost captured in the sales or marketing budgets?

By understating the cost of a process incident, business managers can decide whether it is consistent with the value of the process. If this is not the case, the process has to be modified by eliminating tasks that do not add value, increasing the performance of certain steps, or redirecting a higher proportion of processes to less expensive resources. For example, a Purchase Order process may be designed such that a director must approve any order more than $5,000. Based on the distribution of order size, it could turn out that 30% of the orders are routed to a director. If the cost of this process is determined to be excessive, perhaps the rules could be modified so that only those orders that are in excess of $10,000 need a director's approval. This will reduce the number of orders routed to a director to perhaps 10%, thereby reducing the cost attributable to the Director step by 67%. Using the related reports the user may determine how many times the Director step was activated, thereby providing statistical information about what happens in actual execution of processes. These reports, therefore, enable a business analyst to understand what goes on inside the process with the purpose of providing information to improve the process.

Incident Monitor Reporting

Incident monitor reporting provides information about the status of specific process incidents. One of the BPM user's most basic needs is to find out where requests for product, services or information are in the process, and when these request will come to a conclusion. Whenever users inside or outside an organization interact with its business processes, at some point they almost always want to know where things are. This need to know causes a considerable waste of time as individuals play telephone tag just to find out the status of where things are. In public-facing organizations such as service companies, utilities, municipalities or government offices that deal with tens of thousands of public clients, just to respond to the need-to-know status requires significant resources in call centers. Many BPM systems provide tabular feedback about the status of incidents. Advanced systems also provide graphical, color-coded views of process maps so that simply by looking at the maps users can determine the status of the incidents and how far and where they have to go before they will reach their conclusions. Incident monitor reporting saves time by providing status information at users' fingertips. These reports can also provide indications of how long it will take given incidents to complete based on information generated from other metrics reports. With this information, the workload on the organization can be further reduced as users will know when to expect the conclusions of incidents without having to request its status.

Process Monitor Reporting

While incident monitor reporting provides the status of specific incidents, process monitor reporting provides graphical status reports of collections of incidents. This is accomplished by overlaying the number of tasks at various states (active, completed, aborted) of each step in the process on top of the process map being monitored. As tasks are completed and new tasks are generated, the process monitor report changes to indicate the current count of tasks at each step. This enables a process owner or manager to graphically view the activity levels at each stage in the process. These reports provide an excellent way to determine the level of activity at each step in the process, and quickly point out bottlenecks at steps where the number of active tasks is increasing. These reports therefore provide a live "pulse" of the process by quickly and graphically providing an indication of the activity flow in a process. It can be used by managers to allocate resources and optimize the performance of the organization.

Step Volume Reporting

Step volume reporting provides statistical information about the level of activity at a specific step in a business process, as well as the status of tasks at that step. It enables business managers to answer the following types of questions:

1. How many tasks are currently active at the Order Approval step?

2. How many tasks were completed at the Invoice step in the last week?
3. What is the number of tasks returned everyday at the Order Configuration step? If this number is unreasonable, then perhaps there is a problem in training or in the previous steps of the process that is capturing order information.

Step volume reporting can by used by managers to estimate a particular job function's or department's level of activity or performance. This information can then be used to allocate resources to ensure that bottlenecks do not develop. They can also be used to manage the workload in an organization.

Step Time Reporting

Steps time reporting provides information about the time used for the completion of tasks at specific steps in the process. They are used to answer the following types of questions:

1. How long does it take on the average to complete the Order Configuration step?
2. What is the average and standard deviation of the total elapsed time for the Review step?
3. What is the typical time a task waits in the queue at the Invoice step before it is processed?

Business managers can use this report to determine the average time it takes to complete a task. This information, coupled with step activity reporting, provides information about how much time, and therefore resources, will be required for this specific function. They can also be used to determine if bottlenecks exist or may develop at the step.

Step Cost Reporting

Step cost reporting provides information about the cost of completing a particular step in the process. When used in conjunction with the cost of performing all steps in the process, this report provides valuable information to understand where cost is being incurred and how it can be reduced. It can provide information about which steps in the process contribute most to the cost of the process. By analyzing this information, business process owners can determine which steps of the process provide the most opportunity for reducing the overall cost of the process. By changing the process design, distribution of tasks or business rules associated with the process, the business analyst may be able to reduce the cost of the most expensive steps and thereby reduce the cost of the entire process. In many cases it is useful to be able to aggregate the cost of various steps into a single number in order to provide useful information. For example, a process may have many steps that are performed by individuals in different departments such as marketing, sales, order entry or manufacturing. By aggregating all the steps belonging to various departments into a single number, one can use this report to determine the distribution of cost by department rather than by individuals.

Figure 12.1 shows the cost of a simple purchase order process as a pie chart.

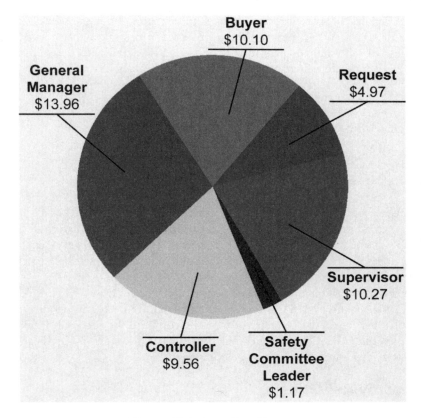

Figure 12.1. Step Cost Report

From this chart it can be determined that the overall cost of processing a purchase order is $50.03. Furthermore, the single most expensive contributor to the cost is the General Manager step with a contribution of $13.96 to the overall cost. This is not surprising because the general manager is an expensive human resource whose time must be used wisely. The company's business rules stipulate that any purchase order over $5,000 must be approved by the general manager, and about 20% of all orders are over $5,000. However, maybe only 5% of all orders are over $10,000. Changing the business rules so that only purchase orders exceeding $10,000 need general manager approval will result in reducing the cost of the General Manager step by 75%.

User Workload Reporting

User workload reporting provides information about the workload of users or teams. While step reporting provides information about steps regardless of who actually performed the tasks associated with the step, user workload reporting focuses on individuals. They can be used to monitor individual performance or estimate resources required or manage the distribution of work. The types of questions they can be used to answer are:

1. How many active tasks are there for John?
2. How many tasks did John complete in the previous week?
3. How many overdue tasks does Susan have?
4. How many tasks did David return yesterday?

User workload reports can be defined very broadly to cover all processes and all steps at which a particular user participated. Conversely, they can be defined for very specific criteria such as a specific step. Advanced reporting solutions can also predict the estimated time it will take to complete the tasks that are currently pending. For example, the BPM system knows that on the average it takes a person so many hours to complete a task. By also knowing the number of tasks that are currently pending in a person's inbox, the BPM system can easily compute the time it will take to complete all tasks. This further enables the BPM system to predict how long it will take for new tasks to be completed.

Jeopardy Reporting

Jeopardy reporting provides information about tasks that are late and which may jeopardize the timely completion of workflow incidents. These reports give management a preview of the tasks that must be completed to ensure that process incidents do not become late. They enable management to answer the following types of questions:

1. Which process incidents are in jeopardy of being late this Friday?
2. Which steps of the jeopardized incidents are causing the incidents to become late?
3. What additional resources are needed to ensure that all jeopardized incidents are completed on time?

Jeopardy reports can also be applied to steps or tasks instead of incidents. This allows supervisors to determine which steps are at risk of becoming late by a specific deadline. They can then take corrective actions to ensure that their teams are able to complete their responsibilities on a timely basis.

Proactive Notification Reporting

Proactive notification reports are generated by the BPM system on a proactive basis. They are alerts that can be configured by users to notify them when specific sets of conditions arise. The currently preferred method of notification is e-mail, but could also be instant messaging as this becomes more widely deployed in organizations. Since proactive notification reporting serves as an alert, the information contained in these reports is summary in nature. They can be used in conjunction with process metric reporting described earlier. Proactive notifications inform the business managers about the occurrence of a special set of conditions. The user can then use process metric reporting to investigate the situation in depth. BPM systems can generate a variety of proactive notification of the types described below.

Incident Alerts

These reports provide alerts about the activity of incidents or cases that are being processed by a BPM system. They can be used to notify business process owners or managers when process incidents of a particular category exceed a defined threshold. Incident alerts can be configured to generate the following types of alerts:

1. Number of active incidents of one or more processes exceeding a

threshold
2. Number of new incidents of one or more processes exceeding a threshold within a specified time frame
3. Number of completed incidents of one or more processes exceeding a threshold within a specified timeframe
4. Number of late incidents of one or more processes exceeding a threshold

For example, incident alerts can be used to notify process owners under the following types of conditions:

1. The number of late loan applications exceed 10
2. The number of incoming orders within the past five days exceeds 50
3. The number of ongoing change requests exceed 25

Incident Alerts can be configured by establishing a query with the following parameters:

When incidents of [Process Name] with status [Status] between [Start Time] and [End Time] exceed [Threshold]
    Where:
        [Process Name] = Name of one, more than one, or all processes
        [Status] = Active, Late, Completed, Aborted
        [Start Time] = Start of time window
        [End Time] = End of time window
        [Threshold] = any positive integer

Step Alerts

Step alerts can be used to notify business owners or managers when the number of tasks at one or more steps of one or more processes exceeds a given threshold. They can be used to alert managers about abnormal situations that may need corrective actions. The following are some examples of the types of step alerts that could be configured:

1. The number of active Buyer steps exceeds 10
2. The number of late Performance Review steps exceeds 5
3. The number of all late steps in the engineering department exceeds 30
4. The number of completed Order Steps within a day exceeds 100. This is directly proportional to the number of new orders coming to the

company every week.

Step Alerts may be configured by establishing a generic query as follows:

When [Step] with status [Status] in [Start time] and [End Time] exceed [Threshold]
> Where:
>> [Step] is one or more steps or tasks of the same or different processes.
>> [Status] is Active, Completed, Aborted, or Late
>> [Threshold] is any positive integer
>> [Start Time] is the start of the counting period
>> [End Time] is the end of the counting period

Note that since this allows users to combine steps from different processes that may belong to the same department or group, one can configure alerts to measure the activity levels on departments, teams or groups.

User Alerts

User alerts can be used to notify business owners or managers when the activities of one or more users related to one or more processes exceeds a given threshold. They can be used to alert managers about abnormal user situations that may need corrective actions. The following are some examples of the types of user alerts that could be configured:

1. The number of active steps in John's inbox exceeds 10
2. The number of late steps in Jane's inbox exceeds 5
3. The number of all returned steps in John and Jane's inbox exceeds 30
4. The number of completed Order steps completed by John within a day exceeds 100. This is directly proportional to the amount of work completed by John.

User alerts may be configured by establishing a generic query as follows:

When step for recipient [User] in [Start time] and [End Time] exceed [Threshold]
> Where:

[User] is one or more users participating in the same or different processes.

[Status] is Active, Completed, Aborted, or Late

[Threshold] is any positive integer

[Start Time] is the start of the counting period

[End Time] is the end of the counting period

Note that since this allows the combination of steps for different users that may belong to the same department or group, one can configure alerts to measure the activity levels on departments, teams or groups.

System Notifications

System notifications are a class of proactive notifications that provide alerts about system-level events and situations that could affect the performance of business processes. They are generally designed for the workflow manager or system administrator who can take corrective action to ensure the smooth execution of business processes. Some examples of system notifications include the following:

1. *Stalled Processes:* If the logic of a business process is poorly designed and does not account for all possible situations, it is sometimes possible for a process incident to be unable to proceed. This generally happens in processes that have parallel branches with conditions associated with each branch. If the condition for all the parallel branches evaluate false, the incident has no way to progress and will remain in this state forever. Such a process incident is called "stalled." If an incident stalls, it is necessary to send a notification to the process owner to apprise him of the situation so that corrective action can be taken. Otherwise, the only way a stalled incident will come to light is if it becomes late, in which case it is probably too late to take corrective action to salvage the situation.

2. *Unavailability of Participants:* If a participant at a step in a business process is no longer available and the business process has not been modified to account for this change, the BPM server will have no person or resource to perform the task. In this case, the BPM system needs to send out proactive notification to the process owner who may be able to take corrective action by naming a substitute.

3. *Over utilization of system resources:* A BPM system consumes resources such as memory and disk space on the computer hosting it. If the BPM server's resource needs become too large, it is likely to exceed the

capacity of the server computer and therefore cause it to degrade in performance or shutdown completely. To avoid these situations, some BPM systems provide the ability to sense resource utilizations and send a message to a system administrator when the resources used exceed a specified threshold.

Conclusion

Modern BPM systems provide a number of reporting capabilities for monitoring business processes and measuring their effectiveness. These reports can be used by business owners to improve their processes by reducing cost or response time. They can also be used to manage the workload of the employees who participate in processes and ensure that proper resources are available to meet performance expectations of internal or external customers who benefit from these processes. When BPM reporting tools are combined with business intelligence solutions, the resulting combination provides powerful Business Activity Monitoring (BAM) capabilities. BAM provides information that combines process metrics and volumes with other economic parameters that are of interest: order volumes, seasonality, regional distribution, product distribution and financial metrics. This feedback enables business owners to monitor and control the overall performance of the organization and respond quickly to changes in internal and external conditions.

Chapter 13

BPM and
Application Integration

A BPM system is the central nervous system of a modern organization that binds its human and IT assets into business processes that deliver goods, services and information to internal and external customers. IT assets include a large number of software applications that are commonly found in a modern organization. These include everything from desktop applications like word processors and spreadsheets, to infrastructure applications such as e-mail and databases, and enterprise or back-office applications such as ERP, CRM, and financial systems. The need to integrate all of these systems is one of the major challenges that must be faced in order for BPM to become an organization's central nervous system. Integration becomes a challenging and complicated because of the variety of technologies used and the lack of industry standards.

This chapter explores the need for integration in substantial detail, with emphasis on the modes of integration required for business process management. The chapter also provides a discussion of the technologies commonly used for integration and their pros and cons. It describes the techniques and challenges for integrating the most common types of desktop and enterprise applications. A new Internet technology, Web Services, provides one of the most promising methods of application integration that is likely to become a widely used and open standard. Because of the significance of Web Services, Chapter 14, "Web Services, BPM and the Internet," offers a more detailed discussion of Web Services and how this technology will transform BPM and application integration.

The Need for Integration

A BPM system is an electronic production line of information. Its basic purpose is to flow information from one stage to another in order to enable decisions and actions for the delivery of goods, services or knowledge to internal and external customers. At each stage it can involve users for knowledge input or third-party computer applications for the purpose of acquiring or saving information, or using an application to make decisions. A BPM system therefore must be able to interact with a variety of computer applications and people for purposes listed below:

1. *Desktop personal productivity applications such as Microsoft Word, Microsoft Excel or Adobe PDF.* These applications are used during the course of the business processes to create, print and save documents, perform calculations and analyze information. They are used by a BPM system to

replicate and replace the functions performed by humans in order to improve productivity.

2. *Databases such as Oracle, Microsoft SQL Server, IBM DB2 and Sybase.* BPM systems use databases in two different ways. First, databases are used to save information gathered by the process, or to enable process participants to make effective decisions based on information that already exists in databases, or a combination of the two. Second, databases are used to save the information used by the BPM server to control business processes.

3. *E-mail applications such as Microsoft Exchange, Lotus Notes Mail, or Internet SMTP/POP Mail.* E-mail is used in two significant ways. First, it can be used by the BPM system to send proactive notifications of process events such as a new task or a late task. Second, e-mail can be used as a part of a process to send messages and attachments as specific actions in the process dictated by process requirements.

4. *Document/Image Management Systems such as those offered by Documentum, Docuware and Hummingbird.* Many business processes depend on supporting documents that are routed as a part of the process for the purpose of justifying or clarifying decisions made in the process, or for the editing or approval of the documents themselves.

5. *Enterprise applications such as ERP, CRM, Human Resource and Sales Force Automation.* These applications are used in conjunction with business processes. An order that is approved by a business process must be transferred to the ERP system. A financial system determines that an invoice is past due. It can trigger an instance of a receivables process in order to collect funds.

6. *Legacy systems such as IBM AS/400 and other mainframes.* These systems are widely used for banking, manufacturing and financial control functions in large corporations. They are not likely to be replaced in the foreseeable future. Business processes have to interact with these systems so that they can effectively use the information and knowledge already in existence.

There are two main reasons why integration is a major challenge for the success of BPM. First, as we have noted above, there are many different types of applications that have to be integrated. Second, there are as yet no industry standards or technologies for integration. Therefore, each application has to be integrated in unique ways, and it is necessary for a BPM system to provide many different interfacing options.

Modes of Integration

In addition to different applications and technologies used for integration, there are a number of different ways in which these applications interact with BPM systems, further increasing the number of permutations required. The five major modes of integration are listed below and discussed individually in the following sections:

1. Pre-process integration
2. In-process integration
3. Post-process integration
4. Real-time client-side integration
5. Real-time server-side integration

Pre-Process Integration

This mode of integration is used before a process incident is active. Its purpose is to allow a third-party application to trigger a business process in order to perform a service. This is illustrated in Figure 13.1.

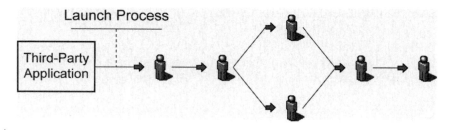

Figure 13.1. Pre-Process Integration

There are many examples of the use of pre-process integration where external events or applications trigger a business process:

1. A new invoice is received from a vendor. It is scanned and placed in an image management system. This triggers a business process whose purpose is to route and pay the invoice after obtaining the necessary approvals.
2. A customer visits the company's Web site and places an order using a Web page. As soon as the order is submitted from the Web site, it triggers a business process to process the order.

3. An HR system determines that a performance review for an employee is due. It triggers a business process to conduct a performance review.
4. An accounting system determines that a customer accounts receivable is past due. It triggers a business process to initiate the collections process.
5. The quality manager of a company updates a quality policy document and places the new version in a specific folder in a document management system. This triggers a business process that attaches and routes the document to various managers in the company for their review and approval.

In-Process Integration

In-process integration refers to the fact that a BPM system may need to use a third-party application at a particular step in the process, hence the term "in-process." It is important to note that there is no human involvement in this mode of integration, for the required tasks are performed entirely by the third-party application. This enables companies to implement what is also called "straight-through processing (STP)," which provides some of the highest return on investment opportunities by fully automating aspects of end-to-end processes. For example:

1. At a particular step in the process, a word processor may be invoked to print a document based on the information passed to it by the process.
2. At the last step of the process, all the data gathered by the process is written to a database.
3. After an order has been processed and shipped, the customer is notified via e-mail containing information about the shipment.
4. If a purchase request is denied, the requestor has to be notified about the reasons for the denial.

In these examples the BPM server, using third-party applications, performs all the tasks described. A BPM solution can deliver maximum productivity improvements by eliminating needless human involvement from routine tasks.

Post-Process Integration

This mode of integration is used at the end of a business process. Its purpose is to enable a business process to transfer information collected by the process, or decisions made during the course of the process, to a third-party application. This is illustrated in Figure 13.2.

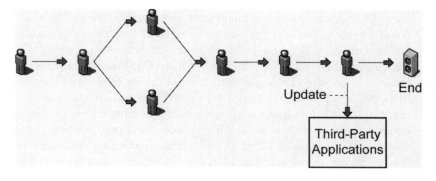

Figure 13.2. Post-Process Integration

Some examples of using post-process integration are:

1. A new customer order is processed and approved as a part of a business process. At the end of the process the order is posted to a manufacturing system.
2. A business process is used to route a new HTML document to various individuals in the company for marketing, quality and legal approval. At the end of the process, when all approvals have been obtained, the process deposits the document into the company's Web content management system.
3. A company uses an Annual Performance Review process to approve salary increases for employees. At the end of the review process, the new salary for the employee is submitted to the company's accounting or human resource system

Real-Time Client-Side Integration

Real-time client integration is used for making process participants more effective in performing their tasks during the course of the process. Process participants use some form of a workflow client and interact in real-time with the BPM server and third-party applications. When users are involved, it is necessary for the integration to be "real time" since the user is waiting for an immediate response from the third-party application. Examples of real-time client integration are:

1. A participant in a business process uses an electronic form to search for a particular account or part number in the company's accounting database. This requires real-time integration with a database.
2. A participant has to reassign one of his tasks to another user in a different department. To do this he needs to browse the company's employee directory and select the name of the user. This requires the integration of the workflow client with the company's employee directory.
3. A user at a step in a process needs to search for and attach a document that resides in a document management system. This is possible only by integrating the workflow client with the document management system.
4. A user filling out an order needs to determine the ship date for a particular item in the order. Ship dates are computed by a legacy system (for example, an ERP system running on a mainframe). This requires integrating the workflow client with a legacy system.

It is possible to have two types of client-integration topologies. In the direct client-application topology shown in Figure 13.3, each workflow client communicates directly with the third-party application.

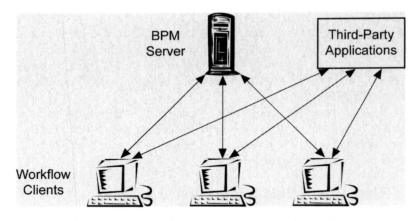

Figure 13.3. Direct Client-Application Integration

From a development viewpoint this is easier to accomplish, but it has a high cost of ownership. That is because if there are a large number of client users, each will have to connect to the third-party application. Maintaining and managing these connections is not easy and the cost of ownership rises exponentially with the number of clients, making it prohibitive.

In the client-server-application topology shown in Figure 13.4, there is only one point of integration between the BPM server and the third-party application.

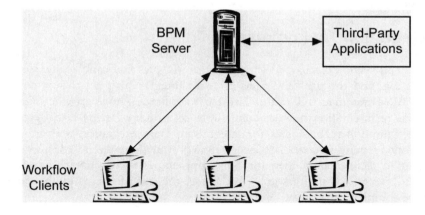

Figure 13.4. Client-Server-Application Integration

All connections between the BPM server and the third-party application are made at a single point. The workflow clients communicate only with the BPM server, just as they already do for other process-related activities. Integration becomes simply another feature of the workflow client. This type of integration, while more difficult to develop, is easier to manage and maintain in the long run. It is therefore the recommended topology for real-time client integration.

Real-Time Server-Side Integration

A BPM server has to support real-time interactions with a variety of third-party applications or systems for the purpose of performing basic functions. These include at least three important ones:

1. Directory services for the purpose of user authentication and obtaining information about users
2. E-mail systems for sending e-mail messages
3. Databases for keeping process status and related information

Notice that all these applications fall in the category of *infrastructure*. A BPM system relies heavily on these infrastructure applications to the extent that they should be considered prerequisites for business process management. Furthermore, the interaction between these applications and the BPM server must be robust and capable of supporting high transaction volumes.

Integration Technologies

This section discusses a variety of technologies that can be used for integration, and the pros and cons of each. Integration is a two-way street. The BPM system as well as the third-party application must provide suitable means of integration that are compatible with each other. If both systems share common technologies for integration, then integration is easier and does not require intermediary layers. However, if there are no common integration technologies, then the only approach is to rely on intermediary layers, also called "middleware." In this case the task of integration becomes more complex and costly.

Text Files

Text files are the most rudimentary form of integration. Almost every application and operating platform can recognize text files that use the ASCII character set. Furthermore, the use of comma or character delimited text files to export and import information between various applications has become very common since it was first popularized by spreadsheets in the early 1980s. Text files can be used for simple integration with BPM systems. For example, a third-party application can use a text file to trigger a process and pass context information for the new process incident. A BPM system may also create a text file to output data that is then captured by a third-party application.

While text files are simple to use, they have several limitations that are a consequence of this simplicity:

1. Integration via text files must be customized and programmed. A BPM system and a third-party application have no way of automatically determining the format of the text file and the meaning of the information that it contains. Integration requires one application to specify the format of the file it will output, and the other application then has to be programmed to read and understand the data.
2. It is not possible to impose and control a data structure when using text files. While two applications might agree upon the format of a text file used to exchange information, there is no way to enforce this

agreement. If one application does not produce the data in the agreed format, it may produce unpredictable or erroneous results that can be resolved only by reprogramming. This typically happens when an application is updated with a new version. It is difficult to maintain the integration.

3. Text files are good for exchanging text data. They are not suitable for other types of information such as numeric, images, voice or video.

4. Using text files means reliance on a shared file directory for exchanging files. Thus, using text files as a means of integration can be used only inside the firewall and for applications running on the same network.

Because of these limitations, text files are used only for the simplest integration needs.

E-Mail

E-mail is a popular means of sharing information by users on an ad hoc basis. E-mail messages are basically text files. It is relatively easy for applications to send pre-formatted e-mail messages and also receive e-mail and parse the contents of the message for specific information. Thus, e-mail can be used by BPM systems for integration in two ways:

1. A third-party application can generate an e-mail message and send it to the BPM server to trigger a business process. Figure 13.5 illustrates a configuration where a Web page is used to capture customer registration information. This information is composed as an e-mail message and sent to the BPM server that triggers a process on its receipt.

2. A BPM system can use an e-mail automation agent at a step in the process and send an e-mail message with specific information to a third-party application. The application can then parse the e-mail message and extract the information that it needs.

The major benefit of using e-mail is that it is widely used, standards based, uses text that is readily understood by people and by applications if properly formatted, can reach long distances over the public networks, and is designed to go through firewalls. The latter means that e-mail can be used to integrate disparate systems.

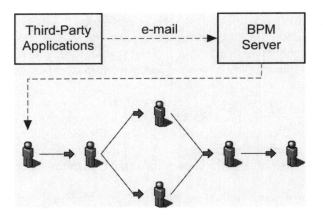

Figure 13.5. Using E-mail to Launch Processes

While there are many useful applications of e-mail integration, it also has limitations:

1. E-mail was designed for free format text. There is no standard format or schema for sending data via e-mail. The sending and the receiving parties have to agree in advance about the format and then ensure that their applications comply with the specification. This drives up the cost of integration and maintenance.
2. Like text files, e-mail does not provide any means of enforcing data structure.
3. E-mail is not the most reliable means of communicating mission-critical business information. If a problem does occur during transmission, it is not easy to detect or recover from it. Furthermore, there is no "handshake" mechanism to confirm a transaction. One application sends an e-mail and assumes that the other application has received it, but, in reality, it may never have reached the destination.

Database Connectivity

Almost every business application uses databases for two primary reasons. First, they use databases to search, consume, update and massage business information. This is the core function of business applications. Second, they also use databases to store information that is used to control the application itself. This may include information such as access rights, configuration of the application, or its current state. Business applications that rely heavily on databases include document/image management, record management, ERP, CRM, accounting/financial applications and many others. It is therefore possible to enable the interaction of BPM applications simply by providing access to the databases used by business applications.

In some cases business applications expose their database schema. This allows other applications and developers to understand the structure and meaning of the information used by the business application. In these cases it is possible for a BPM system to simply read or write information to the databases of these applications for the purpose of simple integration. While this is feasible, its use must be limited for the most basic integration needs, and extreme caution must be exercised. For example, if a BPM application simply needs to read a list of accounts and their owners from a financial application, this can be done safely through direct database connectivity. However, if the BPM application wants to create a new account, it is not recommended that the process application simply write to the database of the financial application and create a new record. This is because the business logic of how to create a new account is a part of the financial application. Any incorrect update of the database could damage the integrity of the database in unforeseen ways. It is for this reason that many business applications do not allow third-party applications to directly access the databases they use, or they allow only very restricted direct access.

Application Programming Interfaces

Many applications provide Application Programming Interfaces, or APIs, for the purpose of enabling third-party applications to interact with them. An API is a structured method, offered by the application developer, to control how other applications can interact with it and what they can and cannot do. It is a programmatic interface, meaning that it requires software coding to interface with the application using an API. The API is in a sense the "gateways" into the application. By offering an API, the application vendor exposes some or all of the core functionality of the application to third-party applications. In most cases vendors also provide a Software Development Kit (SDK) that includes documentation for the APIs and examples of how to use them, often with source code of sample interface examples. For example, SAP R/3 offers over 8000 APIs called SAP BAPIs (or business APIs) that allow third-party applications to programmatically interface with SAP R/3 to perform a variety of functions.

APIs provide a practical mechanism for BPM systems to interact with third-party applications for a number of reasons:

1. The APIs control the scope and method of the interface. This means that a BPM system can interact with the third-party application without having to concern itself with the internal workings of the application. It is the APIs responsibility to control the interaction and the integrity of the transaction.

2. APIs are a direct, programmatic interface. A process application is talking directly with the third-party application without any intermediate layer or middleware. Therefore, the integration is fast in terms of performance.

APIs do have some serious limitations. First and foremost is the fact that each application has its own API, and there are no standards. Using APIs for integration is therefore a "point solution." Integration between a BPM system and third-party application has to be customized for all applications. This is a very costly proposition, especially when one considers the large number of applications a BPM system has to interface with, and the many versions of each. Second, to use an API means that the BPM system and the third-party application must be on the same operating system platform. APIs are not suitable for cross-platform integration. The third limitation of APIs is that they are normally used for interaction when two applications are running on the same computer. In many cases a BPM system and third-party applications will be running on different computers for reasons of scalability and isolation of applications. APIs generally do not provide a method of bridging applications that are running on separate computers on a network.

Object Technologies

Object technologies such as COM/DCOM, CORBA and J2EE were developed to address some of the limitations of using APIs. Object technologies provide a framework for one application to use the services provided by another application. There are several important characteristics of object technologies:

1. *Interface Standardization:* Object technologies such as COM/DCOM, CORBA and J2EE provide standardization of the interface between applications that use these technologies. As a minimum they provide a structure for methods and properties. This makes it easy for the calling application to interrogate the service provider for the types of services it provides and the method it uses to transfer data. It is therefore easier

to use object technologies for integrating applications.

2. *Data Standardization:* Object technologies also make it possible for applications to exchange data in common formats. This simplifies the task of integration while making it possible to deal with a variety of data types.

3. *Remote Invocation:* One of the major advantages of object technologies is that they provide a method of remote invocation, variously called Remote Procedure Calls (RPC), or Remote Method Invocation (RMI) by different technology vendors. A calling application can call an object or the service application over the network running on another computer.

4. *Cross-platform:* Applications that use COM/DCOM, CORBA or J2EE generally belong to the Microsoft, UNIX or Java "camps" and generally work only with other applications belonging to the same "camp" and using the same operating system platforms. However, third-party companies such as Iona, provide "bridges" (such as COM-CORBA bridge) that enable applications using one object technology to remotely invoke services using a different technology.

Object technologies are easier to use by BPM systems for integrating with third-party applications. Even though the low-level aspects of integration still require programming, they do standardize the interface at a high level and provide a format for all applications using the same object technologies to interact with each other.

Object technologies can also be used for exposing services provided by a BPM engine to third-party applications. This is the basis of the OEM strategy of these BPM vendors. It enables third-party applications to embed BPM functionality and use them to enhance their own functionality and provide greater value. Many business applications can benefit from robust, embedded BPM capabilities. These include document management, asset management, customer relationship management, enterprise resource planning, accounting/financial, and many others.

While object technologies offer significant benefits over the use of other integration technologies such as APIs, they still suffer from drawbacks. First, while object technologies do provide standardized interfaces between a calling application and service provider application, the interface is still specific to the service provider application and cannot be "discovered" automatically. The integration between the calling application and the service provider application must be developed for a specific purpose. If the service provider application is changed or upgraded, the interface is likely to change also. Thus, object technologies are still a "point integration" solution, albeit an easier point integration than APIs. Second, while bridges between various object technologies are available, they are expensive to deploy in terms of the development and maintenance cost. The world continues to be divided into the COM/DCOM, CORBA and J2EE camps.

Application Adaptors and Connectors

To ease the burden of integration, many EAI companies offer middleware that allows an application to connect to multiple service provider applications. This middleware, also called "adaptors" or "connectors" is illustrated in Figure 13.6.

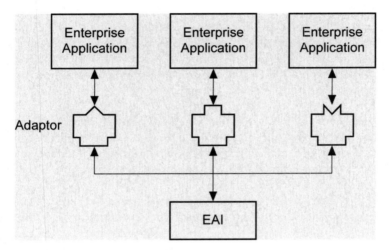

Figure 13.6. Application Adaptors or Connectors

Middleware essentially acts like a "broker" between the calling application and the service provider. The adaptor provides one standard interface to the enterprise application. The key is that adaptors can be developed for many different service provider applications. The calling application has to develop and implement only one interface to the adaptor. The adaptor acts as middleware and connects to several other service provider applications. Thus, integration is simplified since it is limited to only one interface to the adaptor. The adaptor also hides the complexity and nuances of each individual service provider application.

Adaptors can be used by BPM systems to integrate with third-party applications to perform services during the course of a business process.

This is an effective method that is limited only by the number of third-party applications the EAI vendor supports, and the flexibility of the integration in terms of the number of functions that it can perform.

There are some drawbacks of using adaptors for integration. First, adaptors are proprietary to the EAI vendors, and are not based on industry standards. This means that applications that can be integrated are limited to those supported by the EAI vendor. Second, the cost of deploying an integration adaptor and EAI middleware is generally very high. After making this investment, an organization cannot easily switch. Third, adaptors are middleware. They add a layer between the calling application and the service provider application, thus having some impact on performance. And finally, adaptors may be suitable for some but not all the modes of integration that are described in this chapter.

Legacy Screen Scrapers

Mainframe systems continue to be used extensively for finance, manufacturing and accounting functions in large corporations. These systems are expensive to begin with and contain large amount of information that cannot be easily ported to other platforms. This is the primary reason they will continue to be used for the foreseeable feature. In fact, in the past couple of years, there has been a slight shift back towards mainframes as companies realize the difficulties of managing decentralized computing environments created by the personal computing revolution.

Information contained in legacy systems has an important role to play in business processes of any corporation still using such systems. Furthermore, for the purpose of full automation, a BPM system has to provide a way to use the functionality of the legacy system as a part of a business process. For example, if a legacy system is used to create and manage new accounts for new customers, it is important for the pertinent business process to automatically communicate with the legacy system for the purpose of creating the new account as part of the business process. This is challenging because mainframe legacy systems were not originally designed for integration with third-party applications.

Several companies now offer "blue screen scraper" applications. The "blue screen" refers to the screen of the IBM 3270 terminals, sometimes called "dumb terminals." They are widely used as a part of IBM mainframe installations as the means for users to interact with the mainframe. Screen scraper applications replace the "blue screens" and reside between the mainframe system and the calling application. To the mainframe they provide the same interface as offered by the terminal, so that the mainframe can continue to function without any change or reprogramming. For the calling application they provide a programmatic way to perform the functions that a human would have performed using the terminal. For example, using a blue screen terminal, a user would use a menu and type "N" for new account, and then in a particular location of the screen enter the name and address of the new customer. This would cause the mainframe to create a new account. The screen scraper application accepts these same inputs from another application and makes the mainframe "think" that the identical information has been entered in the same location.

Screen scraper applications provided by companies such as Pivotal provide good mechanisms for BPM systems to interface with legacy mainframes.

Automation Agents

Automation agents enable BPM systems to engage third-party desktop or enterprise applications as participants in a business process, just like the workflow client provides the means for people to participate in process. A business process is like an electronic production line for information. In a modern manufacturing production line, workers are used at some steps that require manual dexterity or human knowledge. Other steps are performed by robots or flexible manufacturing systems (FMS). Robots are used in a manufacturing production line because they are flexible instruments; they can be reprogrammed to perform various tasks depending on the part being manufactured. This makes it easy to switch from manufacturing one part to a different part. Likewise, in today's modern office, users or knowledge workers perform some steps in business processes, and at other steps these same knowledge workers use desktop applications (word processors, spreadsheets, databases, e-mail) or enterprise applications (ERP, CRM, SFA). Users perform some steps in this production line, and others are performed by these applications. Like robots, these applications are used because they are flexible and can be used to perform a variety of tasks depending on the process.

BPM systems that use automation agents enable many tasks formerly performed by knowledge workers to be delegated to applications. This eliminates user involvement in the business process that results in reducing cost, decreasing response time and increasing consistency. They facilitate "straight through processing (STP)" which is the implementation of business process with very limited or no human involvement.

Anatomy of a Flobot

The Ultimus BPM Suite uses Flobots™, which are classic examples of automation agents. A "Flobot" is a "workflow robot." Within a process users perform some steps while other steps are performed by Flobots. Flobots are available out-of-the-box for a variety of third-party applications such as scripts, XML, Microsoft Word, Microsoft Excel, Adobe Acrobat, Microsoft Exchange, e-mail, and others. These Flobots have two modes. First, when the business process is being designed, the Flobot can be activated in the "training" mode. In this mode the process designer instructs the Flobot what it has to do. This training is dependent on the capabilities of the Flobot and the purpose of the application. For example, in the case of the Microsoft Word Flobot, training may include the following:

1. Open a word document template.
2. Run a pre-defined Word macro.
3. Transfer real-time data from process variables to specific locations in the document.
4. Run a different Word macro after data has been transferred.
5. Print, save, fax or e-mail the document.
6. Close Word.

Likewise in the case of an E-Mail Flobot, the training may include the following:

1. Compose an e-mail message using data from specific process variables.
2. Configure the "To" field of the e-mail message using pre-defined variables.
3. Configure the "Subject" field of the e-mail message.
4. Insert attachments as specified by other pre-defined variables.
5. Configure the Flobot to send the e-mail message upon completion of the above tasks.

The second mode is the "real-time" mode of the Flobot, which is triggered during the actual execution of the process. When the process incident reaches the Flobot step, the Flobot automatically "wakes up." It takes data from the process variables and invokes the application associated with the Flobot. It then performs all the tasks it has been programmed to perform, then goes back to "sleep." All this occurs without any human intervention.

Flobots can be used for a large variety of tasks that include printing documents, creating Adobe forms, sending messages, reading/writing from databases, performing XML transactions with third-party applications, running customized scripts, etc. The fact that they do not involve people and can use real-time information from a process makes them a powerful solution for automating repetitive tasks.

BPM and Databases

BPM systems must be able to support robust interactions with databases. This is because they use databases for two very important functions:

1. A BPM system requires a method of saving the status of process incidents, definitions of business processes, information pertaining to tasks assigned to various users and the status of this task. This information is best classified as process control information. It is structured information, and the logical place to save this information is in a database. This falls into the server-side integration mode.
2. A business process must have access to business information kept in databases. Participants in a process use business information to make decisions as a part of the business process. Furthermore, the process collects and refines information and decisions that must be kept as a part of the business information. This requires strong links to databases. This falls into the client-side or in-process integration mode.

There are three points at which a BPM system must interface with a database:

1. The BPM server must be able to connect with a database in order to use and maintain the process control information.
2. The workflow client must be able to interact with business information kept in databases.
3. An automation agent used by BPM systems must be able to interact with the business information in databases in order to perform transactions without human interaction.

For robust integration with databases, BPM systems should meet the following requirements:

1. A BPM system must support enterprise-class databases such as Oracle, Microsoft SQL Server or IBM dB2. These databases are designed for high-scalability and performance that support a large number of concurrent connections. Desktop databases such as Microsoft Access are not recommended since they are designed for individual use and do not offer scalability.

2. In almost all cases the database server will be physically different than the BPM server. Therefore, the communication between the two is over a network connection that must be secure, fast and reliable.

3. There are a variety of technologies that can be used by the BPM server to communicate with the database server. These include ODBC, ADO, OLE DB, or JDBC. The choice of a particular technology depends on the nature of the application and the technologies used for the BPM server. Regardless of the technology used, the most important consideration is that the BPM server must be able to perform multiple simultaneous transactions with the database server.

BPM and E-Mail

E-mail has become the de facto method for ad hoc communications and notification between users. It is easy to use, and its usage has become widespread because of Internet messaging standards such as SMTP and POP. A BPM system can leverage e-mail through tight integration. This can provide a number of useful capabilities:

1. A BPM system can use e-mail to send notification to participants when they have new, late or aborted tasks, or when tasks are escalated. This is the server-side mode of integration because the process server acts like a mail client and sends such messages to affected participants. This capability is particularly useful in Web-based BPM solutions. The Internet is a passive communications medium. A user does not know about the change in status of a task or the arrival a new task unless the user points a Web browser to a particular Web site or URL. E-mail makes a Web-based solution proactive. The user receives an e-mail message with the notification, and in many cases the URL of the site they need to visit in order to perform the action specified is incorporated into the e-mail notification.

2. Some BPM solutions provide the capability to trigger a process based

on the receipt of an e-mail by the BPM server. The e-mail message is parsed based upon rules previously agreed upon, and the data in the e-mail message is used to provide the context of the process incident triggered by the e-mail. This is an example of pre-process integration and can be used to trigger business processes from remotely hosted Web sites, mobile devices, or other locations or interfaces outside the firewall where it is not possible to directly access the BPM server.

3. E-mail may be used explicitly as a part of a business process to send notification to consumers of BPM services. This is an example of in-process integration, or post-process integration, and is typically done through automation agents. For example, when an order from an external customer has been processed and shipped during the course of a process, an e-mail message may be sent to the customer with information about the ship date, carrier and tracking number.

E-mail integration is relatively easy to accomplish because of strong industry standards for e-mail. Presently SMTP and POP standards are the most widely use and provide a simple method of integration. In addition, Microsoft offers the Exchange messaging standards, IBM Lotus offers the Notes Mail standard, and Novell offers the GroupWise standard. However, due to the strength of SMTP/POP standards, the proprietary messaging solutions of these vendors now offer SMTP/POP compatibility, and are gradually shifting to the use of the latter.

BPM and Document/Image Management Systems

While databases provide an excellent method of saving structured business information, electronic document managements systems (EDMS) provide an excellent mechanism of saving unstructured information. Unstructured information includes documents, images, voice, and videos. The importance of managing unstructured information is obvious since every organization has a lot of knowledge contained in documents, images and other unstructured information sources. With the move to a digital economy, many other paper documents are being converted to electronic form, thus increasing the demand for managing such information.

The routing of unstructured information for creation, review, approval and distribution is handled by business process. For example, new quality assurance documentation must be routed for approval to all the quality assurance managers and the division manager before they are formalized and published. Marketing, product management and legal must approve new Web content before it is published on the corporate Web server. Incoming invoices must be scanned and routed for approvals before they are submitted to the accounting system for payment. Resumes submitted on the company's Web site must be qualified by human resources and then routed to various hiring managers who are interested in the qualifications of the candidate. All of these are examples of business processes that deal with unstructured information which require effective integration of a BPM system with EDMS.

There are three useful modes of integration with EDMS and BPM systems:

1. *Pre-Process Integration:* Many business processes require scanning of documents, saving the scanned documents in EDMS, and then using a BPM system to route the document for approval or other types of process. For example, an incoming invoice may be scanned upon receipt and placed in the EDMS. This action triggers a business process instance that routes it for approval or some other decision-making activity. Likewise, a user creates a new version of a quality assurance procedure and places it in an EDMS. This action triggers a process that routes the document for approval before the quality assurance procedure is accepted.

2. *Client-Side Integration:* As a part of a process it is often necessary to attach documents to justify an action or provide supporting information. If a company uses an EDMS, the documents are most likely saved in the EDMS. To enable process participants to attach and view documents located in the EDMS, a BPM solution needs to provide client-side integration to the EDMS. Such integration has to support searching for documents, viewing attached documents, updating documents, check-in and check-out of documents, and other functions supported by the EDMS.

3. *Post-Process Integration:* An EDMS typically saves a document with attributes or properties that enable the document to be classified. These properties may include author name, date of creation, version number, key words, or other similar pieces of information necessary to classify the document. At the end of a process it is often necessary to update the properties of the document since they may have been changed during the course of the process. This is why post-process integration is needed, and is typically accomplished through an automation agent for the EDMS.

The previous discussion uses the term "attaching documents" to the process. The word "attachment" is familiar to all e-mail users as the physical attachment of a file to an e-mail message. Physically attaching documents works for e-mail, but does not work for a BPM system. E-mail generally travels from a sender to one or more receivers. If a document is attached, it is up to the receiver to decide what to do with the attachment in the context of the e-mail. However, a business process is very different. If a document is attached to the process, it may travel to many subsequent parallel steps where the users might modify the document. This will result in multiple versions of the document. If the process then converges to a single step, the BPM system ends up with multiple versions of the same document. It is impossible to decide which one of the physically attached copies should be used. Moreover, attaching documents physically and sending them over the network to all the recipients is potentially slow and ineffective, especially when some of the recipients may not even want to view the document.

To overcome this, when an EDMS is integrated with a BPM system, the EDMS passes a "pointer" or a unique reference number of the document to the BPM system. The document always physically stays in the EDSMS. The BPM system routes the pointer to various users in the business process. When a user wishes to view the document, the pointer is used to identify and downloaded the document, then presented to the user. The EDMS is also aware if another user has opened the document at the same time, if the user has proper access rights to the document, and other checks to ensure the integrity of the process. This not only resolves conflict in deciding which documents to use, and who can use it at a given time, but also improves overall performance by eliminating unnecessary network traffic.

EDMS vendors provide a number of different methods for integration. The most powerful integration is done though APIs provided by the vendor, which exposes the core functionality of the EDMS. Many vendors also provide objects models based on COM or J2EE for integration. However, these are all point-solutions that have a high development cost, especially if the BPM system has the option of integrating with several different EDMS. To reduce this cost of integration, several EDMS vendors jointly developed the Open Document Management Interface (ODMA). ODMA is a standard API that sits between the EDMS and third-party application. By using a standardized interface, a third-party application could integrate once with ODMA and then work with any ODMA-compliant EDMS as shown in Figure 13.7. While ODMA is a good attempt at standardization, it is hampered by the fact that it is a compromise between all the participants, and therefore supports only the basic integration features. It is used by vendors to pay lip service to a "standard," while they continue to offer more robust integration capabilities through proprietary APIs. Furthermore, ODMA is basically a client/server integration technology. With the emergence of the Internet, the computing model has changed, and that requires new methods of integration.

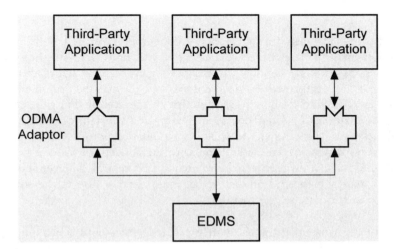

Figure 13.7. Using ODMA for Document Management Integration

To respond to the emergence of the Internet, many EDMS vendors have provided Web-based capabilities for presenting and searching for documents. In this model, the Web browser has become the EDMS client. In many cases an EDMS can integrate with a BPM solution simply by routing a URL as a part of the process. By invoking the URL the user can invoke basic EDMS functionality. This type of integration is limited because it cannot support advanced searching, check-in/check-out and document versioning functions that are at the core of EDMS. Recognizing these limitations the Internet Engineering Task Force (IETF) in association with the World Wide Web Consortium, Microsoft, IBM, Novell and other vendors, have developed the Web Document Authoring and Versioning (WebDAV) standard by extending the HTTP protocol of the Internet. WebDAV provides many of the interface functions needed for EDMS such as file locking, check-in/check-out and versioning. It can therefore be used by

BPM systems to communicate with EDMS systems that support the standard. While WebDAV is relatively new and adoption is still in the early stages, it is likely to grow and become the de facto standard because of the backing of the IETF and major vendors. Wider adoption of WebDAV will make it easier for BPM systems to work with a variety of EDMS and Web content management solutions.

BPM and Project Management

Business process management is sometimes confused with project management (PM) because there are some similarities between the two. A project goes through various well-defined stages. These stages represent tasks that are performed by different individuals in series or in parallel. There are rules and deadlines associated with the completion of each task and the initiation of subsequent ones. The most important of these are dependencies that dictate that a task cannot be initiated before the completion of some prior tasks. All these are similar to the concept of process maps in BPM solutions. However, there are major differences between business process management and project management, and so too in the software that is used for these two domains:

1. Project management deals with the management and scheduling of a limited number of projects that have similar task structure but often require flexibility and changes for each specific instance of the project. For example, every residential construction company has a fairly well defined project structure for building a new house. However, the project manager needs the flexibility to change some of the rules and resources based upon the specific requirements of each house, weather conditions and the availability of subcontractors. These are examples of many ad hoc decisions that are made during the course of each project. The success of the project manager and the project is dependent on the skills and judgment of the former. On the other hand, a business process deals with a large number of cases of a particular type (claims processing, invoice processing, performance reviews, etc.) that have the same rules and tasks, and the rules can be quantified and automated. BPM does not depend as much on the skills of an experienced project manager to make decisions. Project management morphs into business process management if the volume of instances and cases increase and the rules controlling the project can be quantified and automated. The

essence of BPM is to be able to execute a large number of instances without any "project management" to supervise each instance.

2. Project management deals with tasks at a higher or "macro" level. In the construction company example, the project management stages might simply be "Framing," "Plumbing," or "Wiring." Each stage incorporates numerous sub-tasks that are highly dependent on the house being constructed and are too numerous to list. In contrast, BPM deals with lower or "micro" level tasks that are so well defined that most of them can be automated. In a claims process, these might include, "e-mail acknowledgment of claim receipt," "notify appraiser," "create a claim number," and so on.

3. Project management software enables the project manager to understand the tasks that need to be performed, their dependences, current status and the resources available to perform each task. The project manager uses this information to make decisions about what to do next or when to increase or decrease resources. Project management software does not have any provisions for automatically initiating new tasks and taking them to the people or applications that will perform them. Project management is therefore reactive, allowing the project manager to make decisions based on the current situation. BPM, on the other hand, tries to eliminate human supervision by automating the decision-making. It has sophisticated means of starting tasks and taking them to the people or applications that will perform them. It is proactive and self-managing since the rules are better defined.

Figure 13.8 is a BPM-PM matrix that helps understand the types of "projects" that are best handled by project management versus those that are candidates for BPM. This matrix uses the volume of incidents as one axis and the degree of quantifiable rules as the other axis.

1. *Quadrant I:* **High Incident Volume and Quantifiable Rules**: These types of "projects" are excellent candidates for automation by using BPM solutions.

2. *Quadrant II:* **Low Incident Volume and Quantifiable Rule:** These projects are also suitable for BPM. However, because of the low volume, it may not be economically feasible to automate these processes. BPM can be justified for these projects only if the end product or service is of high value.

3. *Quadrant III:* **Low Incident Volume and Unquantifiable Rules:** These projects are ideally suited for project management.

4. *Quadrant IV:* **High Incident Volume and Unquantifiable Rules:** These projects are also best suited for project management. However, the cost of project management will be expensive and justifiable only if the resulting value is high.

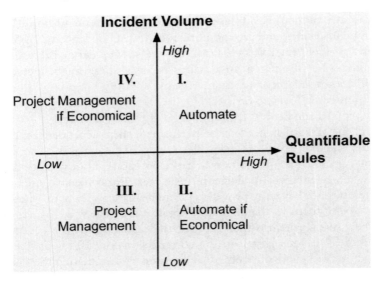

Figure 13.8. BPM-PM Matrix

While BPM and project management are distinct software categories, there are some situations that require the two to interact with each other. These situations arise most frequently as the volume of project instances increase and the rules are standardized so that it is in the grey area between a project and a process. Two natural integration points are:

1. Upon initiation of a business process, the BPM system interacts with the project management software and creates a new project instance using a pre-defined project template. During the course of the business process, the BPM system uses an automation agent at critical points in the process to update the project instance about the completion of various stages. This integration enables the project manager to view the project status in conjunction with other ongoing project instances, and estimate or predict the resources required or the bottlenecks that may be encountered.

2. A large project may consist of some business processes that need to be

executed when the project reaches various stages. These processes would perform some specific set of functions and then update the project status when they are completed. Thus, the project could depend on business processes to perform some set of tasks and people to perform others. To accomplish this, project management software needs to be able to trigger instances of business processes and transfer contextual information to the process (pre-process integration). Likewise, at the conclusion of the business process, the BPM system has to transfer information and status back to the project management software (post-process integration).

BPM and Portals

Web portals are becoming popular in organizations as a medium of communication and providing services to employees, customers and partners. The appeal of portals stems from the fact that they can provide a unique, personalized view to users for information and services that are relevant to their needs. Portals can be tailored to the requirements of various users or groups, and their Web interfaces hide the complexity of the applications that provide services in the background. To the user, the portal interface provides the experience and ease of use of a single application for a wide variety of services and information needs, whereas in reality the portal is only brokering services and information from a variety of applications and sources. Portals also provide other functions, such as single sign-on.

There is a strong need for integration between portals and BPM systems. A business process essentially provides a service to the user initiating the process. Thus, the ability to launch business processes from portals allows organizations to deploy process-driven services that are accessible to the portal users. These could include purchase requests, expense reports, status reports, employee self-service processes, customer self-service processes and many others. All of these have an important place in portals and add much value to the solution. BPM systems that provide pure HTML workflow clients can easily be adapted to work as plug-ins or "portlets" in most Web portals. This is an easy and powerful method of integration. It also can benefit from the capability of modern BPM systems to allow users to easily determine the status of any incident from within the client interface. BPM systems that do not provide HTML clients can also be integrated with portals, but the cost of the integration is likely to be higher. In both cases, the portal becomes a "custom workflow client" for the BPM system.

BPM and Enterprise Applications

Enterprise applications are used in companies to provide solutions for enterprise resource planning (ERP), customer relationship management (CRM), supply chain management (SCM), sales force automation (SFA) and others. Since many business processes involve the use of different enterprise applications, a BPM system must be capable of integrating with enterprise applications using all the modes of integration discussed earlier:

1. *Pre-Process Integration:* A company's financial system determines that an accounts receivable is past due. It triggers a process for launching an incident of the overdue receivables process.
2. *Post-Process Integration:* A BPM application may allow an employee to initiate a request to purchase an item and route it to various managers for approval. When the request is approved, it is necessary for the BPM system to submit the order to the company's ERP or SCM system for the actual purchase.
3. *Clients-Side Integration:* A workflow participant performing a task may need to select a particular customer and determine information about the customer's purchase history maintained in the CRM system. This requires client-side integration with the CRM system.
4. *Server-Side Integration:* A company may be using PeopleSoft or SAP to maintain information about their employees in one centralized directory. The company will want to use the same information for the BPM solution to determine roles and relationships. This requires server-side integration between the BPM system and the third-party directory.
5. *In-Process Integration:* A BPM system routes a customer order for fulfilment. After it is validated and configured, it has to be submitted to an ERP system for manufacturing. This requires the process to interact with the ERP system and wait until the manufacturing step has been completed.

Integration with enterprise applications is the most challenging for BPM systems. This is because there is a large variety of enterprise applications and there are no standards for integration. This increases the cost and the complexity of the integration. In light of this, many enterprise application vendors are developing solutions designed to ease the burden of integration, and BPM systems can benefit from them also. These integration solutions are taking two main approaches:

1. *Adaptors or Connectors:* Some BPM vendors have taken the approach of partnering with major EAI vendors and developing adaptors or connectors to integration platforms offered by the latter. This allows their BPM solution to integrate with any enterprise applications supported by the EAI vendor. This approach is illustrated in Figure 13.9.

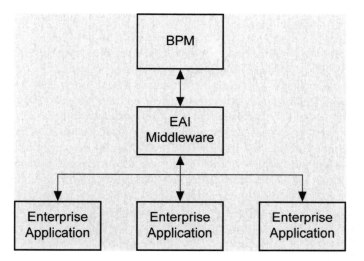

Figure 13.9. BPM Integration Using an EAI Platform

2. *Web Services:* Many enterprise applications are standardizing on the use of Web Services. By providing standard integration they hope to enable any SOAP or XML-compliant application to integrate directly with their application. Chapter 14, "Web Services, BPM and the Internet," describes the significance of Web Services for BPM and how it will dramatically change the nature of application integration.

BPM and Legacy Systems

Legacy systems based on mainframes are still widely used in the industry for mission critical applications in manufacturing, accounting/finance, banking, and others. A BPM system that is designed to automate business processes must be able to integrate with legacy systems in order to be effective. This integration is the most difficult because mainframes were designed for monolithic applications that ran exclusively on the mainframes, unlike today's client/server or Web-based applications that are spread over the desktops. However, mainframes are here to stay and it is important for BPM systems be able to interface with them in order to maximize the benefits of process automation.

There are several ways in which a BPM system can integrate with mainframes:

1. *Message Queuing Middleware:* Technologies such as the IBM MQSeries and the Microsoft MSMQ (Microsoft Message Queuing Server) are designed to enable applications to communicate with legacy systems through asynchronous messaging. These technologies allow a BPM system to compose and send a message to a mainframe.
2. *Screen Scrapers:* Screen-scraping technology was discussed previously in this chapter. This enables a software application to mimic the behaviour of using a dumb terminal. The application then can perform all the functions that a user can perform using the dumb terminal. This offers a convenient method for a process application to requests services performed by a mainframe without requiring any changes in the mainframe that tend to be very expensive.
3. *Web Services:* In the future, companies will be increasingly deploying Web Services middleware between the outside world and mainframe systems. This middleware will expose the services performed by a mainframe as a Web Service, thereby allowing any Web Service-compliant application to interface with the mainframe.

Conclusion

BPM is the glue that binds people and systems into processes for delivering information, goods and services to the internal and external customers of an organization. To play this role, it is essential for BPM systems to integrate easily with a variety of third-party applications and systems. While integration has always been a significant impediment, the emergence of new technologies and standards such as Web Services will go a long way to ease the burden.

Chapter 14

Web Services, BPM and the Internet

The Internet has had a dramatic and ongoing transformational impact on business process management. It has brought BPM to the mainstream and transformed it into an essential enterprise application. The development of industry standards driven by the potential of the Internet, and especially the emergence of Web Services, has elevated BPM and workflow automation products from obscure applications relegated to the back office, to solutions that are gradually finding their way out of the back office and onto the desktops of the front office where the actual conduct of business takes place. In turn, BPM is poised to have a major impact on the Internet. *BPM will transform the Internet into a medium for conducting complex business processes, instead of simply a medium of sharing information.*

This chapter first discusses the impact of the Internet on BPM, followed by a discussion of the factors driving the increasing use of BPM on the Internet, and the role BPM will play in the evolution of the Internet. The chapter then discusses the impact of Web Services to greatly increase the potential of BPM by promising to reduce the cost of application integration, and forcing the convergence or EAI and workflow automation.

The Impact of the Internet on BPM

Before the rise of the Internet, workflow automation was confined to a small group of companies, primarily in the banking and insurance sectors, that used the technology for high-volume business processes such as claims and check processing. Workflow automation was a niche industry that used expensive and highly customized solutions based around production workflow engines and restricted to one or two departments in large companies. The emergence of the Internet in the mid-1990s transformed workflow automation from a high-volume, specialized, business process automation solution restricted to departments, into a broadly used solution that has the potential of eventually reaching every department and desktop. The addition of business process modeling and metrics to workflow automation, and the increasing overlap with EAI under the pressure of Web Services, gave birth to BPM as a discipline and one of the most important investments for any organization.

The Internet and its core technologies of HTTP, TCP/IP and the Web browser, are enablers that have been the catalysts for the rapid growth of many product categories. BPM is no exception. Leading BPM vendors have adopted Internet technologies and the resulting changes have dramatically increased the scope and potential of BPM systems. Indeed, BPM systems are now in lock and step with Internet technologies, and will grow as the latter improves. BPM will become a widely used technology because of the sheer size, ubiquity and the reach of the Internet.

The Network and TCP/IP

An electronic network is an essential prerequisite for BPM without which the latter cannot exist. Prior to the rapid growth of the Internet in the mid-1990s, there were a number of competing networking protocols vying for dominance. These included NetBUEI from Microsoft, IPX from Novell, and SNA from IBM among others. In those days, one of the major challenges for deploying distributed client/server applications such as BPM was the lack of a standard networking protocol, as the proponent of each major protocol vied for competitive advantage. Client/server application vendors had to support different network protocols since their customers did not use a standard network. This drove up the cost of development and deployment of all types of solutions, including BPM.

The emergence of the Internet propelled TCP/IP to its current position as the dominant networking protocol. TCP/IP has now become the de facto standard, and the proponents of the other networking protocols have gradually adopted TCP/IP. They did this because of the TCP/IP protocol's sheer momentum and appeal as well as that it was considered a "public" protocol. It was impossible to compete with TCP/IP. Now software solution vendors do not have to concern themselves with what networking protocols to support. Networking based on the TCP/IP protocol has become a part of the plumbing of the computing infrastructure and is taken for granted. This has made it much easier for BPM vendors to focus on their core application rather than dissipate resources trying to support multiple networking protocols.

The Reach of the Internet

The second major impact of the Internet on BPM is its ability to reach a very large number of potential users at a relatively low cost. By definition, a BPM solution is a distributed application that involves a large number of users who need to participate in business processes regardless of their physical location. The Internet reaches every corner of the globe over the public network. The cost of Internet connectivity is a fraction of the cost of networking in the past, which was so high that only the largest companies could afford them. By adopting Internet standards, BPM vendors can offer solutions that leverage the reach of the Internet and enable participation in business processes from across the globe. This has enabled BPM vendors to offer solutions that enable customers, partners and employees worldwide to participate in business processes. While the reach of the Internet allows BPM to connect disparate users in business processes, the enormous productivity improvement offered by the globally distributed supply chain process increases the demand for BPM.

The Web-Browser Client and HTML

The HTML Web browser has become the de facto standard on every desktop for surfing the Internet. The browser, combined with the use of the HTTP protocol and HTML documents, enables users anywhere to easily find and access a wide variety of information that is interlinked. The number of browser users worldwide has exploded.

Leading BPM vendors have adopted the Web browser as the standard workflow client. This makes their software immediately accessible to a large number of users. Furthermore, the browser makes it easy to train users and to connect them to other information pages for the purpose of obtaining online help or other related information. One of the major benefits of using the Web browser as the workflow client is that BPM vendors do not have to concern themselves the need to install proprietary software for users to participate in business processes. The browser is already on every desktop, laptop, notebook and most PDAs, and can be used immediately.

Another major benefit of using the Web browser as the default workflow client for BPM systems is the use of HTML documents. HTML documents have become the standard for displaying information on disparate systems because HTML is based upon the use of ASCII text. Text can be used on any platform whether it is UNIX, Mac, and Windows and even on handheld PDAs. By the creative use of HTML tags, a Web page can display information while providing structure and formatting. BPM systems that use Web browsers and HTML benefit from the fact that the client can be used on a variety of platforms.

One of the challenges in many distributed applications like BPM is to enable users to quickly and easily connect to the server, performs the necessary tasks, and then disconnect. The Web browser makes it easy because the user simply has to point to a URL. The connection with the server is made automatically and quickly.

Internet Mail

One of the most important benefits of BPM is to reduce lag time. To reduce lag time a BPM system must be proactive: it must constantly push tasks to completion. However, the Web browser is basically a reactive medium. A user does not know that there is new information until the Web browser is pointed to a specified site. Thus, using the Web browser alone would not make business processes on the Internet proactive. This dilemma is resolved by using e-mail, the other ubiquitous Internet technology, in conjunction with BPM systems.

Like the competing networking protocols prior to the emergence of the Internet, e-mail protocols belonged to different camps that were vying for competitive advantage. Not long ago, Microsoft was pushing its Messaging API (MAPI). Lotus had its own proprietary e-mail technology used with Lotus ccMail. Novell was using GroupWise and IBM still relied on IBM PROFS. It was extremely difficult for many of these mail systems to interoperate. Likewise, it was very difficult for BPM vendors to support different mail platforms. BPM was, therefore, restricted to smaller groups of users who shared a common e-mail platform.

The rise of the Internet brought with it the wide acceptance and use of Internet Mail based on the SMTP and POP protocols. Over time, SMTP and POP have become the dominant mail protocols. All major vendors, including Microsoft, now support SMTP and POP. SMTP and POP have provided two major benefits for BPM systems. First, BPM vendors can easily support one e-mail protocol with the knowledge that it will be widely used and accepted. Second, by coupling Web-based BPM systems with e-mail, they can make business processes proactive. When a user has a new task, the BPM server sends e-mail to the user. A URL of a Web site is embedded in the e-mail message along with other descriptive information about the task. By clicking on the URL, the user can quickly point the Web browser to the electronic form for the task and perform it.

XML

As a cornerstone of the World Wide Web, HTML is an excellent method of displaying information on a variety of platforms. HTML uses a number of predefined "tags" that contain formatting information about the text and data in an HTML document. Web browsers interpret these tags and use them to properly format and present the information contained in the document. An HTML page is designed for human users who can use the context of the document to understand the meaning of the data in the document. However, computers or software applications cannot understand the meaning of the information simply by the context or formatting of information. Therefore, an HTML document is not a suitable method of conveying information from one application to another, since it provides no means of describing the data it contains.

XML, or the *eXtensible Markup Language*, is an extension of HTML that is designed to overcome this weakness. XML allows users to define their own tags that can be embedded in XML documents to define the meaning of the data contained in the document. While HTML tags provide formatting information, user-defined XML tags provide descriptions of the information, exposing the structure and meaning of the contents of documents. This provides an excellent mechanism for software applications to communicate information with each other in a standard format and medium that can be easily interpreted. This is why XML is fast becoming the de facto language for business-to-business application integration.

The impact of XML on BPM is profound and far-reaching. As discussed in Chapter 13, "BPM and Application Integration," one of the major challenges of BPM systems is the need to integrate with other applications. Not only are there a large number of applications that a BPM system has to integrate with, but also the technologies used for integration were complex and varied prior to the advent of XML. XML provides a common method for all applications to integrate with each other for the purpose of sharing information. This is because XML is based on ASCII text that can be understood by any application running on any platform. It is already an industry standard markup language, and it allows organizations or industry groups to create their own tags that define data specific to their industry.

One of the significant challenges with XML is the ability to define tags to represent the meaning of data; this may encourage organizations to develop a very large number of tags. Indeed, each company could come up with its own proprietary tags, and in a sense define the language that it uses to represent data. This could lead to a large number of competing "languages" and defeat the very purpose of interoperability and exchanging information. To address this potentially negative outcome, several industry organizations have started creating standard collections of "tags," or "schemas," for the vocabulary and type of information that is commonly used in their industry. These industry-specific schemas make it easy for companies within the industry to start using standard schemas and also participate in the extension of these schemas. One notable initiative is ebXML that was started by the United Nations. Under these initiatives a large number of XML schemas for a variety of industries have been developed and published by groups within the industries. Examples of some of these XML schemas include:

- *GAME Genome Annotation Markup Elements* for DNA
- *Open Financial Exchange (OFE):* for banking transactions
- *Credit Application Format (CAF)* for automotive credit applications
- *Product Data Markup Language (PDML):* for defining product structures and components
- *Real Estate Property Markup Language* for describing real estate
- *Marine Trading Markup Language (MTML)* for conducting marine trading transactions

Web Services

While XML is an excellent document markup language for defining and exchanging data among applications, it does not by itself provide a method for an application to invoke a service performed by another application. To use an analogy, XML is the common language for applications to communicate with each other. However one also needs the "phone system" for these applications to actually engage in a conversation. One of the major challenges in integrating one application with another is the high cost and time it takes using traditional technologies. This is not only a barrier to e-commerce between companies and productivity improvements inside companies, it also locks companies into existing applications and trading partners since the cost of change is very high. Locking trading arrangements reduces competition and creates inefficiencies. While XML does provide an excellent format for exchanging data, it would not be such a revolutionary technology if it were only another one of the many methods of exchanging data between applications. While current technologies such as COM and CORBA rely on manual methods of integration, the next revolutionary technology must provide an easier, and if possible, an automated method of integration. That would dramatically reduce the cost of integration, and enable companies to easily form relationships with partners without being encumbered by the cost.

There are several requirements and steps for fully automated integration between two applications:

1. The client or subscriber application must be able to automatically "discover" what services are provided by the server or producer application, and the business rules associated with the use of the service.
2. The client application must be able to determine the modalities of the interfaces that the server application offers, and configure itself to

interact with the service.

3. The client application must be able to generate a request to the server application to perform a specific service.
4. The client application must be able to send data to the server application in a format that can be understood by the server application.
5. The server application must be able to respond to the client application that it has completed the service.
6. The server application must be able to return data to the client application.

To provide a complete mechanism for a client application to invoke services provided by a server application, the Internet Engineering Committee has agreed on the Web Services standard. Web Services provide standard methods for a client application to request a server application to perform a service, and provide a means to exchanging information between the two. The Web Services standard consists of three parts:

1. *SOAP:* The Simple Object Access Protocol (SOAP) has been designed as an extension of XML to enable a client application to invoke a service in a server application. SOAP is basically a substitute for DCOM, CORBA, and J2EE that provides a method of invoking objects, or services, in a remote system. SOAP is a protocol that contains an XML header for encapsulating information to invoke a service, and the name of the method in the service that is to be used. It also specifies a transport mechanism that can either be HTTP or SMTP e-mail.
2. *WSDL:* The Web Services Description Language (WSDL) is an XML-based standard by which a server application can "publish" the interfaces it offers and the method it provides. WSDL can be thought of as an XML-based "software development kit (SDK)" that a client application can read. By doing so, the client application can understand the modalities of interfacing with it. This Web services description is basically a "schema" of the methods provided by the server application and the data that is received and returned by each method.
3. *UDDI:* The Universal Discovery and Directory Integration (UDDI) is a standard XML-based directory and format where businesses can list the services they are capable of providing online, and the rules, regulations, pricing and terms governing the use of their services. UDDI is in essence the "yellow pages" of online Web Services. The idea is that when a client application needs a service, it will browse UDDI directories to find the business capable of providing the services, and the cost and

business rules associated with each. The client application can then evaluate this information and determine the vendor with whom it wants to conduct business. After selecting the vendor, the client application can use the WSDL for the service to configure itself to subscribe to the service.

In the grand vision of Web Services, companies would be able to set up electronic partnerships with each other automatically without being encumbered by the cost of integration. Once a partnership has been established, the company could electronically invoke services provided by the partner and then pay for these services electronically. Web Services would enable this as follows:

1. A company could deploy a client application that automatically seeks to interface with the types of services or products that the company needs.
2. When a need arises, the client application would search UDDI directories on the Internet for the service or product it needs, and perform "comparison shopping" to determine the quality, delivery and cost of goods or information that it seeks.
3. Once the client application selects a trading partner through UDDI, it would use the WSDL description of the service to determine the modalities of interfacing with that. This would enable the client application to automatically configure itself for interfacing with the Web Service
4. After the interface has been established, the client application would use SOAP to invoke the service and send data as parameters, and then receive the response from the Web Service.

In this grand vision the establishment of partner relationships and the integration of the client and server applications is automated, thus driving down the cost of integration. In addition, the partnerships are dynamic and based purely on economic factors that are not biased by the high cost of integration. Web Services are still in their infancy and many obstacles remain in the realization of this vision. While SOAP and WSDL are beginning to be used for application integration inside companies, the use for inter-company application integration and the use of UDDI are increasing at a slower pace as the industry develops an infrastructure and resolves major issues relating to security, trust, and payments. The grand vision may not be realized in the foreseeable future. Even if that is the case, the benefits of Web Services as an industry standard and an effective means of application integration across platforms and organization are very significant.

BPM systems will leverage Web Services in five major ways:

1. *Process Web Services:* Automated business processes will themselves become Web Services. For example, a company can install an automated business process for order processing, then expose it as a Web Service. They can list and promote the service using UDDI and publish the interface specification using WSDL. This will enable the customer's ordering application to invoke the order process over the Internet. This is also likely to become the default means for a business process hosted on one BPM system to invoke sub-processes hosted on different BPM systems.

2. *Web Services Agent:* A BPM system can provide a Web Service automation agent that can invoke a third-party application at any step in the business process. As more and more enterprise and business applications adopt Web Services as the default interface to expose their core services, the task of application integration will become easier. This enables a BPM system to orchestrate the flow of information in a Service Oriented Architecture (SOA) driven by the logic of the process and its business rules.

3. *Task Web Services:* A BPM system can expose its task-level interfaces as Web Services. While the BPM system controls the business process, specific tasks in the process may be completed by third-party applications. For example, the business process for order processing may use a Web Services automation agent to submit an order for manufacturing to an ERP application. The task of manufacturing might take several days. During this time interval, the business process waits at the next step in the process, called "Wait for Manufacturing." When the ERP system determines that the manufacturing of the order is complete, it can use a task Web Service to complete the "Wait for Manufacturing" step. The business process is then aware that the manufacturing is complete and can proceed on to the next steps in the order process.

4. *Status Web Service:* A BPM system can provide a Web Service that will enable third-party applications and other BPM systems to determine the status of specific process instances. This will enable external applications to monitor and track process instances that are of relevance to them.

5. *Metric Web Service:* A BPM system can provide a Web Service to enable third-party applications to extract metrics about business processes hosted by the BPM system. While many BPM systems provide process metrics, they almost always use proprietary formats and terminology.

Using Web Services will foster standardization in the way metrics are reported.

While Web Services hold tremendous promise for BPM and enterprise integration, there are still major risks that face this emerging technology:

1. While Web Services have received broad acceptance from major players in the software industry, there is still a risk that competing vendors may introduce non-standard enhancements for competitive advantage. If this happens, the scope of Web Services will remain limited.
2. Web Services are in their infancy. They have not been tested as a means of integration in large, mission-critical or high-volume applications.
3. For Web Services to be an effective means of collaboration between enterprises over the public Internet, it is essential that broadly accepted and viable security and authentication models be developed. This has not happened so far, but is expected.

Web Service will likely be adopted in phases and will ultimately lead to a massive shift in the computing infrastructure and the way in which companies conduct business with each other and with consumers. In the first phase, companies will deploy Web Services and SOAP will be used as the means of invoking these services; however, all the integration and discovery will still be manually performed. In the second phase, companies will start publishing and using WSDL to enable automated integration; however, the discovery and selection of services will still be manually performed. In the last phase, companies will start using UDDI to discover and select the services they need, using WSDL to automatically integrate with these services, and SOAP to actually invoke these services.

Impact of BPM on the Internet

The emergence of Internet technologies has had a profound effect on BPM. In a symbiotic and reverse contribution, BPM has the potential of making a major impact on how the Internet is used to address the business and social requirements of a global economy in the early 21st century.

Globalization of the Value Chain

The individual economies of nations of the past have given way to a global economy. In the emerging global economy, companies compete to create value by tapping into the most effective human, material and logistics resources wherever it is practical, safe and economical. In return, companies offer the value they have created to consumers throughout the world. This global value supply chain has created a demand for business processes that are not only fast, but also span the globe. By reducing the lag time and leveraging the Internet to reach users in every corner of the globe, BPM is vital to the global value supply chain. It enables customers, vendors, partners and employees anywhere in the world to participate in business processes that can dramatically shorten response time and increase the agility of the supply chain.

Mobility of Workforce

The workforce in the global economy is becoming increasingly mobile, especially knowledge workers. This mobile workforce demands a means of participating in business processes from remote locations. If they were tied to their desktops for process work, it would be impossible for them to be mobile without sacrificing their ability to respond in a timely manner. The combination of BPM and the Internet provide a means to enable mobile workers to participate in business processes form their homes, remote offices, mobile devices, PDAs and public Internet kiosks. With the emergence of wireless technologies and mobile computing, the demand for accessing business processes by an increasingly mobile workforce will increase.

Specialization

One of the consequences of having a global value supply chain is the increase in specialization. Every company or organization participating in the global economy attempts to increase its contribution by reducing its cost, increasing the value it provides, or a combination of the two. This results in even more specialization. Specialized companies and individuals need to offer their services or value to a larger group of consumers as they increase their specialization. BPM is an effective method for specialists to offer their services to a broader market by seamlessly participating in specific steps in the end-to-end business process. BPM enables them to be integrated in specific stages of the business processes of their customers and provide highly specialized functions or services in those stages. All other aspects of business processes they participate in are essentially transparent to them and not their concern.

Competition and Speed

The modern economy is not only global, but also demands the conduct of business at Internet speed. When long distances separate the participants in the value chain, they cannot afford to act and respond at a speed that reflects the physical distance. This would invariably reduce the value of the supply chain. BPM and other collaborative technologies that leverage the global Internet allow these companies to respond at Internet speed without concern for the distance or time zones. Reducing lag time is one of the most important benefits of BPM, and one of the significant ways of reducing lag time is by eliminating the time it takes for information and decisions to travel from one location to another, regardless of the distance.

BPM on the Internet

There are three industry trends that have been enabled by the emergence of robust BPM solutions. These trends are:

- The growth of e-commerce as one of the primary means of commerce between companies, and between companies and the consuming public;
- The increasing trend towards Business Process Outsourcing (BPO);
- The development of general-purpose Business Process Service Providers (BPSPs).

Each of these is described below.

The E-Commerce Imperative

The Internet has developed in phases, each phase offering more complex and sophisticated means of handling the interactions of Internet users:

1. *Phase I 1992-1996 Web Presence:* In the first phase during the early days of the Internet, companies used the reach of the new technology to announce their presence on the Internet. The Web browser and HTML technologies were at the leading edge during this phase as organizations used the medium to stake out a claim and used the Internet to provide simple information.
2. *Phase II 1996-98 Information:* In the second phase the Internet was used as a medium to distribute complex information. This was the hey-day

of search engines and push-technologies. The complexity and sheer volume of the information provided on the Internet required the development of sophisticated means of searching for information and delivering it more effectively and proactively to the consumer.

3. *Phase III 1998-2001 Transactions:* In this phase companies started using the Web for conducting business transactions, otherwise called e-commerce. However, in most cases the transactions were "one-step." A customer would use the Web to initiate the transaction. The fulfilment of these transactions was generally handled by traditional, manual or legacy systems. Some of the growing pains associated with early e-commerce initiatives were attributable to the fact that while the initial transaction could be automated and implemented quickly, the fulfilment of these transactions became a bottleneck. Many companies began to deploy internal business process automation systems to automate fulfilment processes initiated by e-commerce transactions on the Internet.

4. *Phase IV- Multiple Structured Transactions and Collaboration 2002-2005:* In this phase organizations will use BPM and collaborative technologies to perform complete business processes on the Internet that will include customers, partners and employees. This means the Web will be used to perform series of transactions following the structures dictated by the business process and negotiated by the partners. The business process will handle the entire fulfilment process of an e-commerce transaction.

5. *Phase V- Dynamic Structured Transactions 2006-:* The next major phase will be facilitated by the combination of BPM and Web Services. In this phase, trading partners will engage in structured transactions based on business processes and the dynamic selection of trading partners. Instead of *a priori* business relationships, the companies will be able to select the optimal trading partners for each step in the business process. To establish new trading relationships, companies will describe their available services using private or public UDDI directories. They will then automatically create integration with new trading partners using WSDL. Finally, they will execute their transactions with trading partners using SOAP.

As can be seen in the above phases, the role of BPM is fundamental to the Internet and its growth in the future. E-commerce initiatives will increasingly rely on automatically enabling trading relationships among partners and performing transactions entirely using the Internet. BPM will become the core and essential technology for the realization of such solutions that will fundamentally change the nature of business.

Business Processes by Application Service Providers

In 1999 and 2000, at the height of the DotCom phenomenon, the concept of offering common automated business processes using the Application Service Provider (ASP) model emerged. Sales force automation, customer relationship management and other key functions could be offered using the ASP model. Likewise, it became possible to offer commonly used business processes using the ASP model. Indeed, several companies started offering simple workflow applications like time sheets and expense reports as ASP applications. However, none of these were very successful for a number if reasons:

1. Business processes deal with business information or data. In the ASP model, the data would be located at the ASP and removed from the organization. In addition to concerns about security, this raised significant issue about losing the value of real-time data and separating the organization from its information. Only unimportant processes were left as potential candidates for Workflow ASP. Companies are not willing to pay a lot for these unimportant processes.
2. Business processes must be tightly integrated with the internal business systems and applications of an organization. If the implementation of business processes is outsourced to an ASP, it is very difficult to integrate with the internal system. Such integration invariably requires customization of the ASP-hosted business process. However, the whole idea of an ASP is to offer a standard business process at a reduced cost since it is shared among many companies. As soon as the business process has to be customized, the cost becomes high. At that point it becomes more attractive for companies to deploy the solution internally rather than delegate it to a third-party ASP whose stability may be uncertain.
3. For obvious reasons, organizations do not want to use public networks for mission-critical processes that contain privileged information. Therefore, until a reliable PKI-based security infrastructure is deployed and widely adopted, organizations will be unwilling to use ASPs for important business processes.

While the ASP model has not been successful to date, it will likely emerge as a trend for specific types of business processes in the future because of the following factors:

1. As BPM and Internet technologies mature, it will be possible to offer business processes that can be easily configured to the unique needs of each customer.
2. Web Services will make it easier for ASP applications to be configured for easier integration with the internal systems of the company.
3. Continued proliferation of high-speed Internet connectivity will enable ASPs to provide solutions integrated with internal company databases.
4. The development of sophisticated PKI-based security infrastructure will enable ASP providers to create a "firewall" between the business data of different organizations.
5. Companies will realize that there are certain business processes that are worth outsourcing to ASPs. Leading candidates include document routing, resume reviews, HR processes and others.

Business Process Outsourcing (BPO)

Business Process Outsourcing (BPO) is the latest trend in the IT and business community. Companies are beginning to take important business processes that are IT-intensive and outsource them to competent third parties for implementation and execution. Many of these business processes include workflow as a major component. The use of BPM to facilitate BPO for such processes will be at the core of such BPO offerings in the future. The importance of this is the fact that unlike, ASPs (as discussed in the previous section), a BPO vendor hosts the entire application including the vital business data. Therefore, concerns about separating an organization from its data are not as significant.

BPM Related Standards

The emergence of the Internet as the universal network has had a profound impact on BPM. A fundamental reason for the Internet's universality is that the Internet is based on widely accepted standards. The BPM industry also needs standards that are unique to the requirements and use of this new category of software. If BPM is going to play a major role in the growth and use of the Internet for commerce and collaboration, it is important to develop appropriate standards. The most important standards will address the semantics for business collaborations among trading partners. Standards for business interactions have already been developed in specific industries. For example, RosettaNet's PIPs in the high-tech supply chain and Acord in the insurance industry.

When it comes to technical standards, the story becomes more interesting as technical standards are often shaped by competing interests within the IT industry. There are de facto standards set by IT industry giants along with many du jour standards that have come and gone over the years. While technical standards will become very important in the world of BPM, companies must not wait for the ultimate technical standards to emerge before beginning the journey to process management. The goal is to use the best available tools and adopt relevant standards as they emerge. It is also important to understand that the primary purpose of standards is *technology interoperation*, and they should not be confused with *innovations*. There is much debate about standards and many articles and papers are being published on the subject [14].

What standards should be watched? Certainly companies should keep an eye on industry-specific collaboration standards—and participate in the development of those standards. With regard to technology-related standards, companies should keep an eye on W3C, BPMI.org, Oasis-open.org, OMG.com and WfMC.org. Some of the technology standards of note include BPEL, BPMN, BPQL, XPDL and WS-CDL. While waiting for any of these standards to emerge and gain traction, remember Admiral David Farragut's command in the American Civil War, *"Damn the torpedoes! Full steam ahead!"* Farragut would no doubt instruct companies not to be distracted or torpedoed by technical standards, but to charge full steam ahead with their BPM initiatives, for the payback is here and now in the battles for competitive advantage.

Web Services and Convergence of BPM

One of the important consequences of Web Services will be the reduction in the value proposition of enterprise application integration (EAI) solutions. As discussed in the previous chapter, an EAI solution is middleware that sits between enterprise applications and provides connectors that are specific to each application (as shown in Figure 13.6, "Application Adaptors or Connectors"). Once the connectors have been developed or acquired, enterprise applications can communicate with each as a part of a business process orchestrated by a process engine. EAI solutions are proprietary, very expensive and require long deployment cycles. Once companies have invested in an EAI solution, they cannot easily change. Enterprise application vendors also do not like to involve EAI solutions as the "middleman" since in many cases the success, cost and timelines of their deployment depends on the success, cost and timeliness of deploying the EAI solution.

By adopting Web Services, enterprise application vendors can offer an easier and standardized method of integration. They may no longer require EAI middleware for many deployment scenarios where the capabilities offered by increasingly robust Web Service offerings may be sufficient. The focus and resources of adopting companies will shift quickly from integration to business process management and workflow. Just like the Internet is reducing the role of middlemen involved in commercial transactions, such as mortgage, automobile or real-estate salespeople, so will Web Services reduce the role of EAI middleware.

The emergence of Web Services will force a convergence in the BPM space, which is currently segmented into EAI and workflow vendors specializing in application-centric and human-centric processes, respectively. Pressured by the diminishing value proposition of integration due to Web Services, EAI vendors will expand into human-centric processes to provide complete BPM solutions. Conversely, workflow vendors will benefit from several trends that will position them well as BPM vendors:

1. Web Services will make it easier for workflow automation applications to integrate with third-party and enterprise applications. Previously, customers first had to purchase EAI applications before moving on to business process management. Web Services will allow workflow automation applications to automate processes that involve individuals, enterprise applications, or a combination. In some cases, customers will no longer need EAI middleware.
2. The increasing performance of CPUs and the development of sophisticated server clustering technologies will enable workflow automation applications to scale and perform at very high transaction volumes that are typical for EAI applications. Speed and transaction volume, which used to be one of the distinguishing characteristics of EAI applications, will be marginalized as an issue.
3. Workflow automation applications have to deal with the complexity of human-centric business processes resulting from the need to handle people-related exceptions. These were not a significant consideration for EAI solutions that managed application-centric processes. Successful workflow automation solutions may be better positioned to address the broader needs of BPM.

Convergence in BPM means that BPM solutions in the near future will be equally adept at EAI or workflow automation. Consequently, these two sub-categories will morph into a single category of BPM solutions that can effectively manage all types of process automation requirements.

Wither Application-Specific BPM

There are a number of enterprise applications with some integrated BPM or workflow capability. Application-specific BPM capability is designed to enhance the core functionality of the application by enabling users to automate processes that are common to the application domain. For example, enterprise document manage systems may offer workflow automation for document routing and approval, financial applications may offer business process automation for routing and review of financial reports, and Web content management systems may offer workflow for editing, reviewing and publishing documents. In the majority of these applications, the application-specific BPM does not extend outside the scope of the application or the people who use the application. They are simply not designed with general-purpose BPM in mind.

Application-specific BPM does cause considerable confusion when companies are considering deploying BPM. This is especially the case when a company has already deployed an enterprise application from a software powerhouse, such as SAP R/3. After investing considerable resources and effort to deploy such an application that has embedded BPM capabilities, the first instinct of the IT and business management of the company is to use the embedded BPM capabilities for all their BPM requirements. The problem with this thinking is that application-specific BPM is optimized for the specific needs of the enterprise application and is rarely designed to extend to other applications or to meet general-purpose BPM requirements. This would be akin to saying that since the company has bought a fleet of trucks for transporting goods, the same fleet can be used for taking the salesmen on customer calls. Trucks can indeed take the salesmen on customer calls, but this is not practical from a cost or usability perspective. The same is true if a company tries to use embedded BPM in an enterprise application for general-purpose BPM requirements.

If it is accepted that application-specific BPM is limited to the domain of the application, the next challenge is posed by companies that may have a number of enterprise applications from different vendors. These may include applications for ERP, CRM/SFA, financials, asset management, and

EDMS. If each of these applications has embedded application-specific BPM, the company will end up owning multiple systems for managing business processes, as shown in Figure 14.1.

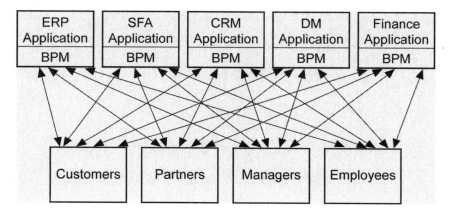

Figure 14.1. Enterprise Applications with Embedded BPM

Each of these systems has its own user interface, business rules engine, security model, administration module and other components. It is challenging enough for companies to manage one robust BPM solution; it is practically impossible for companies to manage multiple BPM solutions. Therefore, deployments scenarios such as those illustrated in Figure 14.1 will be limited with respect to the use of BPM.

Web Services provide a viable solution to this quandary. Enterprise application vendors will adopt Web Services to enable other applications to interact with them. This is consistent with the concept of "Service Oriented Architecture" described by the Gartner Group and others. Basically, Web Services enable an enterprise application to expose the "services" (or group of related functions it can perform), to other applications through XML, SOAP and WSDL standards described earlier. This enables enterprise applications to become a part of business processes managed by a general purpose and robust BPM system as illustrated in Figure 14.2. The major benefit to the organization is that only one BPM system is deployed that will orchestrate processes across enterprise applications. Enterprise application vendors will benefit because they can focus on increasing the core value proposition of their application without having to concern themselves with the nuances and complexities of BPM, which is an application category on its own.

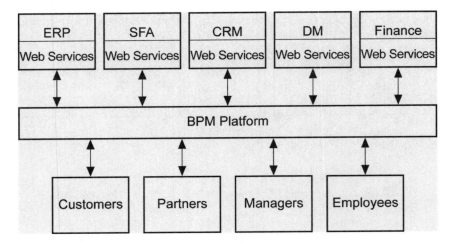

Figure 14.2. BPM integration with Enterprise Applications using
Web Services and SOA

Deployments of BPM and enterprise applications in the future will likely resemble the architecture illustrated in Figure 14.2. However the transition will be gradual and predicated by two considerations. The first is the speed at which Web Services standards evolve, adopted and proven by software vendors and their customers for mission-critical applications. The second is the ability of BPM vendors to offer increasingly powerful solutions that can span the requirements unique to the domain of each enterprise application.

Conclusion

The Internet and BPM will continue to have a synergistic relationship that drives each to the next level. The Internet has played a powerful role in providing a global network as a standard platform for deploying business processes. The emergence of XML and Web Services has contributed to the growth of standard languages for disparate BPM systems to communicate with each other and with third-party applications. BPM is gradually increasing the value of the Internet by providing the ability to conduct sophisticated, multi-step transactions inside and outside the enterprise regardless of the geographical separation.

Chapter 15

Case Studies in BPM

Previous chapters of this book have focused on the features and capabilities of BPM systems from a business perspective. These chapters have explained why some technical features make business sense, and how business needs drive BPM architectural decisions. This final chapter presents two case studies about companies that have adopted BPM. The focus is not on the particular technology or solution that was used. Instead, it pertains to the business requirements that drove the need for a BPM solution and the selection of specific approaches from among the variety of alternatives that were technically feasible. Furthermore, the case studies deliberately do not focus on the economic benefits or ROI of the solutions presented. The ROI case for BPM is very strong, and many other authors have amply documented the significant ROI and economic benefits of BPM. Instead, these case studies focus on the significant intangible benefits of BPM that enable companies to become process-centric and conduct their businesses using this new paradigm to succeed in a highly competitive and fast-paced environment.

In selecting the case studies the primary objective was diversity. The focus is on two companies in different industries and with different cultures that have adopted BPM for reasons that are unique to the companies, but yet reflect the shared experiences of many other companies. The companies are Bernstein AG, a medium-sized, family-owned German manufacturing company, and Microsoft Corporation, the largest and most successful high-tech company in the world. While Bernstein and Microsoft are totally different in their worldviews, their reasons for adopting BPM and the benefits they accrued as a result are remarkably similar.

Bernstein AG: Introducing BPM in a Traditional Manufacturing Environment

About Bernstein AG

Bernstein AG (referred to henceforth as Bernstein) is the quintessential, mid-sized, family-owned German company. Established in 1947, it is located in the small German town of Porta Westfalica. The company has about 500 employees and is 100% owned by the Bernstein family, with Mr. Hans-Joachim Bernstein as the Director. In 2002, the company's annual sales were about $50 million.

Bernstein manufactures markets and sells a large variety of products for industrial control, safety and sensing. These include position sensors, contact sensors, switches, enclosures and a variety of similar products that are used in manufacturing factories and other products for control and safety. In many cases the company's products are used as part of other equipment, either sold to original equipment manufacturers (OEMs), or designed-in as a part of specialized equipment for specific customers. While the company has a large number or products, no single product accounts for a significant portion of its revenue. While most of the products belong to a "standard" category that can be purchased from a catalog, many of them are in some way configured for the needs of specific customers. The development and manufacturing challenges for the company arose from the need to develop and upgrade a variety of products, and be able to configure them to unique customer needs in a cost effective and timely manner. This challenge was compounded by the fact that the products were used for industrial controls and safety in many different countries. Therefore, the original design of the product as well as customer-requested changes had to comply with safety standards and requirements in each of these countries.

While Bernstein product development and manufacturing facilities are located only in Porta Westfalica, Germany, the company sells its products through a number of its own sales offices and agents (manufacturer representatives). Its distribution channel includes 12 regional sales offices in Germany, and international sales offices in the US, Denmark, UK, Holland, France, Austria and Italy. In addition, the company has a number of sales agents in many other countries such as France, China, Australia, New Zealand, the Middle East, South Africa and Japan. The customized nature of many of these products drove the need for collaboration between the remote sales offices, employees and partners of the company.

IT Infrastructure

The IT infrastructure of Bernstein can best be described as a combination of modern and classical. Like many small- and medium-sized companies worldwide, it is a mixture of proven IBM technologies in the back office on which the corporate systems operate, along with newer Microsoft technologies on the desktop. These are connected through a network that reflects the widespread use of the Internet and the TCP/IP protocol. Bernstein's IT infrastructure is shown in Figure 15.1.

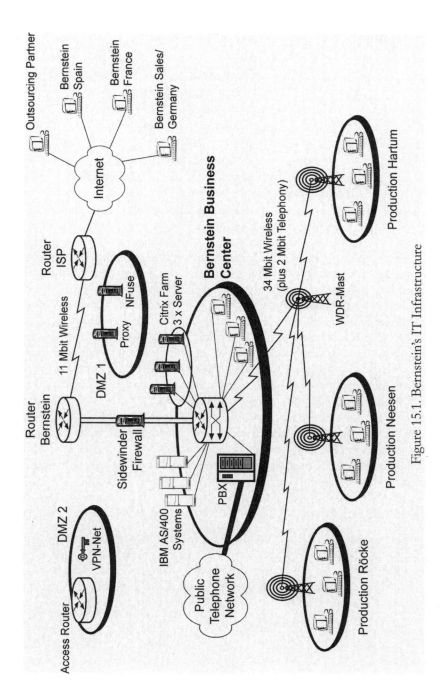

Figure 15.1. Bernstein's IT Infrastructure

Their IT infrastructure consists of the following components:

- Modern building cabling systems in all locations in Porta Westfalicia based entirely on TCP/IP and supported by various 34 MBit/sec wireless connections between the buildings
- IBM iSeries 820 for enterprise legacy applications (ERP/PPS, HR, etc.)
- Microsoft desktops with Windows 2000/XP, Office suite and Exchange, based on a complete Active Directory framework
- Citrix XP installation with a server farm, NFuse and Citrix Secure Gateway for remote access to applications
- Secure Internet communications for all authorized employees and partners achieved through the use of Active Directory and single sign-on

Bernstein's application structure is represented in Figure 15.2. Again, it is not atypical of many other companies of similar size and business. Important to note about the applications is that they are fairly complete and cover the major functional requirements of a company. These include applications for ERP, Human Resources, Supply Chain Management, and reporting solutions. However, as is typical for almost every company, these applications are vertical "islands of automation." They are excellent at providing specialized functions that are in their domain. The application stack parallels the organizational structure of the company that is also along functional lines. However, these applications provide very little interaction with other applications and function in more or less isolation from each other. At Bernstein, as in many other similar companies, what was missing was a focus on processes that span these applications and the people who use them in different departments, and the technologies that might engender such a process focus.

The Need for BPM

The challenges of process automation and the complexity of integrating employees, partners and customers in business processes faced by Bernstein were not unique. The vast majority of companies of all sizes face similar challenges. For Bernstein the most important and significant challenges were the following:

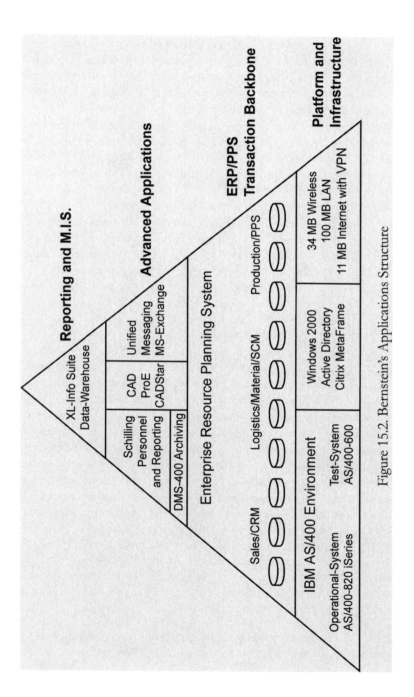

Figure 15.2. Bernstein's Applications Structure

- The company was facing increasing market pressure for efficiency and shorter process times. Major customers of a product line that represented 20% of the company's business were threatening to change vendors unless Bernstein was able to provide them significantly faster turnaround time on custom product configurations.
- There is an ever-increasing demand for the collaboration between customers, employees and partners that is driven by the custom nature of many of the products. Unless Bernstein could add value by significantly reducing the time taken for pricing and delivering custom product configurations, they ran the risk of losing to competitors that have aggressively adopted the Internet for reaching out to customers.
- The company culture and internal organization was based on a traditional functional model. Each function was optimized for doing an excellent job in its domain of expertise. However, this focus on functional efficiency was a barrier for the development of process-centric thinking that cuts across departments. Sales, support and product development processes took longer to complete since each department operated in its own silo without being aware of the priorities, workload, cost and dependencies among all the departments.
- As the company grew so did the number or product lines and the complexity of their products. This increase in product variety and complexity, coupled with the market pressure for shorter response times, accentuated the need to improve the processes in the company.
- As the customer base grew and the competitive situation intensified, Bernstein and all its competitors were faced with the prospect of decreasing product-differentiation and customer loyalty. In this environment, success depends on increasing quality, driving down cost, and becoming highly responsive to customer needs and changes in these needs.
- Finally, while the demand for collaboration and communication posed ever-increasing challenges for the IT department at Bernstein, the budget for the department was being reduced. The IT department simply could not afford new systems. Therefore, their best hope was to preserve their considerable investments in existing systems and applications, but integrate them through a BPM backbone. This would enable the company to become process-centric while at the same time maintain their existing IT investments.

In light of these challenges, Bernstein's owners authorized the IT manager in late 2001 to explore the use of BPM software. As the IT manager recounts, he told the owners that, paraphrasing Winston Churchill, "Your business processes are too important to be left in the hands of your IT department."

Since BPM is relatively new in general and a very different concept for a company such as Bernstein, their initial approach was cautious and exploratory. The company was not prepared to make a huge investment on new technology and a transformation without validating the benefits of BPM in its specific IT environment and company culture. After narrowing the search to a leading groupware solution and a pure-play BPM solution, the company finally selected the latter for its initial pilot.

The Goals

After selecting a BPM platform, Bernstein started the implementation of a pilot project with four major goals:

1. Achieve transparency and control of core business processes.

This goal included educating all the participants and developing a clear understanding of interdependency among employees and departments, regardless of the department to which the employees belonged. Furthermore, it was deemed important to be able to quantify the true costs that were incurred by these processes. The purpose of process automation was not automation alone, but to discover and expose the cost of processes so that the focus would change to the benefits of the process and how to reduce cost.

2. Reduce the response time of customer-facing processes.

It was normal for customers and the sales team to ask the factory for the time and cost of specific modifications based on customer needs. This process would take so long that in many cases the customer was likely to take his business to another vendor. The goal for process automation was to shorten the response time to customers on initial inquiry, followed by reducing the time it took to deliver the quoted item. It was envisioned that process automation could accomplish both these tasks.

3. Create an enhanced understanding and awareness among Bernstein employees about the inter-dependency of the tasks that they perform.

This goal aimed at reducing the company's response time by using BPM and changing from a functional focus to a process-centric focus. A by-product of this goal was to inculcate the employees a sense of the importance of their roles in the customer-facing business processes and the value they delivered to end customers.

4. Develop seamless integration of the BPM system with the existing IT infrastructure, applications and databases.

Bernstein had a lot invested in their IT infrastructure, which performed many of it functions very well. Therefore, Bernstein's goal was not to displace its IT infrastructure, but to integrate it so that their existing applications and systems would work even better in a process-centric environment.

Methodology

One of the most important factors contributing to the success of Bernstein's effort to adopt BPM was the methodology they used. In a company with a strong culture and a way of working that had been very successful in the past, introducing a new product that would be widely used is always a risk. Introducing a solution such as BPM that will fundamentally change the way in which people work is likely to be even riskier. While methodology is not rocket-science, and no single recipe works for all companies, the adoption and use of a methodology means that the advocates have thought about the issues and developed a systematic approach for adopting a new technology that would change the way people worked. If the methodology does not work, then it can be corrected, changed and improved. However, if adoption follows no specific approach or guidelines, the opportunity of learning from mistakes is diminished.

The methodology used by Bernstein was based on the following concepts:

1. *The Design Team:* Early in the project, Bernstein made the decision not to seek outside consulting services to design their business processes. The logic was that their own employees knew their business processes better than anyone else. If external consultants were used there would be considerable time and energy wasted simply to explain the nuances of all the processes to them. If outside consultants developed a system, it would appear to the employees that the company was imposing something from outside. On the other hand, if the processes were developed and tested by employees themselves, the new technology and way of working would be considered an internally developed solution and adoption would much easier. It would be easier to find champions

among employees, and the cost would also be substantially lower. With this in mind, Bernstein created a design team consisting of five employees, each from various departments. This design team was provided internal training in process analysis and design. The design team was responsible for helping the process teams develop and deploy processes and resolve technical problems that cannot be handled by the latter. Since the goal was the have the business users, and not the IT department, own their processes, the design team acted like technical advisors to the process teams who owned and developed the processes. Therefore, right from the start, employees from different departments became interdependent on each other and the process knowledge of each department was captured in the overall processes.

2. *The Process Teams:* In addition to the design team, Bernstein created a process team for each process with the idea of turning users into players. The process team consists of end users who work closely with the design team and are responsible for the process analysis within their departments. It is also responsible for promoting an understanding of the complete process-chain and organizational dependencies throughout the company. These teams not only promote understanding of the processes but also produce BPM champions among end users who then come up with ideas for new processes that could be automated. By creating and empowering the process team, Bernstein was able to generate new ideas for using BPM in other areas in the organization that could benefit from process automation.

3. *Process Selection:* The third important aspect of methodology was the selection of the processes that should be automated first. A company such as Bernstein has hundreds of processes that are potential candidates for automation. Simply understanding all these processes and then prioritizing them is a major challenge. Bernstein simplified this selection by making a decision early on that they would first automate and improve processes that are hurting their customers. They believed that customers-facing processes provide the best opportunity for big wins that would enable them to achieve their goals and demonstrate quick wins for the company. As one manager of the company said, "If you can stand the pain, look at your company through the eyes of a customer." This statement is true not only for Bernstein but many other companies. By first automating and improving customer-facing processes, Bernstein not only hoped to reduce customer pain, but also demonstrate the benefits of BPM and workflow automation to key managers and employees across the company, some of whom had their

natural share of scepticism.

4. *In-House Training:* Last but not least, Bernstein made an all-out attempt to sell the project and its benefits internally to the organization. There was a realization that BPM would require a cultural change and a different way of approaching problems and working together. The IT manager and his team presented the project and processes to everyone concerned. This not only created awareness, but also helped sway employees who had doubts about a new technology and a different way of working. User training was also provided to all participants. Moreover, detailed on-line help documentation was developed for all processes in German, French, English and Spanish, the major languages used by the employees of the company in various countries.

Results

Bernstein started using the Ultimus BPM Suite to automate their business processes using the methodology described above in the Spring of 2002 and had automated about 10 business processes in the very first year. They first automated customer-facing processes that are used primarily by sales engineers in all locations both inside and outside Germany to respond to these customer inquiries:

1. *Custom Product Request (Standard):* Bernstein makes a large number of standard products. However, in many cases a customer asks for some modification of a standard product for their specific needs. This modification must be reviewed, approved and priced by individuals in different departments of the company. These departments included engineering (for feasibility and design time estimation), marketing (for pricing and fit), manufacturing (for delivery times and cost), and legal (for ensuring the company has the necessary licenses to sell the modified product in the country of the end customer). This is a time-consuming process requiring much paperwork and interaction, especially since Bernstein offered a large number or products and they can be used for a large variety of applications. On the other hand, the end customer desires a quick response to determine if the price or delivery time will be suitable for their internal needs. This was one of the first processes automated by the Bernstein team. It enabled a sales engineer to electronically fill out a change request form in response to a customer inquiry. Information entered in this form was then routed electronically to the various individuals or departments whose input was necessary

for developing a response to the customer. By automating this process, Bernstein was able to reduce the response time to customer inquiries from three weeks to five days, and at the same time improved the quality of the estimates that resulted in decreased cost and increased customer satisfaction.

2. *Custom Product Request (Enclosures):* This process is similar to the one described above, except that it applies specifically to enclosures. Bernstein manufactures a large number of enclosures for housing different types of electronic and control equipment. Invariably, customers needed changes to the standard enclosures, such as drilling holes in specific locations, different type of hinges, and changes in the size and shape of cut-outs. There are a large number of permutations for each type of standard enclosure. Furthermore, in many cases a customer would require a particular change and later it would turn out that it was not feasible from an engineering viewpoint. This required going back to the customer and repeating the entire process. To automate this process the company developed a workflow process with an electronic form at the first, or initiation step, that allowed the sales engineering to graphically specify the customization required for a specific enclosure type. By using built-in checks, the electronic form is able to control the modifications requested, and allows the customer only those changes that were feasible. Thus, from the very beginning the customer is involved in the design of the enclosure and the system ensures that the customer does not make any choices that are not practical. This greatly reduced the amount of rework and iterations while working with the customer.

This process proved enormously beneficial to Bernstein and its customers. Approximately 20% of the company's business came from large companies in a foreign country. The company was at risk of losing this business because competitive vendors were beginning to offer customers design tools that the customers could use themselves. By offering an automated custom enclosure process, Bernstein was not only able to reduce the cycle time for responding to customers inquiries, but was also able to defend a sizable portion of its business from competitive vendors. This success by itself was sufficient to justify the cost of the BPM software.

3. *Customer Stock Reservation System:* Another important customer-facing challenge for Bernstein was in the area of reserving stock for a specific customer order. It was normal for sales engineers to quote availability and delivery time to end customers. This was based on the availability of parts in inventory. In many cases, after a delivery quote was made to

a specific customer, it took some time for the customer to decide and return with a purchase order committing to buy. During this time, another customer would place an order that would consume the same parts. The company, therefore, would be unable to make the promised delivery date to the original customer. This would inevitably lead to loss of goodwill among customers. To avoid this problem, Bernstein developed the Customer Stock Reservation system. This process would ensure that parts committed to one customer via a price and deliver quote were reserved for that customer for a specific time period. During this period, the reserved parts are locked from being assigned to another customer or project. If the customer does indeed issue a purchase order in the specified time, the parts are available for them. If, however, a purchase order does not materialize, the reserved parts are unreserved after the time had expired, and are available for sale to others.

The adoption of BPM at Bernstein has resulted in the addition of a "process layer" in the IT application structure of the company as shown in Figure 15.3. This process layer has established the foundation for developing other business processes that will span the human and IT resources as shown in Figure 15.4 (on page 308). Bernstein hopes that this can serve the basis for developing a process-centric culture that is superimposed on a functionally-structured organization.

As is apparent from this case study, the use of BPM at Bernstein enabled the company to achieve its goals and accrue six major benefits through business process management:

1. Reduce the cycle time of customer-facing processes.
2. Brings customers and company sales engineers closer to the internal business processes of the company.
3. Deploy processes that involve multiple departments and individuals to deliver goods and services, thus exposing interdependency of all the participants.
4. Provide solutions for mission-critical problems for which there were no other solution but the automation of processes.
5. Demonstrate that even traditional, small- and medium-sized companies can reap significant benefits from BPM and workflow automation.
6. Prove that, given sufficient guidance and training, internal teams of employees with no prior BPM experience can develop viable solutions with significant ROI potential.

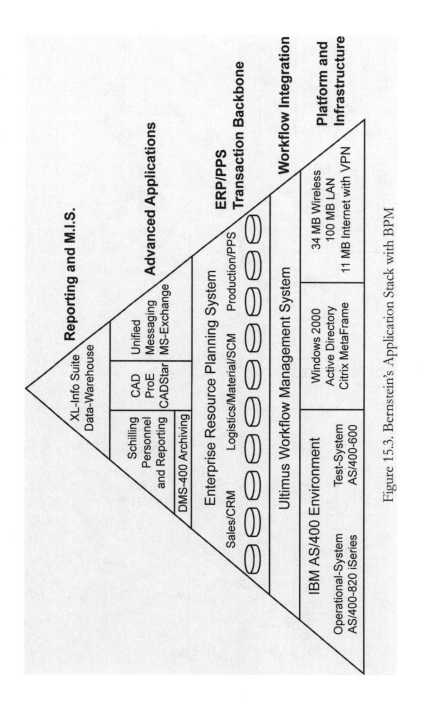

Figure 15.3. Bernstein's Application Stack with BPM

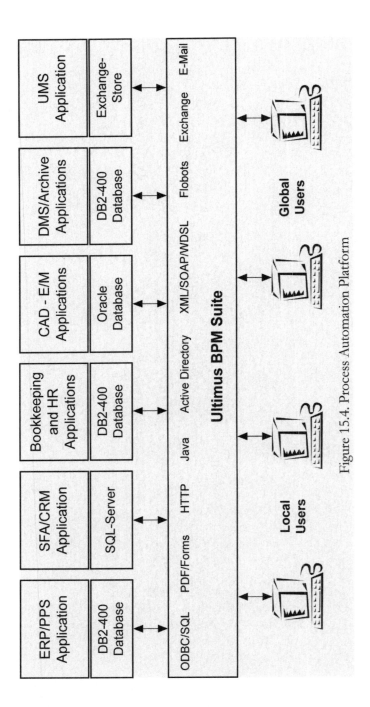

Figure 15.4. Process Automation Platform

Future Directions

Bernstein has been involved with BPM for about two years. During this period it has learned valuable lessons about the technology and methodology that is needed for success. After automating customer-facing processes, it is now shifting focus to internal processes that are also important for its success and reinforce the "process-centric" culture that it is trying to institute. In the second phase of its BPM initiative, Bernstein is working on the automation of a number of processes that include the following:

1. Human resource processes
2. Manufacturing processes
3. Engineering processes
4. Financial control processes

While the automation of a variety of business processes is a major step forward for this company and fosters improved business relationships with its customers, partners and employees, the most important benefit to Bernstein is the emergence of a new way of thinking. This new way focuses on the importance of processes, their impact on responsiveness to the needs of internal and external customers, and the exposure of the inherent dependencies between all the players in business processes. While companies continue to be organized in a traditionally vertical and functional hierarchy, the adoption of BPM has exposed the importance of value chains embodied by business processes that span functional boundaries.

Microsoft: Using BPM for Facilitating Project Management

About Microsoft

Microsoft is the world's largest software company based in Redmond, Washington. While its core business is operating systems and software represented by the Windows, Office and other client and server applications, it also develops and markets computer hardware through its Home Entertainment Division (HED). The Home Entertainment Division's business includes the Xbox gaming console; Xbox and PC games; consumer software; Macintosh software; Microsoft's interactive TV platform business; and sales of hardware products, such as keyboards, mice, and a line of wireless home networking hardware.

Microsoft faces unique challenges because of the variety, leading edge, and highly competitive and global nature of its products. It spends billions of dollars in R&D for the development of new products. The majority of these products are distributed through the retail channel across the globe. Microsoft cannot ship any of these products unless the packaging for each product and new versions is developed and localized in all the languages it supports throughout the world. For the HED, packaging is developed and localized by Microsoft teams in Redmond, Dublin and Singapore. In many cases these teams work with third-party subcontractors and suppliers in different parts of the world.

IT Infrastructure

Microsoft's IT environment is more modern and homogeneous as compared to Bernstein's, which is to be expected given the nature of Microsoft's business. The company has an extensive intranet for its employees, and an extranet that can be used by employees as well as suppliers and subcontractors. All desktops run latest versions of the Windows, and the company uses a number of servers including Windows 2003, Exchange Server for messaging, SharePoint Server as a portal and document sharing, and SQL Server as the database.

The Need for BPM

The HED is responsible for developing and marketing a large number of products through the retail channel. Each product had its own unique packaging designed to create maximum appeal on the retail shelf. These products are sold throughout the world, which requires the localization of the packaging into many different languages. The development of the packaging and localization into different languages for the needs of different markets is a major undertaking. A global rollout of a product cannot be accomplished unless the packaging is ready, regardless of how much money was spent in the development or upgrade of the product.

Microsoft was facing a serious challenge because of the difficulty of coordinating packaging tasks worldwide for eight internal groups across fifteen countries. Their existing workflow tool was inadequate due to lack of flexibility. All tracking was being done with Excel and by using email. This was a manual process managed by a localization program manager that created many problems:

- *Complex Coordination:* The manual process to coordinate a localization project was very time consuming. It relied extensively on the use of e-mail for informing participants about schedules, requirements, priorities and deadlines. Change in any of these required coordination amongst all the participants using e-mail.
- *Limited Visibility:* Project managers did not have an easy way of finding out where a particular project was and when it may be completed. This was compounded by the fact that many of the participants in the localization effort were in different locations and countries.
- *Poor Accountability:* It was difficult to track user accountability. When a localization project was not on time, it was not clear what the reasons for the delay were. This meant that there was no concrete method of improving the process.
- *Lack of Real-Time Information:* Information about the status of a localization project was not real-time so it was difficult to pinpoint why products were not being delivered on time.
- *Inflexible:* The manual process was not flexible enough to handle changes in priority and deadlines. If the priorities or deadlines changed, the localization team had to resort to e-mails and phone calls to coordinate the change.

As the number of products handled by HED continues to increase, the localization effort has become increasingly complex, prone to errors and delays, and reliant on an increasingly larger staff. It was clear to management that such an approach was not scalable. What was needed was a workflow solution that would automate key aspects of the localization effort and reduce human involvement in the process. When the numbers of products to be localized were small, project management methodology and tools could handle the effort. As soon as the number of localization projects increased, the need changed from project management to process management because of the volume of the work, the ability to identify common tasks and working patterns, establish metrics and the need to gain visibility.

The Vision

Microsoft HED's vision for seeking a workflow-driven BPM solution was based on a number of objectives, all driven by the need to reduce the pain and inefficiencies in the localization of product packaging:

1. HED wanted to promote improved accountability for their packaging processes. For the success and timeliness of these projects it was important for the management to assign clear responsibilities for all the players to ensure that no task falls through the cracks.
2. Visibility was the second major objective. At any given time, management wanted to know the exact status of any localization project so that they can determine if it is at risk for delay. Only by knowing that a specific project was at risk could management apply additional resources or corrective action to ensure timeliness. Coupled with this, they wanted the ability to be notified when any task is late, as that may affect the overall product release schedule.
3. HED wanted the management team to have better control of product release schedules by giving them the ability to establish task durations and priorities. For example, localization program managers should be able to change the priority or deadlines of any project and have the change apply seamlessly without recourse to numerous e-mails and phone calls.
4. HED wanted to use workflow automation of the localization process as stepping-stones for improving efficiency throughout all HED groups by eventually automating other processes.

Methodology

Microsoft's methodology from early on was to acquire a best of breed BPM solution that is flexible to meet its workflow requirements and compatible with the Microsoft's environment, but then outsource the development of the solution, preferably to offshore resources that are available at a lower cost. This would ensure that it would be able to make its localization process efficient, minimize the development cost, while at the same time not burdening Microsoft employees with the task of developing and maintaining the BPM solution.

Starting in March 2002, Microsoft conducted a search for BPM/workflow products and identified five vendors that met their criteria. This short list was narrowed to two vendors by June 2002 on the basis of a more in-depth evaluation. These two vendors were selected to run a pilot deployment at Microsoft to demonstrate how each could handle the actual requirements of the HED localization process. After a two-month pilot, Microsoft selected the pure-play BPM solution and delegated the development of the processes to that company. The BPM solution vendor also provided a project manager and offshore developers. The BPM platform was used to create the Microsoft Packaging Workflow to manage the inter-action between Microsoft employees and their localization vendors world-wide. The Packaging Workflow is deployed on the Microsoft Extranet. This is a secure location for Microsoft's external vendors to access Microsoft applications, documents and utilities. Third-party localization vendors worldwide access the Packaging Workflow via this site.

The Microsoft Packaging Workflow went live in December 2002. Since then 12 additional processes have been developed and deployed.

Results

The Microsoft Packaging Workflow uses the SharePoint Portal as the primary user interface that HED employees and localization partners use to interact with the solution. The SharePoint Portal user interface has been expanded to include two or three frames, or "web parts," that allow the user to look at their tasks, start new process incidents and determine the status of the tasks. Tasks are presented on the screen in various categories such as "Due Today," "Over Due," and "Due in Next 14 Days," etc. This makes it easy for each user to determine exactly what they have to do, as well as the priority of the tasks. The ability to check the status of any local-ization project means that managers know the exact status of each and every project. Similarly, if they want to change the priority or deadline of any project they can simply make the change in an electronic form and the resulting changes in priority or deadlines for all pertinent tasks for the pro-ject are automatically calculated and ripple through to all the tasks and their owners. By using the SharePoint Portal as the user interface, the Microsoft Packaging Workflow also enables users to attach and route documents as a part of the workflow that are necessary for the completion of the project. Since the solution is Web-based and resides on the Microsoft extranet, em-ployees and subcontractors in different countries can participate in the process. Furthermore, the solution makes extensive use of e-mail notifica-tions to inform participants about new tasks, delays, or changes in priorities or deadlines.

Since the deployment of the solution, Microsoft HED has derived a number of tangible and intangible benefits by using it:

1. HED employees used to spend a considerable amount of time writing and managing e-mails for managing the localization effort. The Packag-ing Workflow eliminated the majority of the time spent with e-mail. The time saved on e-mail management is approximately 40 hours per

product line. Currently the Microsoft Packaging Workflow manages over 30 product lines, resulting in 1200 hours of time saving from managing e-mails. This saving alone pays for the cost of the BPM software.

2. The Packaging Workflow produces information about every task and the status of a localization project in real-time, regardless if where the participants or managers are physically located. At the click of the mouse, the product manager knows the status of any of the localization projects.

3. Instead of using e-mails for daily management, they are now used for new task notification and escalation to ensure that projects continue to meet the planned deadlines and users are aware of their responsibilities.

4. The HED Packaging Workflow provides much greater user account-ability and visibility. Users know when a task is assigned to them and what additional tasks are coming down the road. Likewise, managers can hold their teams accountable for lapses in the completion of tasks.

5. By analyzing the status of their projects, managers now have better in-formation that gives them the ability to figure out where the bottle-necks are.

6. Microsoft HED has invested in developing the print and online help documentation for the Packaging Workflow that is available to all par-ticipants online. This makes it easier for new employees to get up to speed quickly.

Future Direction

Like the case of Bernstein, Microsoft HED has invested in a BPM platform that enables it to address the immediate point of pain represented by the packaging localization process. Once deployed, the BPM platform can be used to automate and manage a large number of other business processes that are common in the organization. In the case of Microsoft HED, the team expects to automate additional workflows for hardware packaging such as the labels workflow, vendor contracts workflows, hard-ware manuals and others. Once the company has deployed a BPM platform and methodology, and incurred the initial cost of ramp-up, automating ad-ditional processes becomes a matter of assigning priorities and ensuring that the processes are understood and documented from a business perspective.

Conclusion

Bernstein AG and Microsoft are two good examples of how companies in different industries have adopted BPM to achieve objectives that are similar and exemplify the impact of this new way of conducting business:

1. *Speed:* Business can be conducted much faster using BPM. Microsoft greatly reduced the time it took to communicate with all participants in the localization process. Bernstein was able to retain a major overseas customer by providing them with a "self-service" tool for configuring custom enclosures and processing them for quotation and purchasing.

2. *Visibility:* BPM ensures that business managers have visibility into key business processes and the underlying metrics so that they can take corrective actions and improve them. Bernstein is able to track customer inquiries by using BPM. Microsoft is able to get quick feedback about the status of any localization process so that corrective action can be taken for projects that are in danger of missing completion dates.

3. *Accountability:* BPM results in accountability by not only exposing underlying bottlenecks but also by exposing the role of each participant in the success of the overall process. In the case of Bernstein, employees throughout the company become aware of their roles in delivering value to the end customers. When their roles in the supply chain are exposed, they are much more responsive and understand the purpose of their work. In the case of Microsoft, program managers are able to quickly see the status of all the projects and determine where things are slipping and deadlines are in jeopardy.

4. *Flexibility:* BPM solutions allow business processes to adapt to changing needs and situations. As the company evolves, processes can be changed electronically; this is much faster than having to re-train people or change manual processes. Microsoft managers are able to change deadlines and projects priorities, as well as change the sequence of tasks to be performed for each localization process. There is no need to communicate changes via e-mail since the workflow automation system takes care of it. In Bernstein's case, customers can configure the parts they wish to price or purchase, putting flexibility at their fingertips.

Speed, visibility, accountability and flexibility are the essential benefits of BPM that can enable companies to compete effectively, in real time, in the global economy of the 21st century.

Appendix A

A Framework for Evaluating BPM Products

In addition to a growing number of BPM software vendors, many enterprise applications also claim *business process management* is embedded in their products. Organizations seeking to select and implement BPM software face much confusion resulting from the emergent state of BPM, conflicting vendor claims, confusing terminology punctuated by many buzzwords, and marketing hype as vendors try to stake a claim on this very large market. This confusion makes it difficult to sift through all the information and logically evaluate these products.

This appendix provides a framework for evaluating BPM software with the hope that it will make it easier to select solutions that best fit your needs. Its purpose is not to offer any final selection. That can only be done by a detailed evaluation of the products and discussions with their respective vendors. Instead, the purpose is to help create a shortlist of three to five products that can be evaluated in-depth. When evaluating BPM software, two key areas must be considered:

- *Capability:* How capable is the product to meet business process management requirements of your organization, based on your needs and the details provided in this book?
- *Completeness:* How complete is the product for meeting your current and future BPM needs?

In that light, 20 key BPM-related features are offered to assist in evaluating BPM product capabilities. These key features are listed below, and a detailed description of each feature and its importance to BPM is provided afterwards. When evaluating BPM software one must make sure that these key features are included "out-of-the-box." Many products may offer these features through programming or scripting. However, if an organization has to resort to programming or scripting to obtain these features, the total cost of ownership for the product will be very high through its life cycle.

Table A.1. List of 20 Key BPM-Related Features

BPM Capability

1. Robust Business Rules
2. Role-Based Routing
3. Relationship Routing
4. Relative Routing
5. Parallel Routing
6. Ad hoc Routing
7. Queues and Groups
8. Process Rollback
9. Sub-Processes
10. Escalations & Exceptions
11. Flexible Forms Support
12. Web-Based Architecture
13. Automation Agents
14. Custom Views
15. Simulation
16. Process Documentation
17. Status Monitoring
18. Authentication and Security
19. Distributed User Administration
20. Task Delegation & Conferring

To evaluate the completeness of a BPM product, evaluate a list of key modules or components that the software offers. A list of modules is provided below and a detailed description of each is provided at the end. Absence of one or more of these components will decrease the usability of the product and increase the cost of ownership.

Table A.2. List of 10 Key Modules to a Complete BPM Application

BPM Completeness

1. Graphic Designer
2. Collaborative Design
3. Modeling
4. Organizational Charts and Directory Integration
5. Multiple Client Interfaces
6. Business Metrics and Monitoring
7. BPM Administrator
8. Web Services and Integration
9. Database Connectivity and Transaction Processing
10. Scalable BPM Server

By evaluating BPM products against these key features, companies can develop a completeness-capability matrix, as shown in Figure A.1.

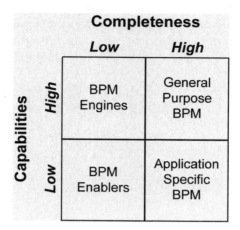

Figure A.1. BPM Completeness-Capabilities Matrix

Each quadrant of the matrix represents a different category of BPM software:

BPM Enablers
BPM Engines
Application-Specific BPM
General Purpose BPM

I. BPM Enablers

Quadrant I of the matrix represents "BPM enablers." Products in this category have low capability and low completeness scores. As such, they cannot be considered BPM products out-of-the-box. Instead, they are infrastructure technologies that can be used to develop BPM solutions via programming. One can take these core technologies and add code and logic to build a BPM solution. These products are generally suitable for independent software vendors or solution builders. Microsoft Exchange and IBM Lotus Notes are examples of BPM enablers.

II. BPM Engines

"BPM engines" occupy Quadrant II of the matrix. These products score high on capabilities but low on completeness. BPM engines, or servers, provide the core logic to implement BPM. Most such products do not provide the workflow inbox or "client" used by end-users to participate in workflow. Nor do they provide reporting and administration tools. Large customers and systems integrators use BPM engines to develop BPM solutions with customized clients. Independent software vendors may also use them to develop complete software applications and services with integrated BPM capabilities. Custom development leverages the capabilities of BPM engines and adds "completeness," but at a high cost associated with software development. Examples of BPM engines include the Microsoft BizTalk Server and FileNet Visual WorkFlo.

III. Application-Specific BPM

Many business applications have built-in business process management capabilities that are designed to add value to the application. These include ERP, CRM, sales-force automation, document/content management, asset management, legal, financial and others. These applications score high on completeness because workflow is built-in and tightly integrated with other functions of the application. However, these applications score low on capabilities because their design goal with respect to BPM is only to add value to the core application, and not to become robust, general-purpose BPM solutions. They typically do not easily address areas that extend beyond the confines of the application. The nature of the processes being automated is an important consideration when evaluating products in this category. If the process will only need to integrate with the core application and users of that application, then application-specific BPM is an acceptable choice. However, if you have processes that will involve other users and applications, the cost of integration and the resulting complexity is often very high, making application-specific solutions less suitable. Examples of "application-specific BPM" include the embedded workflow capabilities provided by PeopleSoft, SAP, Open Text, or Oracle.

IV. General-Purpose BPM

"General-purpose BPM" products score high on capabilities as well as completeness. They are designed to address the entire process lifecycle. These complete packages also provide substantial capabilities since the goal is to be applicable to a variety of business processes out-of-the-box. For most BPM projects, it is prudent to focus on products that fall into this area. When looking at products that claim to handle a wide range of BPM requirements, it is important to verify that the ability to handle processes that involve both people and applications is available. Handling workflows between humans is challenging, with lots of exceptions and routing considerations. If a product does application integration very well, but has limited human-centric process features, it could be limiting. Conversely, if the BPM platform is severely limited in terms of integration, it may not be able to push and pull information to and from enterprise applications. The complete, feature-rich products in this category can be used as platforms for BPM. General-purpose BPM systems are sometimes also called "pure-play BPM," and include products from FileNet, Staffware, Savvion, Ultimus and others.

Scoring Criteria for the Capabilities and Completeness Matrix

The following is a list the 20 key features for determining the capabilities of BPM software, followed by a listing of the 10 modules or components that can be used to determine completeness.

Key BPM Capabilities

1. Robust Business Rules

Every business process has many associated rules that govern its execution. The number and complexity of these rules increase with the size of the organization. It is therefore important for BPM systems to have the ability to embed complex business logic in the business process definition that defines routing based upon real-time conditions and data without the need for programming or scripting.

2. Role-Based Routing

This is the ability to route a task to a job function instead of an individual. If individuals change job functions (which they do frequently), the business process does not have to change.

3. Relationship Routing

Many business processes are based upon reporting relationships. Supervisors do reviews, department managers review expense reports, and so on. Therefore, the ability to route tasks based upon reporting relationships is very important.

4. Relative Routing

This capability allows a task to be routed to a job function relative to the position of the initiator or some other person in a particular organizational group. For example, a company may have three divisions, A, B and C. Each division has a quality manager (QM). For a particular process, a task must be routed to the QM for approval. Since there are three QMs, this cannot be done simply by naming the job function QM as the recipient. If the initiator is in Division A, the task must go to the QM in Division A; if the initiator is in Division B, then it must go to the QM in Division B; and so on. The relative job function feature allows one to specify a relative job function as the recipient. Then the task is routed to the job function that is in the same organization as the initiator or some other "seed" person in the process (i.e., the routing is relative).

5. Parallel Routing

In every organization, there are many tasks that can be performed in parallel to reduce cycle time. For example, if five department managers are required to make a budget forecast, and each forecast is independent of the other, it does not make sense to route the budget forecast from one department manager to another in a sequence. This only adds to the completion time since all of them cannot do their part at the same time. Parallel routing allows the department managers to perform budget forecasts at the same time.

6. Ad hoc Routing

In many situations it is necessary to route a workflow task to a person or job function on an ad hoc basis. When designing a process, one may not have prior knowledge of the recipient of a task. For example, an item in a purchase order is charged to a specific expense account identified by an account number. Company policy dictates that the account owner must approve every order charged to an account. When designing the process one is not aware of what the account number will be for any particular purchase order. Therefore, one does not know who the account owner is. A robust BPM solution must provide a dynamic method of assigning recipients that should include user input, database lookup, call to a Web Service, or some other application-specific method.

7. Queues and Groups

This is the ability to route tasks to shared queues, such as a shared in-box in the purchasing department. Any buyer can select a task from the queue based upon availability. Likewise, in many cases a task must be performed by a group of people simultaneously. This requires the ability to route tasks to a group. A robust BPM solution must support the "push" and "pull" method of assigning work.

8. Process Rollback

In real business situations, people often change their minds. A capable BPM solution must provide a means of handling the situation where a decision was made at a step in the process, and after the process has gone forward, the user changes his or her mind. The process must be "rolled back" to accommodate the change. For example, an order entry clerk has placed a customer order and the order process has gone forward. Then the customer changes his mind about some aspect of the order. Instead of canceling the order process, rollback enables the process to be called back to a known state where changes can be made and the process can then move forward with the new information.

9. Sub-Processes

A robust BPM solution must provide a means for one business process to initiate other business processes. Since business processes can be very complex, this feature ensures that such processes can be implemented modularly. This feature must include the capability of transferring data from the parent process to the sub-process, and returning data when the sub-process completes execution.

10. Escalation & Exceptions Handling

The ability to escalate a task if it is late is a basic requirement of BPM. It ensures that tasks do not fall through the cracks and cases are completed expeditiously.

Exceptions are rampant in every organization. The larger the organization, the more exceptions or special cases there are. A BPM solution must have very strong exception handling capabilities offered as a part of the administrator module, or as a part of the workflow client. For example, the ability to reassign a critical task from one user to another if the original user is absent and his computer is password protected; the task must be passed to the second user for completion.

11. Flexible Forms Support

Forms are the user interface of a business process and are used for gathering and disseminating information. The ability to easily design and use intelligent electronic forms is, therefore, an essential feature of workflow automation. Some workflow products rely upon routing documents only. However, while documents are ideal for carrying free-form information, they are not convenient for summary or control information such as signatures, totals, destination addresses, list of required approvals, etc. Advanced BPM solutions provide tightly integrated support for a variety of forms such as HTML thin forms, Adobe PDF forms, Microsoft InfoPath forms and ActiveX forms.

12. Web-based Architecture

A BPM solution involves a large number of participants. To easily reach all these participants and provide connectivity, it is important for a solution to provide a Web-based interface. The Web browser is available on every desktop and provides an excellent mechanism for connecting easily with the BPM server. Furthermore, for large-scale deployments, it is important to offer other features, such as metric reports and administration, through a Web-based interface. This reduces the overall cost of ownership.

13. Automation Agents

BPM is about integrating people and applications into unified processes. A BPM solution must be enabled to exchange information with other applications to perform tasks. Automation agents provide this capability, which enable third-party applications to become "actors" in the process.

14. Custom Views

A task inbox or client is the application used by process participants. At a minimum, it should provide a task list of all the tasks the user has to perform. In addition, providing the flexibility to customize what data is displayed in the task list, and how it is organized, is also important. Beyond this, in many cases, it is critical that it support custom views of not only tasks, but also other items such as subordinate tasks, status of tasks that have been completed, and more. Modern solutions provide many other useful functions such as the ability to monitor, prioritize, and filter tasks. All of these features should be accessible from custom-defined views available in the client inbox.

15. Simulation

BPM involves a large number of individuals and desktops. Once a business process is designed, it is important to test it before deployment. Since it is not logistically practical to test it by actually going from one desktop to another, the BPM software must provide some means of testing it through simulation on a single desktop.

16. Process Documentation

The ability to document a business process is very important and, indeed, is a key requirement of quality standards such as ISO 9000. BPM software must provide a means of generating documentation. This is a requirement for the proper maintenance and support of the solution.

17. Status Monitoring

This is the ability to monitor the status of process incidents. Ideally, this ability should be available to each workflow participant for incidents they have participated in. This capability must also be available to a central workflow manager in order to enable administration and handling exceptions.

18. Authentication and Security

A BPM system must provide robust authentication and security features since it involves a large number of dispersed users as participants. When a user logs in to a client, the system must be able to verify his identity and determine if he is authorized. When the user approves a document, it is important to know that it was the user and not someone else. And finally, when information is transmitted as a part of the server, it must be secure from interception.

19. Distributed User Administration

In a medium or large enterprise, it is not practical to manage and administer users from a central location in order to handle exceptions or balance workload. It is not practical for a central administrator to be aware of the schedules, priorities or the workloads of all the participants of a process. User administration must be distributed so that managers are aware of the workloads, priorities and schedules of those who work for them. They can be responsible for the administration of their subordinates.

20. Task Delegation & Conferring

In real life business situations, individuals often assign tasks for others to perform. They often wish to discuss a particular task with someone else and get their opinion. A BPM solution must provide some means of assigning tasks to others and conferring with others.

Completeness Criteria

1. Graphical Designer

The ability to graphically design workflow maps for business processes is one of the basic requirements of modern BPM software. A process map represents a business process in a flow chart fashion, with clear indications of the dependencies, conditions, and sequences in which tasks must be performed from initiation to completion. A graphical workflow designer is an integral component of BPM software.

2. Collaborative Design

In many cases, business processes are designed and developed by multiple people who span departments, and even organizations. As a result, there needs to be a system to support collaborative design and development efforts. This system must support not only basic development functionality (like repository functionality that supports the check-in/check-out and versioning of business processes), but also more granular capabilities. This would include the ability for multiple people to work on different steps of the same process and reusing existing processes, rules, and forms. Systems that support collaborative design can greatly increase the speed at which processes are designed, modeled, automated, and deployed.

3. Modeling

For many high-volume, resource-intensive business processes it is often necessary and advisable to model the process and test its performance under various scenarios before it is developed and deployed. This allows the business analyst to determine the resources needed to obtain desired performance, and identify bottlenecks or unproductive use of resources. Modeling ensures that the workflow will behave as expected and is optimized for the business requirements. Since the development and deployment of automated business processes could be expensive and time-consuming, it is better to verify design performance before taking this step. Furthermore, the migration of a process designed and modeled in the modeling tool to the BPM software must be as seamless. This can best be accomplished through integrated process modeling tools.

4. Organization Charts and Directory Integration

Business processes deal with individuals, their job functions, reporting relationships, and the groups to which they belong. Thus, the ability to be "aware" of the organizational structure of a business is an essential requirement. BPM software must provide some method of encapsulating a company's organization chart.

Businesses keep user names, passwords, and access rights in directories such as Microsoft Active Directory, NT Directory, SAP, PeopleSoft, or LDAP. Since BPM software needs information about users, support for standard directories is an essential requirement for reducing the cost of ownership. Without good directory support, customers will have to maintain multiple directories. Maintenance and synchronization of these directories is a major issue.

5. Multiple Client Interfaces

Business processes usually involve people with varying skills and job responsibilities. In most cases, participation in the business process is part of their job, but not their entire job. Therefore, their interface with the BPM system must be easy for them to use and fit within their work environment. A complete BPM solution will provide multiple client interfaces, including support for common e-mail applications such as Microsoft Outlook, portals, and wireless devices. The choice of client application should be driven first by the user, and then by the capabilities they require to participate in BPM.

6. Business Metrics and Monitoring

The ability to produce BPM reports so business managers can measure the time and cost of processes is important for a complete BPM solution. The business manager can then use these reports to modify and optimize business processes based upon their cost-effectiveness and timeliness. They can also be used to set realistic expectations and determine the true cost and time of doing business. The ability to perform real-time metrics and monitoring enables business managers and administrators to take action proactively if inboxes are full, processes stall, or costly exceptions occur. A BPM solution must support both monitoring and metric reporting to get the maximum value out of the system.

7. BPM Administrator

An administrator module is an important component of BPM software because it provides capabilities such as process installation, version control, access rights, and the overall management of business processes.

8. Web Services and Integration

The best way to reduce task time is to take people out of the task. This can be done when automated systems in the corporation can be used to perform the task. Not only does this reduce task time, but it also reduces errors. To make this easy, BPM solutions must support Web services, at a minimum, and other integration approaches. As organizations evolve toward Service-Oriented Architectures (SOAs), the support for Web services becomes mandatory to leverage the flexibility that SOA provides.

9. Database Connectivity and Transaction Processing

Businesses store vital information in databases. Business processes use information from these databases, or massage raw data into useful information, that is then saved in these databases. In either case, connection to databases is essential for business process management. Furthermore, since BPM can involve a large number of users, connectivity to databases must be established on the server-side where it is quick, easy, centralized, and a one-time activity. Connecting BPM participants to databases directly from the client-side poses difficult logistical and administrative problems.

BPM is about secure, reliable, and high volume transaction processing. As each task in a business process is completed, it initiates a transaction on the server-side. This transaction determines what actions must be taken next. It then ensures that the information necessary for subsequent tasks is delivered to the right individuals or applications. As the number of participants and process incidents increase, so do the number of transactions that must be performed reliably by the BPM server. If the transactions are not reliable or fast, the workflow system will fail. Thus, secure, reliable, and efficient server-side transaction processing is an essential requirement of BPM.

10. Scalable BPM Server

A BPM system must be scalable to enable a large number of users to participate or a large number of transactions to be processed. This implies that the BPM server or engine must provide scalability. In modern server architectures, the best method of achieving scalability is through object-oriented design and the use of server clusters on which these objects can be distributed for dynamic load balancing. In addition to these performance-related issues, other scalability concerns include the ability for all users to participate (refer to Item 5 of this list, "Multiple Client Interfaces") and development complexity (refer to Items 1 and 2 of this list, "Graphical Designer" and "Collaborative Design," respectively). It is critical that a BPM solution can scale both in terms of performance and operational issues.

Bibliography

1. "Groupware: Communication, Collaboration and Coordination" © 1995 Lotus Development Corporation, Cambridge, MA
2. "Workflow Imperative" by Thomas Koulopoulos
3. "Business Process Management (BPM): The Third Wave" by Howard Smith, Peter Fingar
4. "Business Process Management: Profiting From Process" by Roger Burlton
5. "Business Process Management (BPM) is a Team Sport: Play it to Win!" by Andrew Spanyi
6. "Business @ the Speed of Thought: Succeeding in the Digital Economy" by Bill Gates
7. "Secure Electronic Commerce: Building the Infrastructure for Digital Signatures and Encryption" (2nd Edition) by Warwick Ford, Michael S. Baum
8. "Modern Operating Systems" (2nd Edition) by Andrew Tanenbaum
9. "Essential COM" by Don Box
10. "Pure Corba" by Fintan Bolton
11. "Object-Oriented Programming in Java" by Martin Kalin
12. "LDAP Directories Explained: An Introduction and Analysis" by Brian Arkills
13. "Understanding and Deploying LDAP Directory Services" (2nd Edition) by Tim Howes, Mark Smith, Gordon Good, Gordon S. Good
14. "Business Process Fusion is Inevitable" by Howard Smith and Peter Fingar, BPtrends.com, March 2004

Index

About the Author

RASHID KHAN is the co-founder and CEO of Ultimus Inc., a pioneer in business process management and workflow automation. Ultimus was established in 1994, without any outside investment, with the long-term vision of bringing workflow automation to every desktop. Today, Ultimus is a leading provider of Web-based BPM software solutions that allow companies across industries to enhance profitability through improved worker productivity. The Ultimus BPM Suite is used by more than 1,200 customers including Dell, Sony, Microsoft and Compaq, and has won several industry awards, including the *eWeek* 2004 Excellence Award, *CRN* Editor's Choice Award and *PC Week's* Best of COMDEX. The company employs more than 200 people in twelve offices across the globe and has consistently achieved profitability and excellent growth in revenue, earning Ultimus positions in the prestigious Inc 500, and Deloitte & Touche's Technology Fast 500 in North America.

Prior to establishing Ultimus, Khan was the founder and CEO of Sintech Inc., a leader in advanced software for mechanical testing. He founded Sintech in 1983, and bootstrapped the company to become a leader in its industry. After six years of rapid and profitable growth, Khan sold Sintech to MTS Systems Corporation in 1989, where he worked for five years as a vice president and general manager. During this period he took the company through ISO 9000 certification. This experience made him aware of the need for business process management and workflow automation.

Khan obtained two undergraduate degrees from MIT in Computer Science and Political Science. He obtained a Masters degree in Computer Science from the University of California at Berkeley, and an MBA from the Harvard Business School. Khan was awarded three technology patents by the US Patent Office, two of them in the area of business process management and workflow automation software. He has published numerous technical papers and business articles.

Other Advanced Business-Technology Books from Meghan-Kiffer Press

Business Process Management: The Third Wave
The Breakthrough That Redefines Competitive Advantage

IT Doesn't Matter: Business Processes Do
A Critical Analysis

Business Process Management: A Rigorous Approach
Copublished with the British Computer Society

The Real-Time Enterprise
Competing on Time!

The Death of 'e' and the Birth of the Real New Economy
Business Models, Technologies and Strategies for the 21st Century

Enterprise E-Commerce
The Breakthrough for Business-to-Business Commerce

MK

Meghan-Kiffer Press
Tampa, Florida, USA, www.mkpress.com
Advanced Business-Technology Books for Competitive Advantage